ZBrush Character Creation

ZBrush Character Creation:
Advanced Digital Sculpting

Scott Spencer

Wiley Publishing, Inc.

Acquisitions Editor: Mariann Barsolo
Development Editor: Pete Gaughan
Technical Editor: Ryan Kingslien
Production Editor: Elizabeth Ginns Britten
Copy Editor: Elizabeth Welch
Production Manager: Tim Tate
Vice President and Executive Group Publisher: Richard Swadley
Vice President and Executive Publisher: Joseph B. Wikert
Vice President and Publisher: Neil Edde
Media Associate Project Manager: Laura Atkinson
Media Associate Producer: Angie Denny
Media Quality Assurance: Josh Frank
Book Designer and Compositor: Chris Gillespie, Happenstance Type-O-Rama
Proofreader: Nancy Bell
Indexer: Nancy Guenther
Cover Designer: Ryan Sneed
Cover Image: Scott Spencer, Hector Delatorre

Library of Congress Cataloging-in-Publication Data:

Spencer, Scott, 1975–
   ZBrush character creation : advanced digital sculpting / Scott Spencer. — 1st ed.
      p. cm.
   ISBN 978-0-470-24996-3 (paper/dvd)
   1. Computer graphics. 2. ZBrush. I. Title.
   T385.S662 2008
   006.6'93—dc22

                              2008009613

10 9 8 7 6 5 4 3 2

Letter from the Publisher

Dear Reader,

Thank you for choosing *ZBrush Character Creation: Advanced Digital Sculpting*. This book is part of a family of premium-quality Sybex books, all of which are written by outstanding authors who combine practical experience with a gift for teaching.

Sybex was founded in 1976. More than thirty years later, we're still committed to producing consistently exceptional books. With each of our titles we're working hard to set a new standard for the industry. From the paper we print on, to the authors we work with, our goal is to bring you the best books available.

I hope you see all that reflected in these pages. I'd be very interested to hear your comments and get your feedback on how we're doing. Feel free to let me know what you think about this or any other Sybex book by sending me an email at nedde@wiley.com, or if you think you've found a technical error in this book, please visit http://sybex.custhelp.com. Customer feedback is critical to our efforts at Sybex.

Best regards,

Neil Edde
Vice President and Publisher
Sybex, an Imprint of Wiley

To my parents, for making all things possible, and to Bill Johnson and Paul Hudson for their guidance, inspiration, and friendship.

Acknowledgments

There are so many people who bring a book like this to life; I would like to try and thank each of them here. This includes those with a direct hand in the editing and layout as well as those whose support makes this kind of endeavor possible. First off I'd like to thank Karl Meyer, Brian Sunderlin, and Gentle Giant Studios for giving me a place to learn and grow as well as make cool stuff; Meredith Yayanos for her loving support, Jim McPherson for his keen eye and expert artistic guidance. Thanks to Richard Taylor, Tania Rodger, and the gang at Weta Workshop for their friendship and constant inspiration. I would also like to thank Andrew Cawres and Freedom of Teach for the tools and assistance to grow as an artist.

Thanks to Ryan Kingslien for serving as tech editor and a constant source of information on the inner workings of ZBrush as well as his keen eye for sculptural form. Ofer Alon, and Jaime Labelle at Pixologic; Kyle Mulqueen who will forever be renaming .tif files in his sleep, Alex Alvarez, and everyone at Gnomon. Thanks also go to Belinda Heywood and the team at Secret Level.

I'd also like to thank Rick Baker and Dick Smith for inspiring me to pick up clay for the first time. I must also thank those friends who have shared techniques and critiques; Zack Petroc, Meats Meier, Scott Patton, Cesar Dacol, Ian Joyner, JP Targete, Mark Dedecker, Stefano Dubay, Hector Delatorre, Nobu Sasagawa, Bill Spradlin, and Ricardo Ariza.

A very special thanks to Eric Keller for his input and bringing this book to me. I also must thank the wonderful team at Wiley who helped me through the process and were always professional, patient, attentive, and helpful to the process. Thanks to Mariann Barsolo for starting the process and helping it along. Thanks to Pete Gaughan for guiding the direction of the book and helping to keep it on track and clear. Thanks to Liz Britten for her masterful copyediting and layout, bringing the final product to light.

Foreword

There are rare moments in history when a renaissance is conceived and the whole paradigm of a particular medium is changed forever. Through the celebration of subtractive carving or additive sculpting, these various art mediums have established a whole new cultural iconography and have created treasures through the art of sculpture.

A new artistic renaissance is quietly unfolding around us, establishing a medium of art no less powerful than those that have developed before it. As the unique artistic tools that are Photoshop, Painter, the tablet, and the stylus have forever changed the conceptual designer's palette of techniques and injected a freedom and spontaneity into artists' work, so has the development of 3D modeling packages allowed sculptors another wonderful tool in their equipment.

As each new renaissance delivers to the world master craftspeople and artisans operating at the pinnacle of their chosen discipline, Scott Spencer has chosen to master the medium of 3D digital modeling and become a master craftsman in his own right. Scott is an exceptionally talented person who draws from an innate gift and understanding of the sculpted form and pairs this with his complete grasp of the technical complexities of software packages, digital technology, and cutting-edge 3D software. Scott has become well recognized for his work within the high-end creative merchandising field, primarily working within Gentle Giant (one of the world's leading merchandising and collectibles business), but he has also carved his own distinct career with the tutoring of 3D digital modeling and sculpture to students and professionals alike.

I have had the great pleasure of getting to know Scott over the past four years and have watched in awe as his skill and artistry has tasked the 3D modeling tools at his fingertips into creating dynamic figurative sculptures worthy of any gallery.

It is, therefore, a wonderful thing to be invited to write a foreword for Scott's book on ZBrush and the art of 3D modeling. I find Scott to be an inspiration as he wields his craft. It is Scott who I have turned to when considering our own artists at Weta Workshop becoming proficient in the field of 3D digital modeling, as I know there is no better tutor from whom we can all learn and who is part of this amazing new renaissance within the art of sculpture.

—RICHARD TAYLOR
Weta Workshop
Miramar, Wellington, New Zealand

Richard Taylor and his partner Tania Rodger began what would become Weta Workshop Ltd. in New Zealand in 1994. Taylor won four Academy Awards for his work on The Lord of the Rings *trilogy, for which Weta performed the gamut of digital production from compositing to animation of CG creatures. Over the past 20 years, the company has provided physical and digital effects for many films, advertisements, and television shows, including the* Hercules *and the* Xena *series, as well as feature films including* Master and Commander; I Robot; Van Helsing; The Last Samurai; The Chronicles of Narnia: The Lion, the Witch, and the Wardrobe; The Legends of Zorro; *and* King Kong.

About the Author

My name is Scott Spencer, I am the Digital Art Director at Gentle Giant Studios in Burbank, California. At Gentle Giant I work in various media, creating digital characters for film, broadcast, and games as well as physical sculptures for concept design, promotion, and other applications. Over the past few years I have worked on various projects in both film, broadcast, and games, from the remake of the classic game "Golden Axe" to the *Iron Man* movie, *Pumpkinhead 3, Species 3,* as well as several collectible figures and statues sold on the commercial market.

In approaching this book I tried to take lessons from the teachers that most influenced my own education. The two instructors are Bill Johnson and Paul Hudson. Bill Johnson is the owner of Lone Wolf FX, a makeup effects company, and my first employer. From Bill I learned an enormous amount not just about sculpting and creature design but also about thinking and seeing like an artist. I also found in Bill a great friend whom I count as one of my closest to this day.

At Bill's urging I went to art school at The Savannah (Georgia) College of Art and Design. I studied animation with a minor in drawing and anatomy, and I met my second great artistic influence. Paul Hudson teaches perspective, anatomy, and illustration; he is an accomplished illustrator, painter, sculptor, and general Renaissance man. Paul teaches his students by example to be passionate about the continuous process of learning that is to be an artist.

While at SCAD I noticed ZBrush and a light went off for me. Here was a program that would let me do what I do in clay on the computer. I had used Maya and 3ds Max but never felt the same seamlessness as in ZBrush. This software helped me be a better artist; it didn't fight me into a technical corner.

ZBrush can be a hard nut to crack. I wanted to learn this program desperately, so I worked many an endless night, with the help of the user base at ZBrushCentral, which is extremely supportive to artists. I wrote what is now the official ZBrush to Maya ZPipeline guide, available with some of my other tutorials on ZBrush.info.

After SCAD I attended the Florence Academy of Art summer sculpting session, then I found my way to California and to Gentle Giant Studios, which seemed to be one of just a few companies seamlessly blending traditional and digital art techniques. It was a fertile ground for ZBrush. In two short years we had built an entire digital sculpting team from the ground up that included many traditional sculptors who migrated from clay into ZBrush. Today we handle a large volume of projects from toys and collectibles to life-size figures and models for video games and film.

In the years since I started using ZBrush, my passion for the program and the approach of applying sculptural approached to a 3D world has led me to teach a selection of classes at the Gnomon School of Visual Effects as well as release several video tutorials for Gnomonology .com and Pixologic.com.

Along the way I have made a lot of sculptures, taught a lot of classes, and met some amazing artists who continue to inspire and influence me. I have taught at the Weta Workshop in Wellington, New Zealand, where I had the rare opportunity to meet and get to know some of the best creature and character artists in the world. Overall I consider myself very fortunate to have the opportunity to do what I always dreamed of doing—sculpting characters for a living.

I have included several guest artists in this book to help offer more variety in style and approach. Here I would like to introduce you to these amazingly talented individuals who were kind enough to include their thoughts and work in this book.

Cesar Dacol

Cesar Luis Dacol has worked in the film industry for nearly 20 years, having started his career in the makeup effects industry and transitioning to computers effects in the mid-1990s. With a background in anatomy and traditional sculpting, he quickly adapted to the 3D world of computers. For the past five years Cesar has worked primarily as lead and modeling supervisor, contributing to many feature films such as *300, Barnyard,* and *Fantastic Four.*

Ian Joyner

Ian Joyner has been a character modeler for more than five years. In that time he has worked on everything from feature films, ride films, and critically acclaimed video game cinematics. Ian's work can be seen in many projects including *BioShock, Marvel Ultimate Alliance, Hellgate: London, Warhammer: Age of Reckoning* and *Halo Wars,* the feature films *Rocky 6 (Rocky Balboa)* and James Cameron's *Aliens of the Deep,* as well as the award-winning short *A Gentlemen's Duel* by Blur Studio.

Jim McPherson

Starting in the 1980s in the makeup and special effects industry, Jim has worked with Rick Baker's Cinovation Studios on *Gremlins 2, The Nutty Professor, Matinee, Men in Black,* and *Planet of the Apes.* Rick's philosophy of sculptural character design has been a huge influence in Jim's work. The opportunity to design characters under his tutelage was an educational experience that cannot be matched. Previous to the dragon tutorial in this book, Jim has sculpted for designer Miles Teves on a dragon maquette for the film *Reign of Fire.*

Jim currently works with the team at Gentle Giant Studios. The digital sculpting team has completed work on many of the characters in Sega's "Golden Axe." The digital artists work in close proximity with a brilliant team of traditional sculptors. This is the correct atmosphere to meet the challenge of applying the principles of sculpture in digital modeling.

Zack Petroc

Zack Petroc has a bachelor of fine arts degree from the Cleveland Institute of Art with a major in sculpture and dual minor in drawing and digital media. Additionally, he studied anatomy at Case School of Medicine and figure sculpture in Florence, Italy. Zack uses his strong design background for both his traditional and digital work. This allows him to contribute to the artistic vision of a project not only during the concept design stage, but also throughout production. Zack is currently working as a freelance art director and concept designer for feature film and video games. He is also a member of the Art Directors Guild Technology Committee.

Alex Alvarez

Alex is founder and director of the Gnomon Workshop and of the Gnomon School of Visual Effects in Hollywood. Having dedicated the last decade to educating students and professional artists around the world, Alex has helped change the face of computer graphics and design education. He has been published in industry magazines, websites, and books, and he has taught courses at several major trade conferences. Alex is president of the Los Angeles Maya Users Group and sits on the Advisory Boards for Highend3D.com and CGsociety. He continues to work on personal and professional projects, recently as a creature development artist on the James Cameron film *Avatar*. Prior to Gnomon, Alex worked for Alias|Wavefront as a consultant and trainer for studios in the Los Angeles area. Alex is an alumnus of the Art Center College of Design and the University of Pennsylvania.

Ryan Kingslien

Ryan Kingslien is a senior Pixoltician at Pixologic, where he works with programmers and artists to fuse art and technology for ZBrush's cutting-edge digital art tools. He studied traditional art at the Pennsylvania Academy of Fine Art and digital art at the Gnomon School of Visual Effects, and earned his degree in liberal arts with a focus on creative writing at Antioch University.

Svengali

As a leading creator of some of the most useful plug-ins for ZBrush, Svengali can be found at www.zbrushcentral.com.

Fabian Loing

Fabian Loing is 26 years old. He was born in Jakarta, Indonesia, and is currently a character artist, living in Canada, and working for Pandemic Studios.

Image Contributors

In addition, I would like to thank the following for consenting to include images of their work in the book. I hope you find these images as compelling and inspiring as I do.

- Alex Oliver, "The Mummy"
- Arran Lewis, "ZSphere anatomy"
- Magdalena Dadela, "Old woman"
- Steve Jubinville, "The darkness monster"
- Joel Mongeon, "Studio Wall series"

Contents

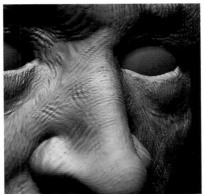

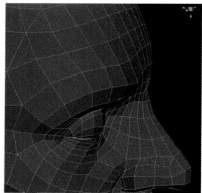

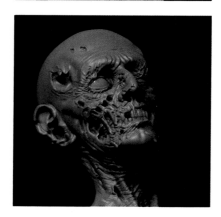

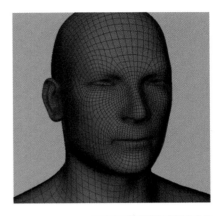

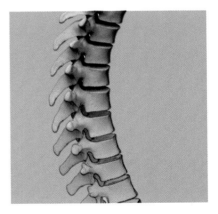

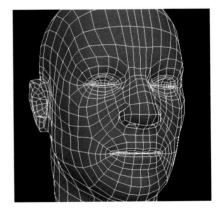

Introduction

Welcome to *ZBrush Character Creation: Advanced Digital Sculpting*. I wrote this book to pull together the tools and techniques I have gathered over the past few years as a digital sculptor from both personal experience and the openness and sharing of other ZBrush artists. It is my hope that this book will help build on your experience with ZBrush and open up new and exciting techniques using the program.

This book focuses specifically on character sculpting and painting with ZBrush. Creature and character work has been the focus of my career for the past 10 years, and since moving into a digital workflow with ZBrush, I have seen the possibilities for artists explode. We will cover topics from basic sculpting to more advanced techniques of building form and character. We will also look at painting skin and adding fine details to our characters. Throughout the book, I have invited some friends to add their own experience with ZBrush in the sidebars. Every artist works differently, and we can learn so much from seeing other approaches to the same problems.

In addition to working as a digital sculptor, I have been an instructor at the Gnomon School of Visual Effects in Hollywood teaching ZBrush for the past two years. In this time I have seen a variety of students, from beginner to advanced, approach ZBrush and learn the toolset. This experience has helped me craft this book in a way that I hope will be most beneficial to you, the reader.

In my experience teaching, I have found that it is important to learn the ins and outs of the software. Knowing how to find the tools is, of course, necessary. I have also seen that just as important is an understanding of what to do with the tools you learn. It is easy to find the Standard brush, for instance, but I illustrate how to use the brushes to build a character with sound structure, form, and an eye toward sculptural anatomy. These foundation artistic principles are the core of good work whether you are making it in ZBrush or in clay.

Who Should Read This Book

This book is for anyone who wants to sculpt creatures and characters in ZBrush. It is best to work from the first exercises through the book if you are new to ZBrush. You may also skip to the section specific to your center of interest. For this reason I have sought to include many examples of how to approach digital sculpting from an artistic perspective in the book. It is not by any means the last word on the subject, but I find that my own experience in traditional media has helped me in ZBrush. I hope that by applying the same principles of gesture, form, and proportion to this book it will help you as well. It is easy to become preoccupied with the technology, so we often need to step back and look at the art itself. Because this is a sculptural medium and a series of still images can only show so much, I have included most of the exercises on the DVD in video form. You can watch these and see the steps performed in real time.

This book is for the intermediate ZBrush user. I assume a certain amount of experience but I have also been careful to include enough information that a new user can grasp the topics quickly. For a more foundational introduction to the tools, I recommend looking at Eric Keller's *Introducing ZBrush,* also from Sybex.

What You Will Learn

In this book you will learn how to work with the ZBrush sculpting and painting toolset to create believable characters. We will also look at how to get your work out of ZBrush into a third-party application for rendering using either displacement or normal mapping techniques. We will look at anatomy and how it affects the form of the head and explore how to use anatomical knowledge to assist in sculpting a human head. We will talk about color theory and how it influences color choices when painting a creature skin from scratch. We will also discuss how to create your own base geometry in ZBrush using ZSpheres, as well as how to remesh a ZTool into an animation-ready base topology. Other topics include posing in ZBrush, using alphas and stencils for detailing, understanding ZScripting, and customizing your interface. Over the course of the book, we will also look at production considerations and how to get the most flexibility from ZBrush in a work pipeline.

Hardware and Software Requirements

To complete the core exercises of this book, you need ZBrush version 3.1 or higher. Some sections also include material related to Photoshop and Maya and using these programs together with ZBrush. Hardware requirements are a PC or Mac running ZBrush with a gigabyte or more of RAM. The more RAM you have, the better results you can get with ZBrush.

It is also imperative that you have a Wacom tablet. While it is possible to use a mouse with ZBrush, it is like drawing with a brick. A Wacom or other digital tablet will open the doors for you to paint and sculpt naturally. Personally I recommend a Wacom Cintiq. There are two variations of this tablet screen available at the time of this writing. The desktop model with a 21˝ screen as well as a smaller 12˝ portable model. The Cintiq allows you to sculpt and paint directly on the screen and can vastly improve the speed and accuracy with which you can use ZBrush. It is essential to use some form of Wacom tablet be it a Cintiq or a standard Intuos with ZBrush.

How to Use This Book

I have structured the text to start from a basic look at the ZBrush toolset and progress through the entire program into more advanced concepts and tools. Although there is an open and thriving user community, there was a need for a physical manual for working with ZBrush. This book seeks to fill that void and offer a training solution for users who prefer to work from a printed material at their own pace. I also recommend you read Eric Keller's *Introduction to ZBrush* published by Wiley.

This book will be especially useful to those who are coming to digital sculpting with no previous 3D experience. I have tried to communicate the ZBrush workflow with examples from traditional sculpting and painting technique. To me, ZBrush is not only its own medium as much as it is an extension of paint and clay, much in the same way that Corel Painter extends and improves on paint and canvas, thus allowing the artist to use traditional techniques in new ways. Because of this, I believe it is just as important to discuss where to find the tools as it is to illustrate how to use them effectively to create compelling creatures and characters.

Chapter 1: Sculpting, from Traditional to Digital introduces the ZBrush interface and working methods. In this chapter we create a doorknocker from a primitive plane.

Chapter 2: Sculpting in ZBrush further explores the ZBrush sculpting toolset. Starting with a ZBrush primitive sphere, we block in the skull, facial muscles, and then skin of the human head.

Chapter 3: Designing a Character Bust applies what we have learned about sculpting in ZBrush to an imported polygon mesh. Using a generic human head model, we sculpt two different character busts. Advanced techniques for transferring sculpted details are also examined.

Chapter 4: ZBrush for Detailing In this chapter we look at creating high-frequency details in ZBrush. By using alphas and strokes, we can detail a character with a realistic skin texture.

Chapter 5: Texture Painting Using PolyPaint we paint a creature skin texture from scratch. This chapter introduces ZBrush texture applications as well as some important color theory to assist you in texturing your own characters.

Chapter 6: ZSpheres explores ZBrush's powerful mesh generation tool. Using basic and advanced ZSphere techniques, we create a biped base mesh.

Chapter 7: Transpose, Retopology, and Mesh Extraction examines the ZBrush posing tool called Transpose. In this chapter we also look at ZBrush's retopology tools for generating new base meshes from existing ZTools. Finally we look at making accessories with retopology tools and mesh extraction.

Chapter 8: ZBrush Movies and Compositing looks at a unique technique of rendering multiple materials passes from ZBrush and compositing them in Photoshop. We also look at capturing video directly in ZBrush.

Chapter 9: Rendering ZBrush Displacements in Maya is an extensive look at displacement mapping with ZBrush. Techniques for exporting both 16- and 32-bit maps are covered. This chapter also examines how to render your displacement map in mental ray for Maya.

Chapter 10: ZMapper covers the robust normal mapping plug-in ZMapper. Techniques for displaying and rendering normal maps in Maya are also covered. Other applications of ZMapper examined here include cavity mapping and blend shape animation.

Chapter 11: ZScripts, Macros, and Interface Customization concludes the book with a look at ZBrush interface customization. Custom menu sets, hotkeys, and custom macros are all examined. The chapter includes an introduction to ZScripting by guest artist Svengali.

The Companion DVD Videos

On the DVD I have included several support files for each chapter. Many tutorials have video files accompanying them. In addition to videos, I have included supplementary text materials expanding on certain concepts as well as sample meshes, materials, and brushes. The video files were recorded using the TechSmith screen capture codes (www.techsmith.com) and compressed with H.264 compression.

The videos included I hope will help further illustrate the sculptural approach I take in ZBrush. Being able to see a tool in use can better illustrate the concepts than still images alone. On my website www.scottspencer.com you will find more tutorials expanding on the content of this book.

How to Contact the Author

I welcome feedback from you about this book or about books you'd like to see from me in the future. You can reach me by writing to scott@scottspencer.com. For more information about my work, please visit my website at www.scottspencer.com.

Sybex strives to keep you supplied with the latest tools and information you need for your work. Please check their website at www.sybex.com, where we'll post additional content and updates that supplement this book if the need arises. Enter **ZBrush Character Creation** in the Search box (or type the book's ISBN: **9780470249963**), and click Go to get to the book's update page.

In conclusion, thank you for buying this book. I hope you enjoy the exercises within as much as I have enjoyed putting this book together. Being surrounded by likeminded artists who all have something to contribute makes every day a learning experience. It is an honor for me to share some of what I have learned with you. I hope you enjoy this book. Happy sculpting!

one

Sculpting, from Traditional to Digital

One of the most exciting *aspects of ZBrush is the way it allows the artist to interface directly with the model and create in a spontaneous and organic fashion, just as if working with balls of digital clay. Thousands of years of artistic tradition have given us a wealth of technique when it comes to the discipline of sculpting. While traditional painters have had applications like Painter and Photoshop to open the doors to the digital realm, sculptors were out in the cold—until ZBrush.*

Gesture, Form, and Proportion

When learning to become a better digital sculptor, you will benefit from the same traditions and tenets that guided traditional sculptors for centuries. Just like drawing and painting, all the fundamental artistic lessons applicable to sculpting are true on the computer as well. Whether we are sculpting an alien, a princess, a warrior, a horse, or abstract form exploration, our primary concerns will always be the same (Figure 1.1).

Gesture

Gesture represents the dynamic curve of the figure. In life drawing, these lines are quickly laid down on paper and do not necessarily seek to describe the contour or form of the figure at all (Figure 1.2). The function of the gesture drawing is to capture the *rhythm and motion* of the pose, the thrust of the figure, and the action inherent in its posture (Figure 1.3). Keeping a sketchbook of quick, loose sketches you don't intend to show is a great way to train yourself to find the gesture and rhythms in a figure. These kinds of exercises help sharpen your eye, and this translates into better figures when sculpting from the imagination.

Figure 1.1: Examples of traditional clay sculpture

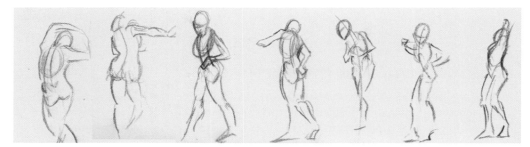

Figure 1.2: A selection of gesture sketches

Gesture is the source of the life of a drawing or sculpture. It must be addressed from the outset—if the gesture is poor, it can be difficult to introduce it later into the process. If you start with a strong gesture, the sculpture will be appealing and alive from the start. A wooden, stiff pose with a poor gesture can have acceptable anatomical form and skin details while still being fundamentally unappealing (Figure 1.4).

The rules of gesture apply to even a sculpture that is not a figure. Notice in the lion's head how the gesture of the lines in the mane serve to create a sense of flowing action down toward the ring (Figure 1.5). These lines are more of a graphic consideration and can almost be considered in the abstract. Their presence serves to strengthen the visual impact.

Figure 1.3: An example of gesture and action

Figure 1.4: This Hercules from the Piazza della Signora in Florence, Italy, is an example of bad gesture in an otherwise good sculpture.

Figure 1.5: Lion head sculpture

Closely linked to gesture is the concept of rhythm. Master draughtsman George Bridgman describes rhythm as "in the balance of masses the subordination of the passive or inactive side to the more forceful and angular side in the action." That is to say, the interplay between the active and passive curves in the body combines to create a sense of rhythm in your sculpture (Figure 1.6).

Gesture is an important consideration no matter what you may be sculpting. It is gesture that makes a sculpture exciting, whether it is a door knocker, a monster, or a human. Especially when dealing with figurative sculpture, a well-executed gesture with special attention to rhythm helps establish a sense of weight and balance to the figure.

Figure 1.6: In this image of Celini's Perseus, I have indicated the alternating curves that establish a sense of rhythm down the length of the figure. Notice how they alternate, as in the inset image.

Form

Although ZBrush excels at adding fine details to a model, form is always of primary concern when sculpting. Many sculptors rush to the detailing phase while overlooking the importance of developing the form, anatomy, and structure of the model. This makes for a weaker sculpture overall. Take Michelangelo's David, for instance; it's a perfect example of a masterful sculpture but there is not a single pore or wrinkle on the body. The figure lives and breathes because the interplay of forms of the surface gives the impression of skin, fat, and bone. David appears to be a living being in an inanimate material. This is true even when you are working on a completed 3D model from a third-party application. There is no replacement for the subtle variations in surface shadow and transitions you can add with ZBrush's sculpting tools. Adding a more organic sense of the artist in the work will create a far more appealing character. It may not seem like much, but taking away the perfect parametric nature of a polygon model can push a character's believability well into the next level before the first wrinkle or pore is applied.

Form in general refers to the external shape, appearance, and configuration of an object. In drawing and painting, you are describing form by directly applying light and shadow—from the highlight to the midtone to the core of the shadow. In sculpture, you are creating these halftones and *value* changes by altering the shadow casting surface. By altering the underlying shape, you can model the way light plays on the surface. Without shadow, there is no form. You can see this if you turn on Flat Render in the ZBrush window, thus removing all the shadows and highlights. Only a flat silhouette remains (see Figure 1.7).

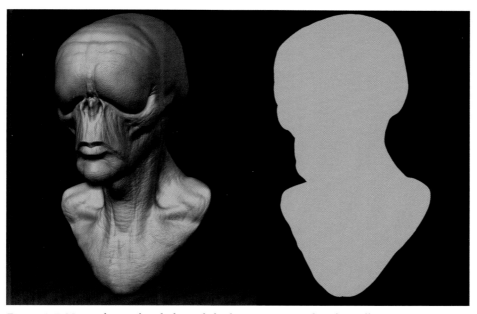

Figure 1.7: Notice how when light and shadow are removed, only a silhouette remains.

It can be helpful when sculpting to remember that the shapes you are making with your brush will affect how light and shadow interact on the surface. That is how the shapes are created. If the light is turned off, all form goes away. Creating good form as you sculpt it requires an understanding of both the shape itself as well as the quality of the shadows created by that shape under different lighting conditions. As a further example of how shadow describes form, we can take a lesson from painting and drawing. Here is a photograph of a face next to the same photo posterized. With all the midtones removed so only the extreme highlights and shadows remain, you can still identify the fact that this is a face. When you're reading a surface, the shadows tell you everything about what you are looking at (Figure 1.8).

Figure 1.8: Even with just the shapes of the shadows, this face is still recognizable.

This gradient between the lightest light and darkest dark is called *value*. Paintings and drawings have what's called a key or value range—the set number of steps from lightest light to darkest dark found within the image. When you're sculpting, it is good practice to be sensitive to these gradations on the surface of your own work. Even though you are not applying value directly, you are affecting the values the eye perceives by the height of the shape you are sculpting or the depth of the recess. Examine how the shadows interact on the surface; to darken a shadow, you may deepen the crevasse or add to the mass of the adjacent shape. Moving the light often as you work can help you spot these value changes from different lighting conditions.

You can move the light interactively in ZBrush. Set your material to one of the standard materials and choose ZPlugin → Misc Utilities → Interactive Light from the main menu. Move the mouse to see the light moving around your sculpture as you work. See the DVD for a video showing this feature in action.

When you're dealing with form, it also becomes important to address transitions that create space between forms and how one feeds into another. Figure 1.9 shows how deepening a crevasse or raising a high point can darken your shadow and give it a harder edge. This will change the character of the transition.

Try to be sensitive to the transitions between your forms and the variation you create. If the transitions between all your shapes are the same hard edged shadows the figure will be visually bland.

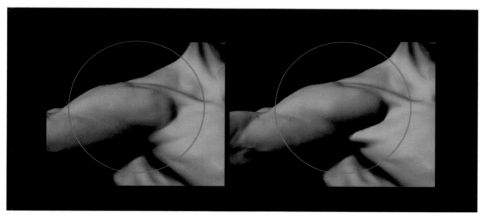

Figure 1.9: By deepening the furrow next to the deltoid, the character of the shadow changes, changing the feeling of the transition. Notice how the relative darkness of the shadow changes from the clavicle to the arm in the first image. Also note how in the second image this value has now become one consistent value and thus less visually interesting.

An important concept to bear in mind while you sculpt is to reduce everything to its base form and work on big shapes first. Just as a painter will tackle the big shadows and big lights first, then work down to details, the same is true in sculpting. This is one of the most important aspects of this section to remember—by working on big shapes and then refining, not only do you ensure that you resolve the major shapes first, but it helps your mind organize the complex forms of the figure into easy-to-manage sections. The final result may appear complex and intricate, but you approached it in small portions one at a time (Figure 1.10).

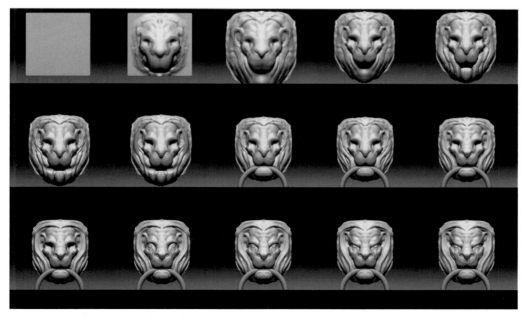

Figure 1.10: These images show the progression of the lion head sculpture from the most basic, broad strokes down to the finer lines.

Figure 1.11: By reducing this creature to its most basic shapes, the form relationships and proportions become apparent.

All forms can be broken down to their base shapes and planes. Complex shapes like the face mass can be reduced to aggregate planes for easier study and execution. This is called *planar analysis*. While sculpting you will find it helpful to always be thinking of what the basic forms are in your character and how they relate to one another (Figure 1.11). The viewer will have different reactions to a character based on the relationships between its basic forms. This relationship between forms is called *proportion*.

The proportions between the basic forms have a visual impact on the viewer. These reactions can change based on how the artist manipulates these relationships. For example, a character with a huge, bulbous head on a small body will create a different reaction than one with a tiny head and an oversized body.

I often get asked how densely to subdivide the model while working. This is never a set number. The subdivisions you can get on your machine will vary depending on how much RAM is installed. The polygon count of your level 1 mesh will also influence how densely you can subdivide.

Artistically the best approach in my opinion is to divide to the lowest level at which you can represent the shapes you are trying to sculpt. By avoiding detailing too early and refining the basic forms of the character you will find that excellent results can be attained from lower polygon counts. Only then, when the form is resolved, are you ready to detail. The fine detail passes need to be done at the highest possible subdivision levels. In most cases this is 2million or more polygons. Later in this book we will look at detailing characters and ways to get sharper details from lower polygon counts.

Proportion

Proportion refers to the relationship between the overall size of an object and the relative sizes of its parts. Many books have been written on the balance of these measures, and the fundamental rules of proportion have been understood as far back as the ancient Egyptians.

When you're sculpting a figure, it is important to understand proportion as it pertains to the human form. Proportional canons are sets of rules to help guide artists in creating a specific type of figure.

There are many systems, or canons, of proportion. Michelangelo often used a heroic eight heads to measure the figure, while a more ordinary human measure is 7½ heads high. No proportional system is "law," and there are variations in all people. These are intended as an idealized system of measure. Straying too far will result in a figure that looks "off."

By understanding the proportional canon you are working with, you can make educated decisions about the character you are creating by changing the proportion.

Best Practices for Digital Sculpting

Use these guidelines as you sculpt:

- Work from big to small; focus on the basic shapes first, then refine the details.
- Move the light often to check the shadows on your form.
- Don't feel the need to outline every muscle or shape with a recess—some shapes can and should be subtler than others. This adds variety and interest to the surface.
- Smooth as you work—by building up form and then smoothing back, you can create a subtler surface and avoid the "lumpy" look.
- Try to use the largest sculpting brush size for a particular shape; this helps keep you focused on the big forms first and ensures you don't get bogged down in details too soon.
- Work at the lowest subdivision that can support the form you are trying to make. This also keeps you focused on big shapes over details, and it helps avoid the lumpy look of some digital sculptures.
- Step up and down your subdivision levels often. Don't work at the highest the whole time unless you are working with the Rake and Clay tools.
- Rotate the figure often and work on all areas at once. You shouldn't finish the head before the arms; each part should always be at the same level of finish. This keeps you from having to match one area of the sculpture to another, creating disconnection between the shapes.

Another Take: Gesture, Rhythm, Proportion

Featured Artist: Zack Petroc

You don't have to worry about gesture, rhythm, and proportion in all of your sculpts—only in the ones that you don't want to look lifeless.

Being aware of these foundational concepts, and what they can bring to your art, marks the first step down the endless path that leads toward perfecting your skills. I say *endless* because the more you learn about these concepts, the more you will realize just how complex and intricate their execution can be. To infuse your work with gesture and rhythm is to give it life, and to give it life is to create a work that can transcend its basic visual concept and become a true masterpiece.

No matter the subject—from animal, to human, to creature, to foliage—I always start by trying to understand its gesture and, more importantly, what its gesture is going to convey about the character. A powerful superhero archetype will have a distinctly different gesture than a cowering villain. There are countless conscious and subconscious gesture cues that give instant insight into the nature of your character. Hero types lead with their chest; from a side view, the character's chest is the farthest point forward on the figure. The head is typically pulled back creating a straighter line from the base of the skull to the upper area of the back where the neck inserts into the torso. By pulling the head back and pushing the chest forward, you are automatically creating a larger distance between the front and back of the arm. This allows our hero character to have wider shoulders and larger-than-life upper arms. It's the setup of the gesture, from the head to the chest, that allows all of these proportional cues to be possible. In this respect, the gesture truly is the foundation for our character to be built on.

Rhythm is linked directly with gesture and refers to the visual lines that flow through your character. Increasing your awareness of this concept is the first step toward mastering it. These rhythms are what lead your eye around the form and, when executed properly, convey a sense of movement and direction, even in a static sculpture.

continued

Proportion is a relative thing. When I stand next to Hulk Hogan, my gigantic and, if you will, super-toned upper body might make him appear small. However, we all know that relative to the general public, this is not the case. He is indeed a large man. The same philosophy about relative size can be applied to individual parts that make up a character. For example, one way to make a character appear taller is to make its head smaller. Other, subtler cues to let our viewer know the innately taller stature of our character might be to widen the shoulders while keeping their overall mass smaller. We can also add a slight downward angle to the clavicle as it goes from the sternum to its end at the top of the shoulder. These cues are all taken from real-life proportions of extremely tall people and are therefore subconscious traits that can help convey the believability that our character is indeed tall.

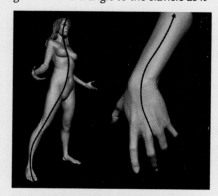

Remember, mastering these concepts can take a lifetime, but becoming aware of them can happen as soon as you would like, and that's all it takes to begin the journey. (Well, that and a gnarly-looking old walking stick. Preferably one with some kind of killer animal head carved into the handle. I would suggest an Orca or some form of rogue badger. This will help get you there in style.)

In the following example, from my sculpting the female figure tutorial on Gnomonology.com, I've drawn black lines over the form to represent the gesture. These long, flowing curves are what the forms were developed around and help give the sculpture character. I typically start by visualizing these curves on screen while I sculpt, then try to push and pull the forms to match them.

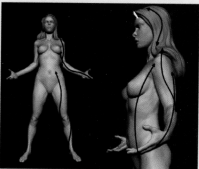

In the next example, we can see the lines of rhythm that flow throughout the sculpture. Note their interaction as they overlap and traverse the form. Even in this somewhat standard pose, the rhythms should be visible and help to indicate a sense of movement.

Proportion plays a key role in defining the "character" of any design. The final image shows how enlarging the head on this sculpture affects the viewer's impression of it. The design appears more childlike, and seems to have a smaller overall stature. An important part of this exercise is to also be aware that none of the finite details were changed. This shows us just how secondary and inconsequential the finite surface details can be if we don't first establish the proper foundation.

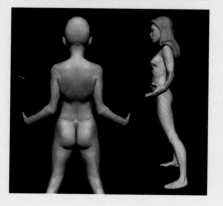

ZBrush Interface General Overview

At first glance, the ZBrush interface (see Figure 1.12) can be a daunting sight, especially if you have previously worked in software like Autodesk Maya, 3ds Max, or XSI. The truth is, it looks far more complex than it actually is. Many menus you won't often visit, and a few will form the backbone of your workflow. In this section, I will give you a brief overview of the interface and the location of some of the major palettes and their functions. This tutorial is designed to introduce you to the sculpting brushes and some of their basic settings. We'll also explore ZBrush's 2.5D Illustration brushes and briefly discuss lighting and rendering within ZBrush. By completing an illustration in ZBrush, we'll touch on each facet of the program and introduce tools and workflows that will be valuable as you progress through the book. We'll delve into each menu in more depth as it becomes pertinent. To begin, it will be good to have a fundamental understanding of what is where and why.

Upon opening ZBrush, you will see the default interface. The central window is called the *document window*. This is where all the sculpting and painting takes place. In ZBrush you import OBJ files as "tools" and sculpt them in the document window. OBJ files are a standard polygon model format most 3D applications will export. For more information on importing to ZBrush see Chapter 3.

Flanking the document window are two columns that contain some quick links to other menus. The left side has fly-out icons linked to the brush, stroke, alpha, texture, and materials menus. Here you will also find a color picker for selecting colors while painting.

The right side contains a selection of icons primarily concerned with navigating the document window and the display of your active tool. It is important to note all these options are available in the top row menus and often the menus (as in the case of Brush, Stroke, Alpha, Texture, and Material) are abridged in the form found here. For all the options, visit the full menu at the top of the screen (the area marked "Brush controls" in Figure 1.12).

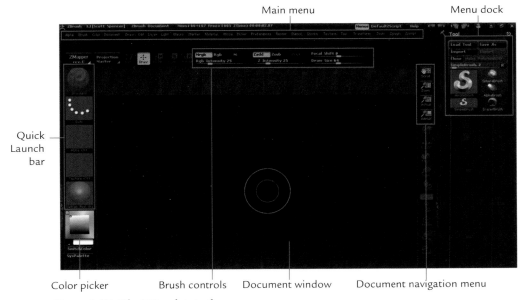

Figure 1.12: The ZBrush interface

The top menu bar allows you to change the various aspects of your active sculpting tool. It contains an alphabetized list of the complete ZBrush menus. The ZBrush interface allows you to work in a circular fashion, picking menus and options as needed. Any main menu can be torn off and docked on the side of the screen by clicking the round radial button. Table 1.1 provides a breakdown of each menu and its major contents.

Table 1.1: ZBrush Menus

Menu	Description
Alpha	Options to import and manipulate alphas, grayscale images primarily used as brush shapes, stencils, and texture stamps.
Brush	Contains the 3D sculpting and painting tools.
Color	Options for selecting colors as well as filling models with color or material.
Document	Options for setting document window size as well as exporting images from ZBrush.
Draw	Settings that define how the brushes affect surfaces. These include ZIntensity, RGB Intensity, ZAdd, ZSub, as well as settings that are specific to 2.5D brushes. This menu also contains the perspective camera setting.
Edit	Contains the undo and redo buttons.
Layer	Options for the creation and management of document layers. These differ from sculpting layers and are typically only used in canvas modeling and illustration.
Light	Create and place lights to illuminate your subject.
Macro	Records ZBrush actions as a button for easy repetition.
Marker	This menu is for MultiMarkers, a legacy ZBrush function that is mostly obsolete with the advent of Subtools.
Material	Surface shaders and material settings. These include both standard materials and MatCap (Material Capture) materials.
Movie	This menu allows you to record videos of your sculpting sessions as well as render rotations of your finished sculptures.
Picker	Options pertaining to how the brushes deal with the surfaces on which they are used. Flatten is one sculpting brush that will be affected by the Once Ori and Cont Ori buttons. For the most part, these options are not used in sculpting.
Preferences	Options to set up your ZBrush preferences. Everything from interface colors to memory management is handled here.
Render	Options for rendering your images inside ZBrush. This menu is only used when doing 2.5D illustration.
Stencil	A close associate of the Alpha menu. Stencil allows you to manipulate alphas you have converted to stencils to help in painting or sculpting details.
Stroke	Options governing the way in which the brush stroke is applied. These options include freehand and spray strokes.
Texture	Menu for creating, importing, and exporting texture maps with ZBrush.
Tool	This is the workhorse of the ZBrush interface. In this menu you will find all options that affect the current active ZTool. Here you will find Subtools, Layers, Deformation, Masking, and Polygroup options as well as many other useful menus. This is the menu in which you are likely to spend the most time (next to Brush). The Tool menu allows you to select tools on which to sculpt as well as select the wide variety of 2.5D tools for canvas modeling and illustration.

continues

Table 1.1: ZBrush Menus (*continued*)

Menu	Description
Transform	Contains document navigation options such as Zoom and Pan and buttons to alter the model's pivot point as well as sculpting symmetry settings and poly frame view.
Zoom	Shows an enlarged view of portions of the canvas. This menu is not often accessed other than to find the Zoom and AAHalf buttons to affect document display size. These buttons are usually available to the screen right menu.
ZPlugin	For accessing plug-ins loaded into ZBrush. Here you will find MD3, which is used for creating displacement maps, as well as ZMapper and other useful utilities.
ZScript	Menu for recording saving and loading ZScripts.

At any time while you are working on a model in Edit mode, right-clicking the mouse will open a pop-up menu at your cursor location. Here you can quickly access your ZIntensity, RGB Intensity, Draw Size, and Focal Shift settings.

Draw Size and Focal Shift control the size of your brush. Draw Size, as is apparent, controls the overall size of the brush, while Focal Shift adjusts the inner ring of your brush icon. This inner circle defines the falloff of the tool or the general hardness of softness of the brush. Falloff means how quickly or gradually the effect of the tool fades at the edges of the stroke. A smaller ring is a much more gradual falloff while a bigger one is an abrupt falloff. If an alpha is selected, the Focal Shift slider acts as a modifier on the alpha softness. Figure 1.13 shows the effects of several Draw Size and Focal Shift combinations. If you want to enter a value manually to the curve, use the slider for brush control at the top shelf of the ZBrush interface.

Brushes can be set to several modes, which determine how they affect the surface. At the top of the screen are buttons for MRGB, RGB, M, Zadd, ZSub, and ZCut. ZAdd and ZSub control whether the brush adds material or takes away with the stroke. MRGB adds material and RGB color, while RGB adds only color and M adds only material. Typically the brushes are set to ZAdd when you are sculpting. It is easy to switch to ZSub by simply holding down the Alt key while you sculpt. This will temporarily swap the modes while the key is pressed. ZCut is used in Pixol (2.5D) mode.

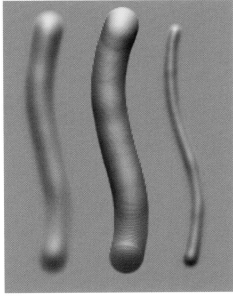

Draw Size 68, Focal Shift 0   Draw Size 68, Focal Shift 68   Draw Size 68, Focal Shift 99

Figure 1.13: Brushes with various falloff settings

Alt and Shift

The Alt key activates the alternate mode for nearly all ZBrush brushes. When sculpting with ZAdd on, holding down Alt will cause the brush to dig in instead of building up form.

Shift serves as a shortcut to the smooth brush. When sculpting, be sure to press Shift to enter Smooth mode. Your draw circle will become blue while Shift is pressed to let you know you are smoothing the surface; typically it is helpful to have a larger smoothing brush than sculpting brush. To change the default size of the Shift smooth brush, adjust the Alt Brush slider at the bottom of the Brush menu.

When a tool is loaded in the document window and you are in Edit mode, navigation is accomplished through a variety of mouse and key combinations.

Rotating is the simplest movement to accomplish. With the mouse off your model in the document window, notice that it becomes a circular arrow. Left-click and drag, and the model will rotate with your movements. To zoom in and out from the model, hold down the Alt key and left-click somewhere on the document window other than the model, release the Alt key, and move the mouse up and down. The object will now appear to zoom in and out. In reality it is scaling, but this differentiation is not important when navigating a ZTool. Panning is accomplished by the same combination of Alt and left-click but you don't release Alt. Simply move the mouse and the object moves with you.

If your model is off center and you want to return to the default view, press the F key to bring it back into focus. Another useful option is the Local button found on the right side of the screen or under the Transform menu. Click Local and your rotations will occur around the last point you edited on the model.

These movements and combinations may take some practice and may seem strange if you are used to other programs, but with a little experience you'll find they become second nature. You can always use the quick navigation icons at the right side of the screen if the button combinations are too difficult.

Customizing the Interface

The ZBrush interface can be fully customized and saved for later sessions. To drag any interface option and dock it elsewhere in the UI, select Preferences → Custom UI → Enable Customize. Now when you hold down Ctrl and click and drag a button from any menu to another part of the interface, you can dock it there for easy access. To save your custom UI for later use, press Ctrl+Shift+I or select Preferences → Config → Store Config. If at any time you want to restore the default interface, select Preferences → Restore Standard UI. For more information on interface customization, see Chapter 4.

Using the ZBrush Tools

In this section we'll explore the ZBrush sculpting tools by creating a lion head door knocker from a 3D Plane tool. This tutorial will expose you to many of the ZBrush sculpting brushes, modifiers, and masking tools.

In ZBrush you can work with models, tools, or documents. For sculpting characters we'll focus on tools and models. When creating final rendered images in ZBrush, you make use of the Document settings.

Creating a 2.5D Pixol Illustration

ZBrush works with essentially three types of objects; models, tools, and documents. Models are geometry that you either create in ZBrush using Primitives and ZSpheres, or obj models imported from third-party applications like 3ds Max or Maya. These models can then become tools when you begin to subdivide and sculpt or paint on the surface. ZTools are a ZBrush file type for storing 3D models with multiple levels of subdivision as well as texture information. Documents are essentially images. Documents are a hybrid between painting and rendering. You can place your ZTools in the document space, light, shade, and render them as a 2.5D illustration.

2.5D illustration is a ZBrush term for an illustration tool that allows you to paint color, materials, and depth. The ZBrush canvas is "depth enabled," which gives ZBrush its powerful image-creation capabilities.

The ZBrush workspace is called the document window. This is where we'll sculpt and paint our characters. The document window has many powerful and unique aspects that are often overlooked when you are not using ZBrush as a purely illustration or concept design tool.

The artist can "drop" tools in the document window, interactively lighting and shading them in 2D. You can even continue to sculpt on your illustration. Although many of the document-based tools are not useful to a production environment outside of the art department, I feel it is important to cover them here as they form the basis of ZBrush's toolset and influence how many of the tools and menus behave.

Documents can make use of layers as well as interactive lighting and rendering, but these cannot be rotated and edited in 3D space; they are composed of *pixols*. Pixols are special pixels that carry color information as well as depth and material data.

For the purposes of sculpting and painting characters, we typically do not use the document settings, but there are some cases where these tools will come in handy. Some brushes, especially those we use in the Projection Master plug-in, are document based, so it is important to understand the distinction between documents and tools as well as how to use them effectively together.

The purpose of this tutorial is to introduce you not only to sculpting in ZBrush but to the different methods of working in the program. While making this door knocker we'll be using primitives, the standard sculpting tools, alphas, and brush strokes. First we'll use ZBrush primitives to sculpt and assemble a door knocker.

Sculpting a Lion's Head

You will begin by sculpting the lion head. For the lion bas-relief we'll use a ZBrush primitive, the Plane3D tool. I want to remind you that I am constantly moving the ZTool as I work, sculpting from all angles. You can see this in the video captures of the tutorial sessions on the DVD with this book. Each tutorial step is cross referenced with the video time code of that section on the video tutorial capture (there is no audio with this video).

1. Under Tool, click the active tool icon and select Plane3D. Click and drag on the canvas with the left mouse button to draw the tool (video time code: 00:00:19).

2. Before we can edit this, we need to enter Edit mode. Press T on your keyboard or click the Edit button at the top of the screen (Figure 1.14). If you neglect to enter Edit mode after drawing a model on the canvas, ZBrush will continue to add copies to the document window, dropping each one to the canvas as you go.

3. To change materials, open the Material menu. ZBrush has several default materials available to you. Typically I use the MatCap White Cavity shader over the default red wax. The translucency in red wax makes spotting surface form a little tricky. Click the current material box at the left of the screen or under the Material menu to open the Material Palette window. From this palette select the icon swatch for the material you prefer. For this tutorial I used the White Cavity shader. It is under MatCap Materials in the Material Browser.

4. The plane is now in Edit mode, but this is a ZBrush primitive and not a polymesh. Polymeshes are polygonal 3D models that can be subdivided and sculpted inside ZBrush. Models imported into ZBrush are polymeshes by default, but meshes we create from primitives need to be converted with the Make PolyMesh3D button under the Tool menu. This converts the ZBrush primitive into a polymesh, which we can now use to sculpt on.

Figure 1.14: Edit mode can be accessed via this button at the top of your screen or by pressing the T key.

At this stage, let's activate sculpting symmetry. This allows you to sculpt one side of the lion's face while the other side automatically mirrors your changes. To turn on Symmetry, press the X key on the keyboard to activate X symmetry. The full symmetry options are located under the Main Transform Menu at the top of the screen. To access the options click select Transform → Activate Symmetry. You'll see a red dot on the other side of your model that mirrors your brush strokes. It is generally a good idea to start a sculpture with Symmetry turned on. Always turn off Symmetry in the final stages to add another level of realism by breaking the perfect balance between the forms, or adding little differences between the sides.

At this time you may also turn on Perspective Camera. By default ZBrush uses an orthographic camera, but if you want a view that is more natural click Draw → Persp to activate the perspective view. Focal length can be adjusted with the Focal Length slider. Figure 1.15 shows the visual difference between Perspective and Orthographic modes.

5. You may now sculpt on the surface of the plane. At the top of the screen select the Brush menu and tear it off with the circle icon so it docks to the side of the screen for easy access. Click the active tool icon and select the Standard brush. You want to make sure your Stroke is set to Freehand and that Alpha is turned off. Set your Draw Size to about ¼ the plane size and leave Focal Shift at 0 and ZIntensity to 20. Your Brush, Alpha, and Stroke settings can also be accessed via the left screen menu shown in Figure 1.16.

Figure 1.16: This menu at the left side of the screen allows you to select your brush, alpha, stroke, and texture.

Figure 1.15: ZTool with Perspective mode on (right) and off (left)

Mouse Average and LazyMouse

Under the Stroke menu you will find several options that affect how your brush is drawn across the surface of the sculpture. The Freehand stroke is the most widely used as it behaves like a paintbrush tool in Photoshop. Mouse Average is used to average the instances of each alpha as you stroke along the surface. This can reduce "stuttering" in the stroke or dotting when working at higher subdivision levels. When working on lower levels, keep this set to 1.

Also in this menu you will find LazyMouse. LazyMouse is another averaging utility that delays your pen stroke so it appears at the end of a red line extending from your brush center. This is very useful when you're trying to sculpt long, sweeping curves that might otherwise be extremely difficult to achieve freehand. The image here illustrates the differences in these two stroke options; the staggered stroke on the left was created without Lazy-Mouse, and the smoother stroke on the right was drawn with LazyMouse.

6. Click and draw on the model surface now, and you will see it begin to pull at the polygons. The effect is faceted because we are currently at the lowest subdivision level (Figure 1.17). You can add geometry by subdividing the model once with Tool → Geometry → Divide to add one subdivision level.

To add a subdivision level use Ctrl+D; to step up your subdivision levels, press D; to step down, press Shift+D.

---

7. Begin to block in the basic form of the lion head (Figure 1.18, video time code: 00:02:17). Remember to add as well as subtract with your brush and rotate often around the shape. Don't get overwhelmed with making little details at this stage. Instead, establish the primary forms of the lion's face and their positions in relation to each other.

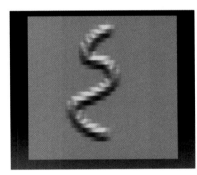

Figure 1.17: When sculpting at lower subdivision levels, the strokes will appear faceted.

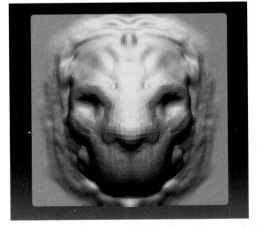

Figure 1.18: Shape roughed in from front and side

This is easier to do by moving often and working the entire sculpture at once. If you spend too long in one view, the sculpture tends to flatten out. If you sculpted entirely from one view, it may look great until you move the model. A single view can be misleading. Looking at the sculpt in Figure 1.19, it is difficult to perceive the flattening, which is obvious when viewed from the side. This is why you want to be sure to rotate often while you work. Figure 1.20 shows how I corrected the flattening from the top view.

> Don't neglect looking at the sculpture from the top and bottom. Typically the viewer won't see it from such an extreme view, but it helps you quickly identify whether the forms of the face are flattening out or turning nicely in space, as shown in Figure 1.20.

Figure 1.19: Objects may look fine from the front while lacking depth when viewed from other angles.

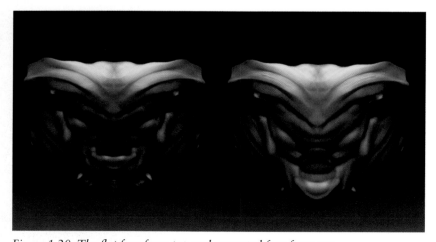

Figure 1.20: The flat face from top and corrected face from top

8. While working, establish the forms that are advancing in space, like the snout and brows, as well as those that recede, such as the eye sockets and mouth (video time code: 00:09:49). You can cut in with your brush by clicking the ZSub button at the top menu bar or by simply holding down the Alt key while you sculpt.

9. To quickly bring the faces of the snout forward and create depth in the head, in a three-quarter view use the Move brush (Figure 1.21). The Move brush will grab and pull vertices underneath the draw radius. Use the Intensity slider to increase the strength of the move. I also use the Move brush to pull the points of the square plane into silhouette with the outline of the lion's mane.

Everyone uses the sculpting tools differently. You find the combination that works for you through experimentation and emulation. Sketching character heads or faces on primitive spheres and planes makes for great practice.

At this stage you can add another subdivision level to allow yourself more material to sculpt on. Continue to use the Standard, Inflate, and Clay brushes to define the head and mane. Notice that I am stroking in a general direction for the sculpted hair as I mass out its form (Figure 1.22).

At this point I begin to carve away the recess where the ring will fit into the lion's mouth (Figure 1.23, video time code: 00:20:25).

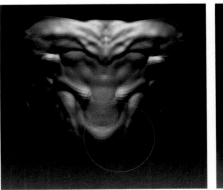 

Figure 1.21: Pulling the snout forward from the top and side views

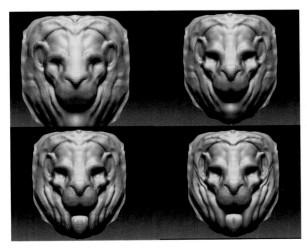 

Figure 1.22: Progress shots

Figure 1.23: Sculpting a recessed area for the ring to sit

Adding Subtools

Now that the basic form of the lion is established, let's add the ring to his mouth. Adding the ring at this stage will allow us to sculpt the forms of his mane and mouth around the ring so it appears that the two parts are interacting.

1. To add a subtool, you must append it into your current ZTool. Save your ZTool and then return to the Tool menu. Select the current tool icon and pick the Ring3D tool. Once again we are dealing with a ZBrush primitive and not a polymesh. While an object is a primitive, we cannot sculpt but we can change the object's parameters. In the case of the ring, we want to make it smaller. Select Tool → Initialize, and change the ring Radius to 21 (Figure 1.24, video time code: 00:21:37).

Figure 1.24: The Initialize menu allows you to change aspects of the ZBrush primitives before they are converted to polymeshes.

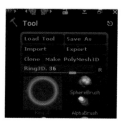

Figure 1.25: Make PolyMesh3D button

2. To make this ring ready for inclusion with the rest of the lion head, convert it to a polymesh. Click the Tool menu at the top of the screen and click the Make PolyMesh3D button (Figure 1.25).

3. To add this to the lion head as a subtool so you can manipulate both models on screen at once, you must append it to the current tool. At the top of the screen click Tool → Subtool. In the Subtool menu is a button marked Append; click it and a flyout menu will appear showing all the currently loaded ZTools. From this menu select the Lion tool. This will add the Lion ZTool as a subtool to the ring (Figure 1.26). Subtools combine multiple ZTools together into one, allowing you to sculpt and manipulate each separately while retaining their positional relationship to each other. Later in this book we'll use them for placing eyes and other accessories into a character while retaining multiple levels of subdivision on each tool.

Figure 1.26: Clicking the Append button will open a menu from which you can select the tool you want to add as a subtool.

Navigating Subtools

You may only sculpt on one subtool at a time. To set your active subtool, select it under the Subtool menu. Alternately you can Ctrl+Shift-click the object in the document window to activate that subtool.

To toggle subtool visibility, use the eyeball icon. You can set visibility on any subtools, active or not. To show all subtools, click the eyeball icon on the active tool to hide all but the current subtool. Ctrl+Shift-click the subtool in the Subtool list.

The ring should now be centered in the lion's head. It must be moved down into the mouth area we created for it. There are three methods of moving objects and faces in ZBrush that are useful for different tasks (described in a moment). To move the ring, we'll use the Transpose tools.

4. Enter Transpose mode by pressing W. You will now have a transpose line on the screen. Click on the 3D ring and drag to a point on the canvas to draw a new transpose line (Figure 1.27). Because we are in Move mode at the top of the screen, this will allow us to move the ring (Figure 1.28, video time code: 00:23:02). Notice that there are two other buttons, for Scale and Rotate, respectively. If these buttons are active, the transpose line will scale or rotate the ZTool instead of moving it. The transpose ring can be repositioned by clicking on the line itself, or to move an endpoint click on one of the three circles. To use the transpose line to manipulate the currently selected subtool, click inside one of the three circles and drag with the mouse.

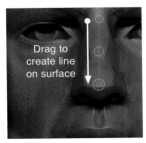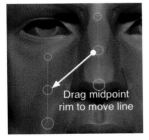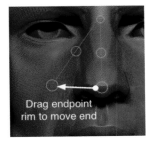

Figure1.27: Using the Transpose tool

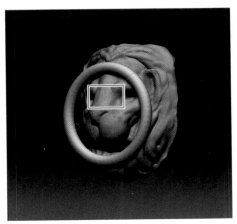

Figure 1.28: Ring with transpose line: click and drag in the center of the indicated circle to move the ring.

Moving in ZBrush

"Moving" in ZBrush can refer to moving ZTools in relation to each other, moving in relation to the canvas, or moving polygons as a group with a brush. There are three methods of moving inside ZBrush:

- Transpose: Designed for posing models
- Move brush: Moves polys and faces with a brush when sculpting large forms
- Document Move gyro: Moves objects in relation to the canvas

5. Click in the center circle and drag. You can see how the Ring3D tool can be easily moved and placed in space. If you need to move it back from your view, simply rotate the model so you are looking down on it. Place it approximately in the lion's mouth. We'll use the Move brush to adjust the shape of the mouth to better grip the ring (Figure 1.29).

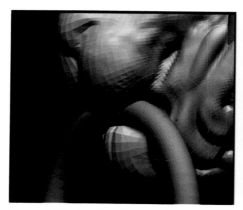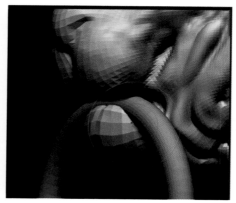

Figure 1.29: Moving the mouth into position with the Move brush

Refining Your Model

Now that we have roughed in the lion head and placed a subtool, we can begin to refine the forms of the sculpture overall. In this section we'll continue to use the sculpting brushes to make the rough shapes relate to each other and create a sense of rhythm in the forms. Before we start, let's take a moment to look at some of the new tools and modifiers we'll use in this section, specifically the LazyMouse Pinch brush and BrushMod sliders.

1. At this stage, let's develop the mane. Add another subdivision level by pressing Ctrl+D. There will be a level of stylization to the planes of the hair. We want to create sweeping arcs that transition from the top of the head to the chin. To create smooth-flowing strokes like this with hard edges, use the Pinch brush. Select the Pinch brush and set your Brush-Mod slider to 60 and your ZIntensity to 15 (Figure 1.30).

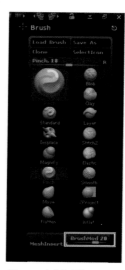

Figure 1.30: The BrushMod slider

As you stroke along the surface, notice how it pulls the edges together and up (Figure 1.31, video time code: 00:27:11).

If you set the brush slider to –60, the inverse happens: it presses in while it pinches. I keep the slider at 60 and use the Alt key to invert my stroke to press in when needed.

2. You can further control the sweep and smoothness in the strokes of the mane by using the LazyMouse option. This technique will average the stroke and help you create a sweeping line. Press the L hotkey or select Stroke → LazyMouse (Figure 1.32).

The red line that trails slightly behind your stroke is the center of the influence (Figure 1.33). This delay built into the LazyMouse stroke is what allows you to make long sweeping motions with the brush tools that would otherwise be difficult, if not impossible, with an unassisted freehand approach.

Figure 1.31: The cross sections show the Pinch brush stroke with different BrushMod settings.

Figure 1.32: The Lazy-Mouse button on the Stroke menu

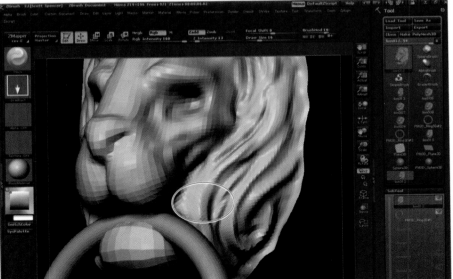

Figure 1.33: Lazy-Mouse in use. Notice the red action line, which offers visual feedback on where the effect of the stroke is on the surface.

Figure 1.34: The mouth and mane sculpted to flow around the ring

3. With the ring in place, return to Draw mode by pressing Q. Change the selected subtool from the ring back to the lion head (select the subtool from the Tool → Subtool menu or by Ctrl+Shift-clicking the lion head in the document window). You will notice the lion head becomes a lighter shade when selected.

4. Select the Move brush from the brush palette and tumble to a side view. Adjust your draw size and pull the lower jaw up and around the ring (Figure 1.34, video time code: 00:25:07). If the Move tool isn't working strong enough, raise your ZIntensity slider to increase its power. You may also want to turn on subtool transparency with the Transp button at the right side of the screen. This allows you to see through subtools in front of your active tool but also allows your tool to sculpt through to the hidden surface.

5. Continue to pull strokes in the mane, keeping in mind the gesture of the lines and how they flow down into the ring. Keep looking for the overall graphic quality of the shapes and trying to maintain a visually appealing rhythm. When using LazyMouse for a long fluid stroke, try setting your ZIntensity lower than necessary and using the Replay Last command to repeat your stroke, building up to the form you want by repeating. Replay Last is found on the Stroke menu, or use the Ctrl+1 shortcut. Each time you use Replay Last, the same stroke repeats and thus builds up its effect on the surface.

Some of the deep recesses could benefit from being tightened. Doing this from the front of your sculpture can sometimes be tricky if the area you want to tighten is small or close to other details you want to remain unchanged. Often you will pinch the faces on either side and inadvertently change areas you wanted to remain unchanged. Masking into tight areas can also sometimes be a challenge. One unique solution to this in ZBrush is that you can sculpt from inside the model as well as the outside.

6. Select Tool → Display Properties and click the Double button to activate double-sided rendering (Figure 1.35). Now when you rotate around the back of the lion head, you can sculpt from the inside (Figure 1.36). This is very helpful in tight areas like the creases in the hair or the eyelids.

Figure 1.35: The Double button in the display options allows you to turn on double-sided rendering in the display.

7. From the front, draw a masking line by Ctrl-clicking and dragging to mark the area you want to pinch. This is just a visual note so the same area can be seen easily from the inside. Masking displays on both sides of a face (Figure 1.37).

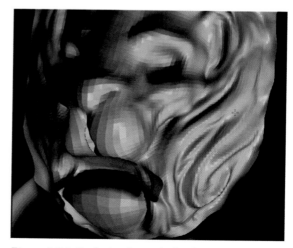

Figure 1.36: Sculpting from the back

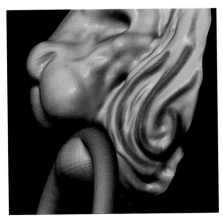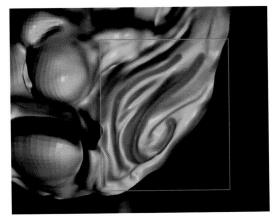

Figure 1.37: With double-sided rendering on, you can sculpt from inside the model as well as outside for reaching tight areas (the right image shows the mask stroke as seen from the back of the mesh).

You can mask out areas you don't want to affect with your strokes by pressing the Ctrl key. Your cursor turns yellow to let you know you are in masking mode. To paint out part of a mask, use Ctrl+Alt-click. To mask large areas, Ctrl-click outside the model and drag a masking rectangle. Also experiment with the Lasso tool for making more specific and complex mask selections. Turn on Lasso with the Lasso button ▣ at the right side of the screen or under the Transform menu. The Lasso button alters the way both masks and hide selections are drawn. Instead of a single rectangle, you can freehand draw a lasso around the desired area.

8. Rotate to the back and locate your masked line. Clear the mask by Ctrl-dragging on the document window or by choosing Tool → Masking → Clear and using the Pinch brush to deepen and sharpen the line. Use a BrushMod setting of 60 and a small Draw Size and Focal Shift of 0. I also use the Pinch brush to refine the planes in the head. I want to add a stylized planar feel to the lion's face while still maintaining the character of a lion.

9. To sculpt eyes directly into this mesh, begin with the Inflate brush at a low intensity and build up the spherical shape of the eyeball (Figure 1.38, video time code: 00:58:58).

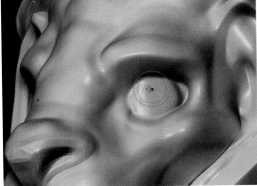

Figure 1.38: Inflating the eyeballs from the mesh

Adding the eyes is easy with masking. While holding down Ctrl, draw a mask in the shape of the eyelids over and around this basic sphere shape. Once the shape of the exposed eye is masked in, you can invert the mask by Ctrl-clicking the document window somewhere off the model (Figure 1.39).

Your eye is now unmasked while the rest of the head is masked. Use the Move brush from the side view to pull the eye in slightly (Figure 1.39). This will create the thickness of the eyelids. Using the Inflate brush, build out the sphere of the eyeball and corneal bulge.

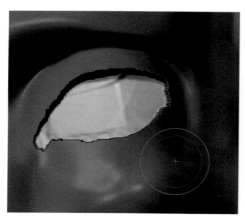
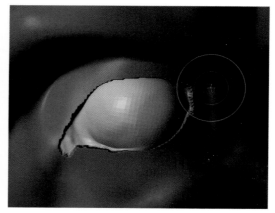

Figure 1.39: Using Masking to help sculpt an eye from the mesh

10. Ctrl-click off the model to invert the mask so the eye surface is masked. Refine the edge of the eyelid with the standard brush and LazyMouse, adding some thickness here.

> While you sculpt, be sure to move between the subdivision levels. Always work at the lowest level that can support the form you are trying to add. If you sculpt the entire time at the highest level, it becomes very hard to make big changes to the shape without creating a lumpy surface.

11. With the Pinch brush and LazyMouse on, pinch the outer edge of the eyelid (Figure 1.40). Be sure to reduce your draw size. At this stage, I also alternate to pinching in with the Alt key to add some subtle wrinkles around the upper eyelid and indicate the furrow at the bottom of the eye where the sphere of the eyeball dips into the skull (video time code: 01:06:36).

12. Pinch the inner edge closest to the eyeball (Figure 1.41). Hold down Alt to pinch in instead of out. Add the medial canthus of the eye and tear duct with the standard brush. Mask out the little dot of skin in the corner of the eye to create the membrane. Invert the mask and inflate slightly with a low intensity.

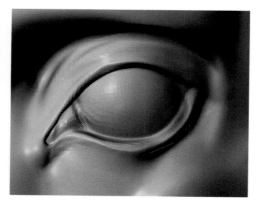

Figure 1.40: Pinch the eyelids to crease them and create sharper transitions. Notice the thickness added to the eyelids in Step 10.

Figure 1.41: Pinching the inner eyelid edges

Finishing Your Model

The following list represents some of the edits to this sculpture to bring it to completion:

- Add the tear duct to the eyes. These little details are extremely important, even on a stylized eye such as this.
- Raise the ears higher on the head to give a more feline-like appearance.
- Increase the slope in toward the jaw and pull the side curls out at an angle. While I made these edits I was looking for a visually pleasing stylization to the lines in the head and hair. The gesture of the curves implied by the mane leads your eye in a figure-8 around the sculpture.

Creating a 2.5D Pixol Illustration

At this stage, the basic sculpture of the lion's head is complete, but so much more is possible here. If you would like to see how this sculpture is incorporated into a 2.5D illustration—with additional details like a backing plate and with the door textured and stained—please see the DVD for a PDF file which continues this project as an illustration (Figure 1.42). I encourage you to look at this material since ZBrush is a powerful illustration tool and many of its sculpting techniques are built on this foundation.

These techniques are useful to the digital illustrator as well as when conceptualizing a character with ZBrush. Even though you can export your work to external renderers for animation and rendering I wanted to show the power of ZBrush as a rendering and illustration tool in itself. These are often overlooked aspects of the program but they are powerful tools to have in your arsenal even if you never do 2.5D illustration. Many of these tools are usable on 3D models in edit mode using the Projection Master script. Projection master will allow us to blend 3D sculpting with the 2.5D tools to create highly detailed models for export to other applications. In Chapter 2 we'll look more in depth look at sculpting a bust in ZBrush.

Figure 1.42: The final 2.5D illustration created in the bonus section on the DVD. By sculpting the lion head knocker as a 3D object and combining it with canvas elements, a complex scene is created.

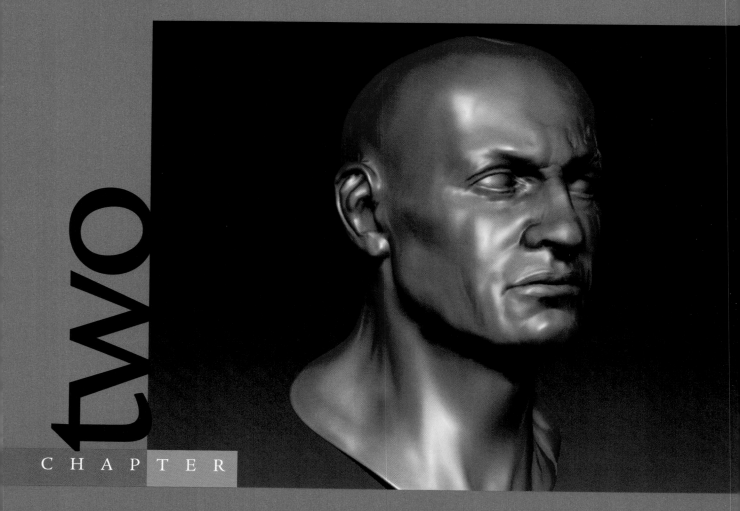

two

Sculpting in ZBrush

In this chapter *we'll continue to explore the tools and techniques for sculpting in ZBrush. We'll start by using a ZBrush primitive sphere as a base to sculpt a human skull. During this process, we'll pay special attention to the anatomical forms and relative proportions of the skull. Once the skull is roughed in using the Rake and Clay tools, we'll mass out the muscular tissues and build a human head.*

In this chapter I'll introduce many of ZBrush's powerful sculpting tools as well as some important aspects of human anatomy. It is important to inform your character work with real anatomy—even if it is a fantasy character. If you understand the bone and muscle that influences surface forms, your creature and character work in ZBrush will be all the more convincing.

An Approach to Sculpting

Starting a head from a simple sphere primitive has several benefits. Sculpting character heads from spheres in ZBrush is a valuable exercise, similar to sketching on paper or with a digital ball of clay. Also, approaching a complex form in ZBrush from such a simple primitive helps to illustrate how topology in ZBrush is not a major concern, provided that the polygon count of your base model is low enough that it can be subdivided to the maximum level. The higher your subdivision levels, the more polygons you will have to push and pull into the shapes you need. Please see the DVD for a video of the head sculpture from this chapter. You will also find a bonus DVD of an alien sculpture which was created from a ZBrush primitive sphere.

At this time I'd like to introduce you to the concept of multiresolution editing. Multi-resolution editing means that changes you make at level 1 on a ZTool telegraph all the way up to the highest subdivision level; changes at the high levels are telegraphed down to level 1 (Figure 2.1).

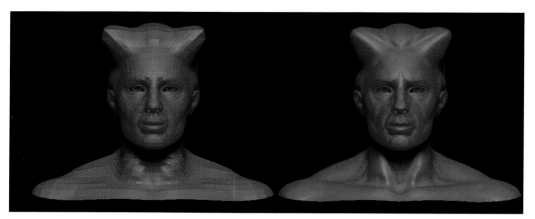

Figure 2.1: The head on the left was altered with the Move tool at level 1. Stepping up to level 3, the changes are telegraphed through each subdivision level and affect each one. (Head by Ryan Kingslein)

Because of this interaction between subdivision levels, when the artist works at the lowest possible level, any forms made will translate to the higher levels. This workflow helps reinforce the "big shapes to smaller details" we discussed in Chapter 1. When you create the big shapes first and work down to the details, your sculpture maintains a solid sense of form. By working at lower subdivision levels, you won't deal with enough geometry to become lost in details. This ensures that you focus on big shapes first and then add details as you begin to subdivide. This is the process we used in Chapter 1 for the lion head. This kind of approach also helps create a smooth and organic surface without the "lumpiness" seen in some ZBrush models.

Although it is desirable to work at the lowest possible subdivision level for the form you are creating, some ZBrush brushes work differently at the higher subdivision levels. The Rake and Clay brushes, for example, are more effective at the higher subdivision levels. The kind of form that these brushes build is rough, so the focus is still on building basic large shapes first and then working down to the details. This is closer to sculpting in actual clay, as you use larger rakes and broad strokes to create base forms and then refine them with tighter and smaller strokes until the surface is smoothed and finished. This latter process is the one we'll use for the human head sketch in this chapter. I use a combination of both working on the lowest levels with some brushes and then higher levels with Clay and Rake tools, but it is important to understand each approach and its merits. Most of all, always remember to work on the biggest shapes first and work your way down to the details.

The Brush Manager

The Brush menu contains all the real-time sculpting tools that you will use while working on an active tool in the document window. These brushes can be used on the model at multiple subdivision levels while you freely rotate in Edit mode.

Figure 2.2: The Brush Manager window

You may notice there are brushes available under the Tool menu. One of these brushes is called the Simple Brush. We explore these in the bonus Chapter 1 on the DVD. These are 2.5D painting brushes and are not to be confused with 3D sculpting brushes, which can be found in the Brush palette. In this chapter, we'll focus on the Brush palette tools, which can be used on a model that is in Edit mode. The Brush palette contains a versatile selection of brushes and brush modifiers (see Figure 2.2). It also allows artists to create and store their own custom brush variations that are loaded each time ZBrush starts. Several specialized masking options are also available, as well as control curves to facilitate altering the way the brushes interact with the surface.

At the top of the Brush Manager window you will find a selection of brush icons. These represent the most recently used brushes and are not representative of the full brush set. To access the complete selection of brushes, click the active brush icon. The active brush icon is the large button in the upper left of the Brush menu as well as the upper left of the standard interface. This opens the brush fly-out menu (Figure 2.3).

Figure 2.3: Clicking the active brush icon expands the Brush menu fly-out.

Beneath the brush icons are several sliders, curves, and icons. These represent the many different modifiers you can apply to your brush. The most important is the BrushMod slider. The BrushMod slider affects each brush differently depending on the brush selected. For instance, when Pinch is selected BrushMod determines whether the brush pinches in or out (Figure 2.4); however, when you're using the Smooth brush, BrushMod controls the height of the smoothing effect (Figure 2.5). We used this slider to affect the Pinch brush when working on the lion head in Chapter 1.

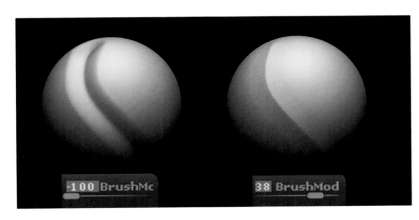

Figure 2.4: The BrushMod slider changes each brush differently. When using Pinch, the slider determines if faces pinch in or out.

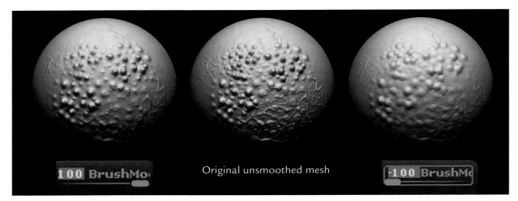

Figure 2.5a: The BrushMod slider determines if the smooth brush affects the recesses or the high points of the sculpted detail. (The center image is the original, unmodified mesh.)

Table 2.1 describes the most frequently used ZBrush sculpting tools.

Table 2.1: The Essential ZBrush Sculpting Brushes

Brush	Description
Standard brush	The default ZBrush sculpting brush. Pulls faces directly out in the direction of the surface normal under the center of the brush.
Move brush	Moves faces as a whole beneath the brush falloff.
Elastic brush	Similar to Inflate but the Elastic brush retains more of the underlying surface forms.
Displace brush	This brush works similarly to the Standard brush, but keeps the details intact in such a way as to suggest that the form underneath has swelled or been displaced.
Inflate brush	Pulls faces out along their surface normal direction as opposed to one normal direction as with the Standard brush.
Magnify brush	Magnifies the faces underneath.
Blob brush	This brush is particularly good at producing certain organic effects very quickly. In contrast to other brushes, the uniformity of its stroke is affected by irregularities in the surface under the stroke, which means that it typically produces short, irregular blobs (hence the name). This won't be so apparent if it is used on smooth surfaces. The Blob slider determines whether the brush pulls the surface out or pushes it in.
Pinch brush	Pulls faces together. The BrushMod slider affects whether the faces are pulled in to a peak (100) or down in a valley (–100) or together in a flat (0).
Flatten brush	Pulls or pushes faces to a single plane depending on the BrushMod slider setting.
Clay brush	This is a general-purpose brush for sculpting with alphas. The Clay slider scales the alpha as a whole; this affects not only the intensity of the sculpt, but also the size (width and height) of the brush stroke. The standard ZIntensity control affects the magnitude of the alpha up/down displacement effect, but does not affect the size of the alpha.

continues

Brush	Description
Morph brush	Blends between the current mesh and a stored morph target.
Layer brush	Adds a single layer of depth. ZIntensity determines the amount the Layer brush displaces a surface outward (if ZAdd is selected) or inward (if ZSub is selected).
Nudge brush	Slides edges along the surface.
SnakeHook brush	Pulls faces out into a tapered horn-like shape.
ZProject brush	Projects depth or color onto the current mesh.
Smooth brush	Smoothes the underlying geometry: BrushMod 100 smoothes recesses, BrushMod –100 smooths high points.
Mesh Insert brush	Inserts other meshes into the current tool.

For more information on the brushes, visit the ZBrush wiki:
`http://www.zbrush.info/docs/index.php/Brush_Types`

The Difference between the Standard and Inflate brushes lies in how the faces are pulled out from the surface. The Standard brush pulls all faces beneath the brush out or in a single direction. The Inflate brush pulls faces out along the normal of the face. The surface normal is the direction that points straight out from any 4 points. The image in Figure 2.5b illustrates this difference.

Other brushes such as Mallet Gouge and Stitch are available. These are specialty brushes, which are created by combining existing brushes, strokes, and alphas. These specialty brushes are based on macros from ZBrush 3.0. Experiment with these brushes on a sphere or plane to see the effect they have.

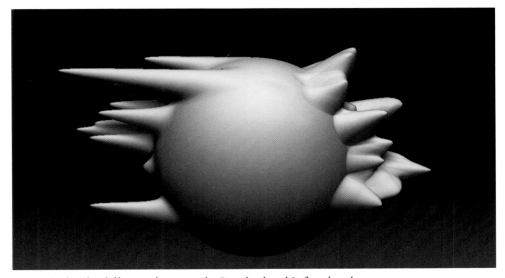

Figure 2.5b: The difference between the Standard and Inflate brushes

The Brush Modifiers

In addition to BrushMod, the Brush menu contains several more options for modifying brush behavior. See Table 2.2 for descriptions of these other options.

Table 2.2: The Brush Menu Options

Brush Menu Option	Description
Mesh Insert button	Selects the mesh used by the Mesh Insert brush.
BrushMod	Modifies brush behavior.
AlphaTile	Tiles the currently selected alpha through the stroke.
AllignToPath	Controls how closely the selected alpha follows your brush stroke.
WrapMode	Wraps your sculpting from one side of the mesh to the other as well as tiling your sculpting within a 1 to 1 ratio.
AccuCurve	Accurate Curve mode forces ZBrush to follow the Edit curve for the brush effect.
Samples	Controls how much of the surface beneath the stroke is affected.
Gravity Strength	Using the Gravity direction arrow caused the stroke to pull faces in the set direction, helping to create the effect of gravity or wind.
Cavity Mask	Masks recessed areas of the model from your strokes; this option is also available under Tool → Masking with Visual Feedback.
BackFaceMask	When you're working with thin models like clothes or wings, this option prevents brush strokes from affecting the opposite side of the model.
Color Mask	Masks by color intensity.
Edit Curve	Allows finer control of the brush curve.
Smoothing Curve	Controls the strength of the smooth brush.
AltBrush	When you press the Shift key, this is the alternate brush size. Use it to make a slightly larger smooth brush.
AutoSmooth	Smooth while sculpting. Usually best to leave this option set to 0.

Brushes are further modified by alphas and strokes. *Alphas* are grayscale images that are imported into ZBrush or selected from the default alpha set. They serve as the shape of the brush itself. Alphas can also serve as stencils or texture stamps, which we'll cover in Chapter 4. Figure 2.6 illustrates the effect of various alphas combined with different strokes.

Alphas are grayscale images that control the shape of the brush. Strokes control how the alpha is applied to the surface by the selected brush.

The Edit curve controls the strength of a brush over the course of its center to the outermost falloff ring. The point on the left of the curve represents the brush strength at its outer radius, whereas the point at the right represents the strength of the effect at the brush's center. Manipulating the Edit curve can create many interesting brush effects, as you can see in Figure 2.7.

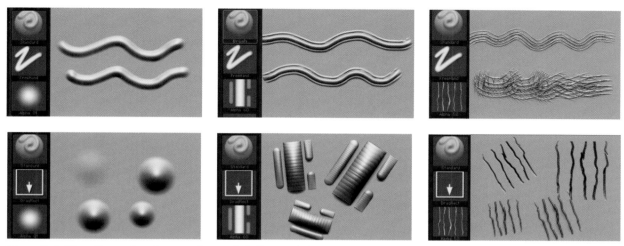

Figure 2.6: The effects of various strokes with different alphas

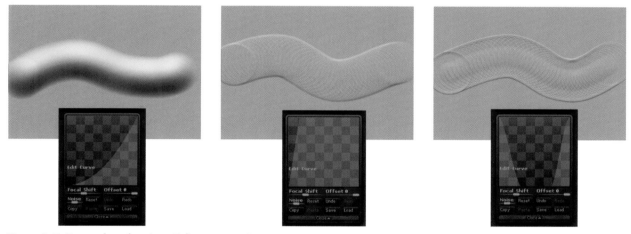

Figure 2.7: Examples of various Edit curve settings

One common edit I make to the Edit curve is what I call creating a "plateau" with the brush curve. By selecting the Inflate brush and changing its Edit curve to that shown in Figure 2.8, I can drastically alter the manner in which the brush adds form to the surface. By giving the brush a more subtle falloff, strokes build in a more gradual fashion, thus making it easier to create changes in the surface that are less pronounced.

Backface masking is useful when you're working on thin meshes such as clothes, wings, or other objects where the front and back faces are close together. If you are dragging a stroke on an object where the thickness is less than the size of the brush, often the stroke will carry over to the opposite side. Backface masking eliminates any faces other than the ones on the side on which you are working, thus reducing this problem.

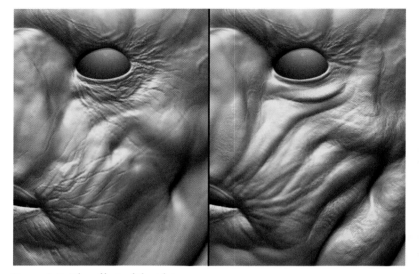

Figure 2.8: The effect of the plateau curve

The Gravity modifier helps reproduce the effect of gravity or wind on a surface. Faces are shifted in the direction of the arrow in relation to the model's current position on screen. To use this modifier, select the Gravity arrow and position it in the direction you want the force to pull. Then, adjust the slider for the correct strength. This works well for folds of skin with the Inflate or Elastic brush; it helps introduce the effect of weight on hanging folds of flesh. The Gravity modifier is also helpful when you're sculpting drapery—positioning the arrow horizontally can create the impression of wind billowing in a fabric. In Figure 2.9, the elastic brush was used to create the strokes on the top. On the bottom, the same brush was used with the addition of a Gravity modifier. Notice how the weight

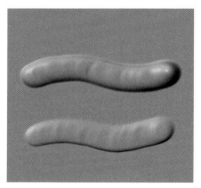

Figure 2.9: The Gravity modifier mimics the effect of gravity on the stroke.

of the stroke is along the bottom edge as if it is being pulled down. Keep in mind that this effect is relative to the model's position on the canvas at the moment of the stroke, not its pivot point.

Cavity masking masks out the recessed areas of the sculpture, allowing you to paint and sculpt only on the high points. This effect can be blurred or inverted with the options available in the Cavity Masking menu. This same mask is also available under Tool → Masking → Mask by Cavity. Figure 2.10 illustrates the effect of this button. The difference between the cavity masking in these two areas is that the Cavity Masking command in the Brush menu is controlled by the curve but there is no visual indication of what areas are masked. Brush-based cavity masking is a real-time masking function that updates and changes as you sculpt the mesh, whereas the command in the Masking submenu is applied once and does not change in real time. When using Tool → Masking → Mask by Cavity, you'll see which areas are masked; however, the lack of a curve offers less control over the strength and spread of the masking effect. In addition, there is no real-time update as you sculpt (Figure 2.11).

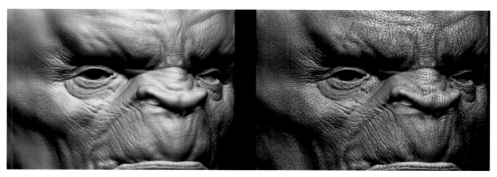

Figure 2.10: Cavity masking isolates the high or low points of the surface from editing.

Figure 2.11: A cavity mask from Tool → Masking → Mask by Cavity

Saving Custom Brushes

The Brush Manager makes saving your own custom brushes simple. In this section, you will create a custom version of the Smooth brush. This brush will be saved in the default ZBrush brushes folder, where it will be loaded each time ZBrush starts.

In Figure 2.12, notice how the Smooth brush can overpower the surface, removing much more form than you might intend. By adjusting the Smoothing Curve and Smooth brush settings, we'll create a brush that does not have this effect. We can then save it as a custom brush for later use.

On the book's DVD you'll find a selection of custom brushes, including this one, called softSmooth. Experiment with these brushes and make your own. After getting some experience with the ZBrush toolset and customizing some brushes, you can build a personal library of brushes. Follow these steps to create and save your own custom brush.

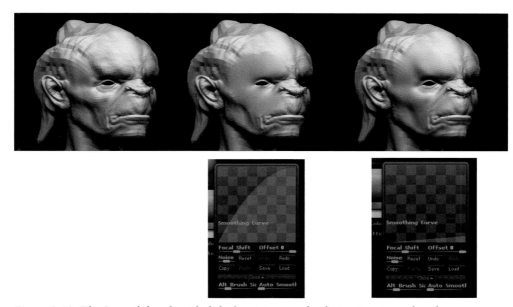

Figure 2.12: The Smooth brush with default settings can be destructive to surface forms.

Here are the steps to create a custom brush:

Figure 2.13: Modify the Smoothing Curve to look like this to create our custom soft-Smooth brush.

1. Select the Smooth brush from the Brush palette. Set BrushMod to 0 and click the Clone button. This creates a copy of the Smooth brush that we can alter rather than replacing the brush.

2. Scroll to the bottom of the Brush menu. Expand the Smoothing Curve window by clicking on it. Select the farthest right point and drag it down. The curve should look like Figure 2.13.

   This ensures the brush will be weaker at its center of influence than the default Smooth. The far-left point represents the strength of the brush at the outermost ring; the right point represents the strength at the center of the brush. Try this brush on a surface. Notice how the effect is much softer and less destructive.

3. To save this brush, click Save As and name the new brush **softSmooth**. If you save in `Zbrush/Zstartup/brushPresets`, the brush will be available each time you start ZBrush. The Brush Manager will also save any alpha and stroke settings when you save the brush.

The Clay Brushes

ZBrush 3 includes several brushes designed to take advantage of the ability to interactively sculpt millions of polygons. These brushes work on the highest subdivision levels of the ZTool; I call them the Clay brushes. They include Clay, Claytubes, Snakehook, and Rake, as well as several brushes that are variations on these, such as Mallet, Slash, and Gouge.

The Clay brushes are designed to take advantage of the capability to manipulate millions of polygons in real time. Unlike the Standard, Inflate, and Layer brushes, the Clay brushes function best when the mesh is at a higher subdivision level. These brushes add material in a loose organic stroke, which feels like actual clay. Figure 2.14 shows the difference in the same stroke on a low poly sphere and a higher subdivided one. The sphere on the left is 8,000 faces while the one on the right is 2 million. ZBrush will allow you to subdivide any mesh to a level that the current machine can handle based on how much physical RAM is installed. In Chapter 3 we'll discuss base meshes and optimizing for ZBrush in more detail.

The Rake tools in ZBrush are based on a real-world sculpting tool. In clay sculpting, rakes are small, serrated blades that are used to scrape down clay at levels determined by how sharp and deep the teeth are (Figure 2.15). Rakes allow the sculptor to rough in forms in a loose manner, then refine them by using smaller and smaller rakes until the whole surface is smoothed. In Figure 2.16, I started the ogre bust with basic planes using rake strokes; as I work the surface, the rakes become smaller and the surface finer.

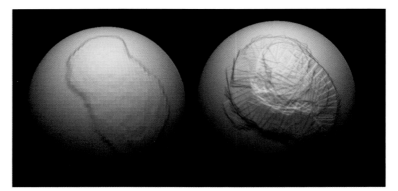

Figure 2.14: Claytubes and rakes on both a low-res and high-res mesh. Notice the increased fidelity of the brush effect on the higher-resolution mesh.

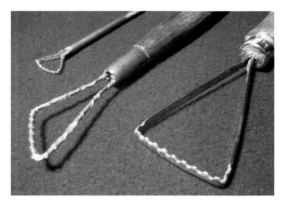

Figure 2.15: Real-world rakes

Figure 2.16: The ogre on the left consists of just the basic forms with prominent rake marks; the right image shows the ogre bust after the rakes have been refined and the surface detailed.

The procedure for working with rakes is to crosshatch across the form you are trying to refine, using smaller draw sizes with each pass. Figure 2.17 shows how this is done in water-based clay. With a combination of crosshatching and stroking along the direction of the form, you can attain a pleasing surface and easy transitions between forms.

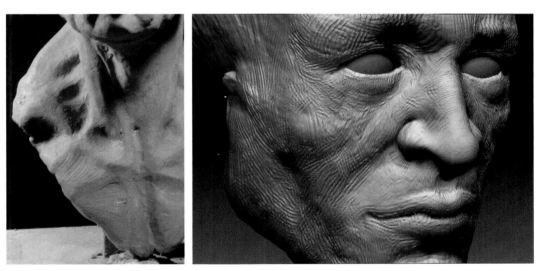

Figure 2.17: Close-up of rake strokes in water-based clay on the left and ZBrush on the right

Typically, forms are built up with any combination of the Claytubes, Standard, and Inflate brushes and then raked down into more specific forms with the Rake tool (Figure 2.18). This may be a difficult concept to fully grasp without seeing it in action. To see rakes in use, watch the video files included on the DVD for this chapter.

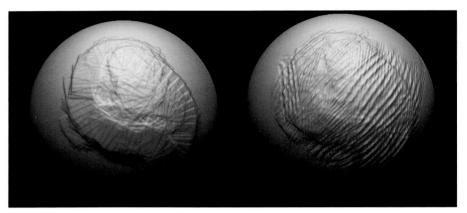

Figure 2.18: An example of Rake and Claybrush strokes at different levels of refinement

What Is a Rake?

Featured Artist: Cesar Dacol

A *rake* is a tool used by sculptors to remove excessive material, such as clay, from a sculpture. By employing the rake, we are able to shape and define the forms of our creation.

In sculpture, there two methods of creation. One is additive in the form of clays. The second is subtractive, as in marbles. Each method utilizes the rake in its sculptural process. With marble, we use various chisels with ever-refining teeth to form, shape, and polish the piece. We use clay rakes in a similar manner to define the silhouette and curvature of our forms, refining them to a smooth finish (if that is the desired effect).

Here we have a sphere in which I have dragged two opposing strokes across the surface. It is where the two strokes meet that the most material is being removed (*below left*).

By pulling the brush in the direction of the form we want to express and countering the stroke in the opposite direction, we'll slowly shape the contour. As we repeat this technique over and over, we create the desired form or shape (*below right*).

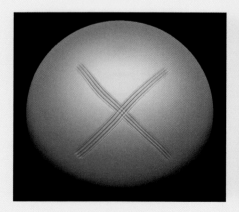

continues

We continue this process with smaller and smaller diameters or brushes. The finer the teeth and density of our mesh, the closer the surface will resemble flesh (*below left*).

In the following image, we have a sphere with a wavy line down the center. Notice how the bounce of light is enhanced by the directionality of the rake groves. This effect creates a tidy path for light to travel down and within (*below right*).

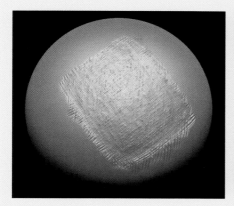
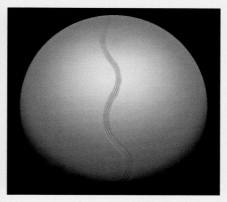

This idea of strokes and patterns manipulating light patterns is not a new one and in fact has been utilized by oil painters on their canvases for centuries. Strokes are an essential part of sculpture and drawing, and you should pay attention to them. Whether we intend it or not, we are sending a message with the quality of our strokes.

Here we see the same form with two different stroke patterns. Notice how the light is perceived differently. Also notice how your eye follows the direction of the strokes.

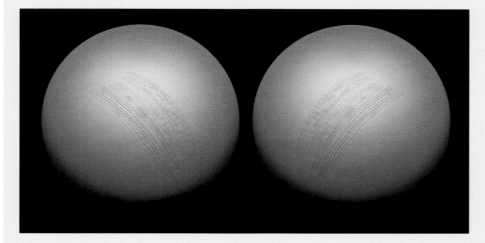

continues

What Is a Rake? *(continued)*

Directionality is obviously the goal here. Observe your face in the mirror. Notice how there is a natural tension to the surface of your skin as it is stretched over fat, muscles, and bones. There is a directionality to your pores, which in turn are affected by gravity and such.

If you are aware of these rules, you can employ them in your sculpture and have light travel over your forms.

Of course, if you use this method, avoid smoothing your model completely or removing all the Rake tool markings. Such markings lend an energy to the sculpture. By utilizing finer rakes and or smaller diameters, you can define the forms more precisely, eventually reaching a point where you're defining the most minute surface patterns of the skin. Rakes were not the only tool and brush utilized to create our final image, but they were the foundation.

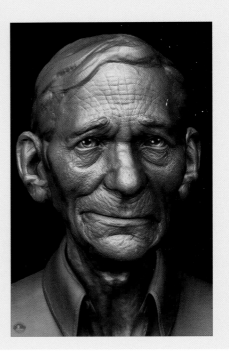

The Ecorche Approach to Sculpting

The approach used to sculpt the head in Figure 2.19 is called ecorche. Ecorche is derived from the French word for "skinned" and generally refers to a sculpture of a human or animal with the skin and subcutaneous fat removed so the muscle and skeletal systems are visible, as in Figure 2.19. As a method of anatomical study, ecorche sculpture involves a constructive approach to building the figure by sculpting the bones and overlying muscles layer by layer, working up to the surface forms. This allows the artist to gain a deeper level of insight into how bone, muscle, and fat combine to create the human form.

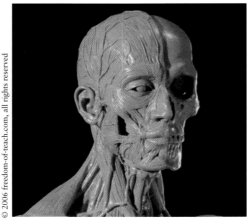

Figure 2.19: Examples of ecorche sculpture sculpted by artist Andrew Cawrse, available at freedom-of-teach.com. © freedom-of-teach 2008

A Note on Anatomical Terminology

Although it is not necessary to know the names of all the bones, muscles, processes, fossa, and epicondyles of the body to be a good sculptor, I find that learning the names is helpful when developing a knowledge of anatomy. Knowing the name of a part gives you a kind of mental box to store the information in. Learning the names also helps you communicate specific information about your figure.

I have found it expedites the process of retaining information about anatomy when you have the names of the shapes you are trying to understand. For this reason, I am including some of this information in this chapter (although this is by no means an in-depth look at the anatomy of the head and neck).

ZBrush layers and clay sculpting tools allow us to use this same approach in a digital medium. Starting with a PolySphere tool, we'll mass in the forms of the skull, add the major facial and epicranial muscles, and then add the skin and fatty tissue that fills out the transitions. This exercise is inspired by a video produced by digital sculptor Ryan Kingslein, available at www.zbrushcentral.com.

In this exercise I approach the head, neck, and ear separately for the sake of clarity in illustrating the steps. In reality I would sculpt all parts simultaneously, thus keeping a unified level of finish to the whole head as it progresses. See the DVD for a video of this sculpture from start to finish.

Before we begin sculpting, let's take a moment to look at the human skull and note some particulars about its shape and the proportion of the masses to one another. The skull can be divided into the cranial mass and the facial mass; these are color-coded in Figure 2.20. The cranial mass is an ovoid shape that forms the protective covering around the brain. Hanging off the front of this ovoid shape is the wedge of the facial mass.

A common mistake is to make the face too big on the head by neglecting the cranial mass. We as humans are constantly focused on the faces of those around us, particularly the eyes. Because of this, our natural inclination is to enlarge these parts. By paying special attention to bony landmarks, proportions, angles, and measures between each part of the head, we can ensure the shapes maintain their proper relation to each other.

In the following sections I'll provide a few guidelines for you to follow. In Figure 2.21 notice that the skull can fit in a box. The centerline of the Y-axis of the skull passes through the auditory meatus, also known as the ear hole (Figure 2.22). This is a key landmark when sculpting the head because it represents an immobile point from which you can make all your comparative measurements. The lateral midline of the skull passes through the eye sockets and nasal bone (Figure 2.23).

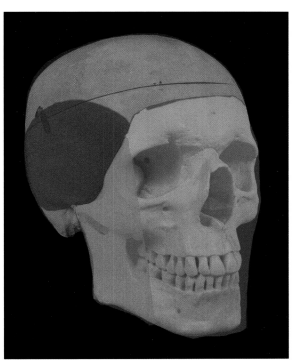

Figure 2.20: The two head masses, cranial and facial

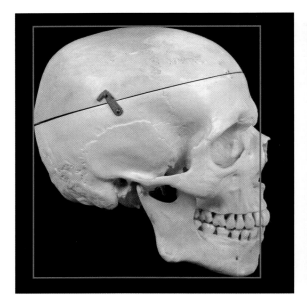
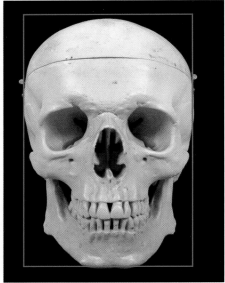

Figure 2.21: The skull in profile notice it is two-thirds as wide as it is deep.

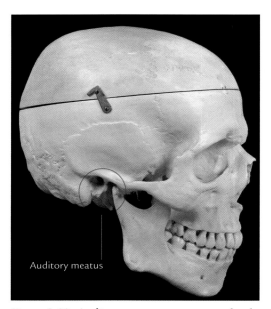

Figure 2.22: Auditory meatus represents a landmark which sits just behind the centerline of the skull in the side view.

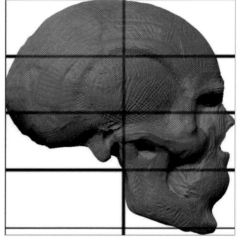

Figure 2.23: The human skull from the side divided into quarters.

Sculpting the Skull

To begin, you will sculpt a generalized human skull from a ZBrush primitive sphere. This exercise describes a high-resolution sculpting method. The sculpting process begins at a higher subdivision level, and the form will be built using the Claytubes and Rake brushes.

As discussed in Chapter 1, complex shapes can be broken down into simpler forms for easier study and replication. The initial shape you want to strive for is shown in Figure 2.24. Notice the rounded facial plane and the overall simplification of the head into a single basic shape. By working toward this first step and building all the secondary forms on it, you can maintain a sense of structural integrity throughout the sculpting process.

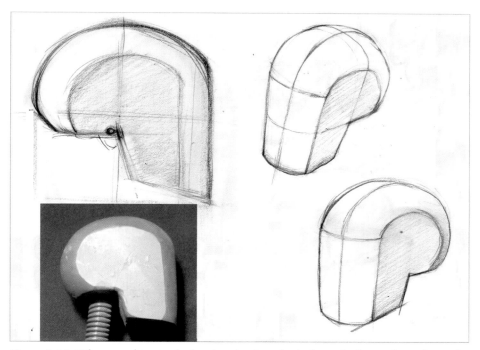

Figure 2.24: When roughing in the head, strive for a basic form similar to those shown here.

During this exercise there are several bony landmarks that will be of interest. These are points that we want to find in the sculpture and ensure are in correct spatial relationship to each other. Failure to find these points or keep them consistent makes it easy to drift off proportions and make a head that appears strange. Figure 2.25 shows several major landmarks labeled on a skull.

1. Create a sphere by selecting the Sphere3D tool—be sure not to select the ZSphere but the Sphere3D tool. Draw it on the canvas and enter Edit mode with the T key. Rotate the sphere so the poles are at the top and bottom. You can see the poles clearly in frame model by pressing Shift+F. Poles are the points at the top and bottom of the sphere where all the edges meet. Often this will be the place where you will get a pinch or strange tweaking in the mesh while you sculpt. By ensuring they are at the very top and bottom of the head, you'll make them easy to avoid. Remember to convert the sphere to a polymesh by clicking the MakePolyMesh3D button on the Tool menu.

You may choose to use the PolySphere.ztl tool for this demonstration instead of the Sphere3D tool. You can find the PolySphere tool in the ZBrush3/ZTools folder; it is not loaded by default. Take care not to select the Sphere3D or the ZSphere tool. The benefit of using the PolySphere ZTool is that the model has no poles. To Load this tool, click the main Tool menu and select Load Tool. Browse to the ZBrush3/ZTools directory and select PolySphere.ztl.

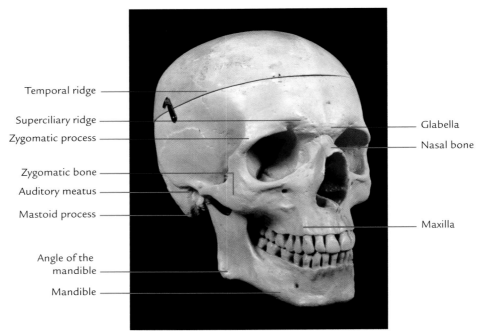

Temporal ridge

Superciliary ridge

Zygomatic process

Zygomatic bone

Auditory meatus

Mastoid process

Angle of the
mandible

Mandible

Glabella

Nasal bone

Maxilla

Figure 2.25: Skull with bony landmarks labeled

2. From the Brush menu select the Move brush. Turn up ZIntensity to 90 so the move effect is stronger. Begin to create an egg shape from the sphere. Make sure X symmetry is turned by choosing Transform → Activate Symmetry.

3. Rotate to a side view, hold down the Shift key while you click, and rotate to snap to a side orthographic view. From the side, rough in the plane of the face and the rear of the cranial mass.

4. Finally move to a top view and make sure the head tapers slightly toward the face.

5. At this point, Ctrl-drag from a point off the model to drag a mask marquee over one half the head from a side view. This helps you determine the halfway point and ensure the masses are the same on either side (Figure 2.26). Based on this midpoint, correct the masses at the back of the head.

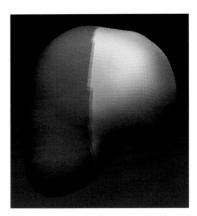

Figure 2.26: Masking one half of the side view to help spot proportions between the two parts

To create a mask marquee, hold down the Ctrl key and drag from a point off the model. A dark marquee will appear. Anything inside this box when you release Ctrl will be masked. If you have an alpha selected, the mask will be shaped like the alpha unless you release Ctrl. If you press Ctrl+Alt, the mask will invert and you will be unmasking what is within the marquee.

Roughing in the Shape of the Skull

At this stage we have roughed in the form of the head, taking into account its most basic shape from front, top, and side views. These changes were made at a lower subdivision level since it is easier to make large form changes when the model has fewer faces. In the next series of steps we'll subdivide the model and start adding secondary masses with the Rake and Clay brushes.

1. Subdivide the mesh so there are enough faces that the Clay brushes will be effective. Usually 500,000 or more faces will suffice. Press Ctrl+D to divide the mesh three times, or choose Tool → Geometry → Divide.

2. Now switch to the Rake tool. Using the Rake set to ZAdd, begin to mass out the side planes of the head. Work around to the lower-back portion of the skull. Then move to the front and crosshatch across to create the plane that will ultimately become the face. There should be a slight curvature to this plane.

3. Once these surfaces are indicated, switch to ZSub by pressing the Alt key and start carving back and defining the edges between the planes with more clarity. Throughout this process we are alternating between ZAdd and ZSub with the Alt key (Figure 2.27).

4. Using the Rake, place the zygomatic bone, also known as the cheekbone (Figure 2.28). This is a major bony landmark on the face. Be sure it angles back and up on the side of the head. This bone will point to the center of the ear.

Figure 2.27: Refining planes with rakes

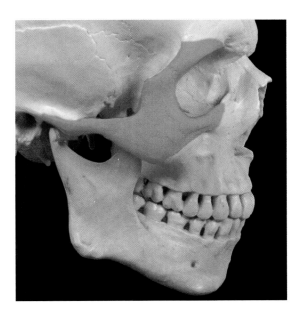

Figure 2.28: The angle and placement of the zygomatic bone

5. From the side, continue the curve up the side of the skull suggesting the temporal ridge. Switch to ZSub and start to hollow out the temple of the skull (Figure 2.29).

6. Note that the skull tends to look sad because of the slight downward angle to the eye sockets (Figures 2.30). Switch to the Standard brush and with ZSub active begin to carve out the hollows of the eye sockets, keeping this ovoid shape in mind.

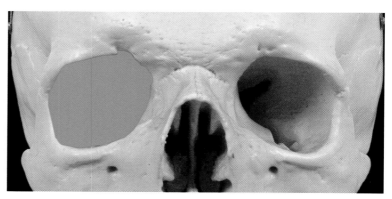

Figure 2.29: Reinforcing the cheekbones and temporal ridge

Figure 2.30: The eye socket

Sculpting the Forms of the Facial Mass

Now let's move on to sculpting the facial mass:

1. Carve away the shape of the nasal cavity from the front. Now move to a side view and tug the area between the nose and eyes back to create the ridge of the nasal bone. This is an important landmark in the profile, so be sure to introduce it now to avoid flattening of the face (Figure 2.31).

2. From the side, tug the cheekbones back with the Move brush.

3. From the front, adjust the angle from the cheekbones up to the corners of the eye sockets so they taper back as they move up. This area is called the zygomatic process and is visible as the lateral upper corner of the eye socket on the finished head (Figure 2.32). Make sure the mouth area has a slight curvature to it. Consider this a cylinder shape on the head. This is important because later

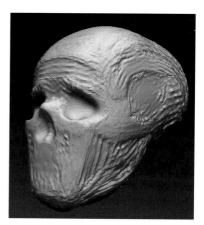

Figure 2.31: Adding the nasal cavity and nasal bone

when you add lips to the head, they will lie more naturally on the face if they are sculpted around a curved base (Figure 2.33).

4. Using the Standard brush with ZSub on, carve away the hollows at the sides of the head (the temples). This region is called the temporal fossa, and we'll fill it with an important muscle in the next section.

5. Don't worry about the rough surface—we'll refine that later. For now, focus on the integrity of the shapes you want to create. Remember that these rake marks will be refined later with a combination of smaller, finer rake strokes and the Smooth brush.

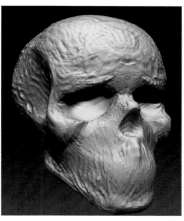

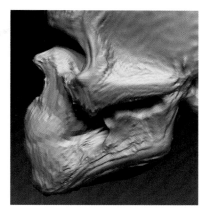

Figure 2.32: Adjusting the angle of the cheekbones to the brow ridge

Figure 2.33: Barrel of mouth seen from the front

Figure 2.34: Cheekbone hollow pulled back into the head

Using the Move brush, pull the underside of the cheekbones in to create the deep hollows seen there. This area is empty on the skull, but in this case tuck these faces deep into the head (Figure 2.34).

6. The glabella is a raised trapezoidal shaped formation between the brows. It wedges into the nasal bone from between the superciliary arches and creates the shape of the center of the brows (Figure 2.35). Mask the bridge of the nose so you can create a hard line between this form and the one we'll now add. Create the shape of the glabella by sculpting against the mask (Figure 2.36).

7. Using the Move brush, create the ear hole, or auditory meatus. Remember that this hole in the side of the skull lies just behind the halfway line between the front and back halves (you can see it in Figure 2.22). It should be placed just below the end of the zygomatic bone. Using Move, hold down the Alt key to move in and out from the point under the brush. This constrains the movement and makes it easy to slide the faces into the head, creating the deep hole.

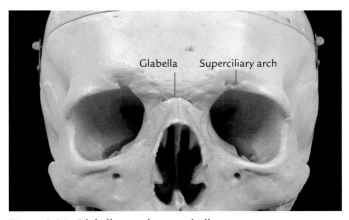

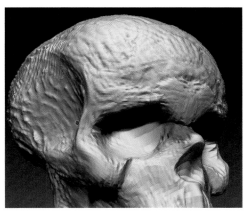

Figure 2.35: Glabella on a human skull

Figure 2.36: Roughing in the glabella

8. From beneath the auditory meatus comes the mastoid process (Figure 2.37). This is a small mound protrusion just behind the jaw. Using the Move brush again, pull the mastoid process down from the auditory meatus. The mastoid process will serve as a landmark later on when we sculpt the neck; this is the insertion of the most prominent neck muscle, the sternomastoid.

9. Delineate the cheekbone from the jawbone with the Standard brush set to ZSub. Carve away between these two shapes to help separate them. Begin to sculpt the shape of the mandible or jawbone.

10. Use a mask again to check proportions between the halves, adjusting the face to compensate for the angles of the profile. I take this moment to correct the angles in the face as well as the length of the jawbone (Figure 2.38).

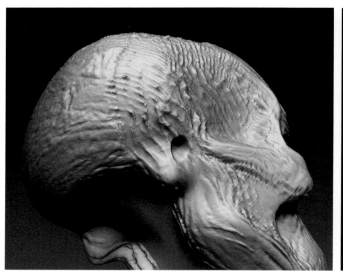

Figure 2.37: Mastoid process, beneath the ear hole

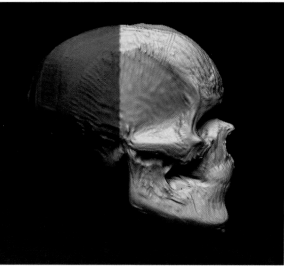

Figure 2.38: Checking proportions with masking on one side of the head

The zygomatic bone should be the widest part of the skull when looking from the front. To move this part out from the rest of the sculpture without disturbing the other forms, mask the zygomatic bone, then invert the mask by Ctrl-clicking somewhere off the model on the document window. Using the Move brush, pull the form out. Remember to hold down Alt while you use the Move brush to pull the faces out in the direction of the surface normal.

Check the width from the bottom as well as other angles to ensure it is correct (Figure 2.39).

11. Select the Rake brush and lower the draw size. This has the effect of making the rake smaller and the strokes finer. Using this tool, crosshatch the strokes already on the model. Crosshatching strokes helps to bring together the forms sculpted so far (Figure 2.40). If you use the rakes with ZAdd on clay, add in the recessed areas first. This reduces the roughness of the surface and begins to tie the shapes together.

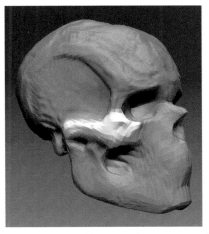
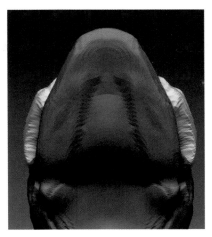
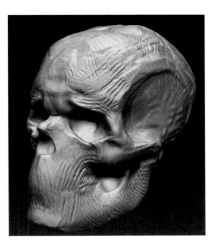

Figure 2.39: Pulling out the zygomatic bone

Figure 2.40: The rake strokes on the mouth area have been crosshatched.

12. Using rakes over the entire skull, resolve the forms to a point that the major shapes are clearly defined. Since we'll add muscle and skin over this skull, don't be concerned with taking it to a smooth finish. We won't add details like individual teeth since we just need the rounded shape of the mouth to serve as a basis for lips later. If you want to take the skull to a finer level of finish, use the Smooth brush with a BrushMod setting of 100 to smooth the recessed areas and reduce the rake marks on the surface. Figure 2.41 shows the skull to this point.

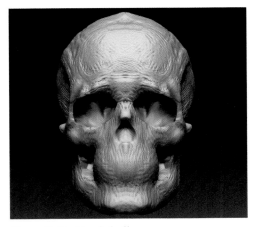
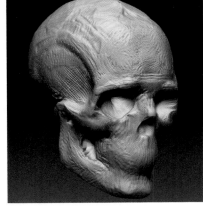

Figure 2.41: Final skull

This skull remains rough since we are only interested in the gesture form and proportions not the surface quality. In the next step this skull will guide us in placing the muscles of the face as we work toward a realistic human head from a sphere.

Sculpting the Muscles

In this section you will add the muscles to the skull. We'll take a simplified look at the muscles of the face, focusing on those major muscle groups directly influencing the surface forms. The muscles we'll add are shown in Figure 2.42.

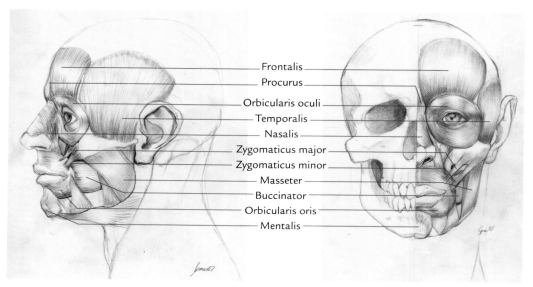

Figure 2.42: The major muscles of the face

For the muscles let's change to the Red Wax material to help you see the placement of each muscle as it is sculpted. To paint on a second material while preserving the first, fill the ZTool with a base material; otherwise, when you select the Red Wax material the whole ZTool will change to display the new material.

Although we're using multiple materials for clarity in this lesson, filling objects with a material is also useful for keeping subtools the same color. When a subtool is inactive, it changes to a darker shade compared to the active one. If you fill a subtool with a material, this overrides the default behavior and all subtools display with their full material settings. To fill a model with a material, follow these steps:

1. From the Material menu, select the White Cavity material. At the top of the screen in your brush controls make sure that MRGB, RGB, ZAdd, and ZSub are off. Only M should be active. With the White Cavity material selected in the material swatch, choose Color from the main menu and click the FillObject button. This will fill the skull with the White Cavity material.

2. Change to Red Wax in the Material Browser, and the material on the skull remains unchanged.

3. Set the Rake brush to M and ZAdd. Now when you rake the surface of the model, the brush will add form as well as change material.

Begin by opening the Skull ZTool from the first lesson (Figure 2.43). Add the masseter muscle (the chewing muscle that fills out the space between the lower jaw and the cheekbone; see Figure 2.44). Its form can be simplified into the shape shown in the second image in Figure 2.44.

4. Use the Clay brush to mass out the width between the zygomatic bone and the mandible. Make sure the Claytubes brush is set to ZAdd, and use M Taper to move this shape down to the lower jaw.

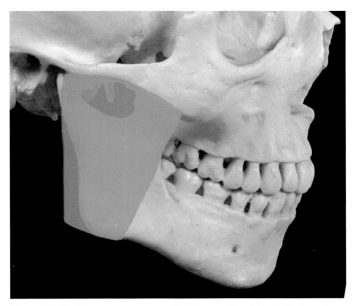

Figure 2.43: The masseter muscle fills out the side of the jaw from the cheekbone to the lower jaw.

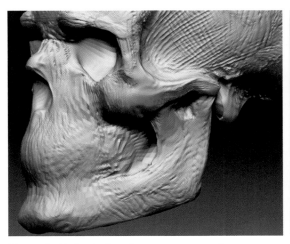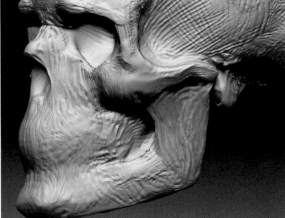

Figure 2.44: Sculpting the masseter muscle

5. Now add the temporalis. The temporalis muscle fills out the hollow at the sides of the head (Figure 2.45). This large muscle actually feeds under the hollow of the zygomatic bone and has a hand in moving the jaw. Mask out the zygomatic bone and the temporal ridge by using the Rake with ZAdd on.

   From the front view, notice how when these muscle forms are added you can begin to see the front profile of a human head begin to take shape (Figure 2.46).

6. Step down a subdivision level and smooth out the hollow under the cheekbone; we'll use this area to add the buccinator muscle later. Masking out the surrounding areas can help isolate and pull those deep faces back to the surface (Figure 2.47).

7. Mask out a shape similar to a clown mouth for the Orbicularis oris muscle. The Orbicularis oris is a circular muscle that surrounds the mouth and lips. Invert the mask and rake in a circular motion (Figure 2.48).

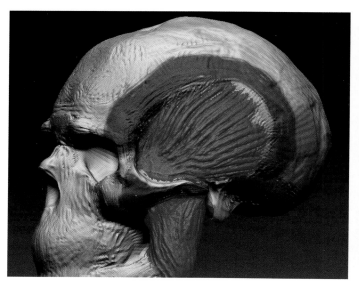

Figure 2.45: Adding the temporalis

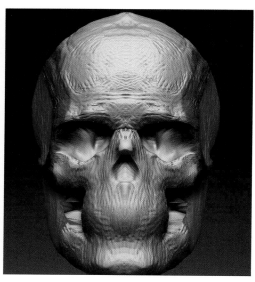

Figure 2.46: These muscles from the front view already begin to give a recognizable shape to the head.

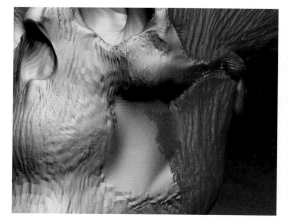

Figure 2.47: Pulling out the cheek hollows to sculpt the buccinator

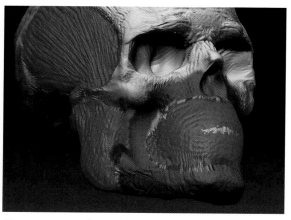

Figure 2.48: Sculpting the mouth muscle called Orbicularis oris

8. Add two triangles of muscle on either side of the chin. These are called the triangularis muscles. These muscles pull the corners of the lips down in a frowning expression. Add a dot in the center of the chin to represent the mentalis muscle. These shapes combined with the bottom of the Orbicularis oris create the subtle W-shaped form changes seen in the chin.

9. Add the buccinator. The buccinator emerges from beneath the jaw and the masseter to insert at the corners of the mouth. This muscle serves to pull the corners of the mouth back. The step down between the masseter and the buccinator creates an important plane change at the cheek, which is often visible in very built individuals (Figure 2.49).

10. The forehead is covered by a thin pair of muscles called the frontalis. These muscles have the main function of raising the brows. Be careful not to lose the shape of the frontal eminence of the structure of the skull. Notice that the frontalis has a small "tail" that inserts into the medial of the eye socket (Figure 2.50).

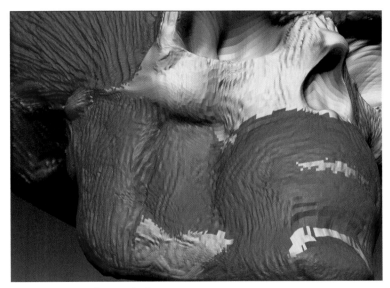

Figure 2.49: Sculpting the buccinator

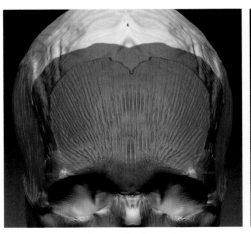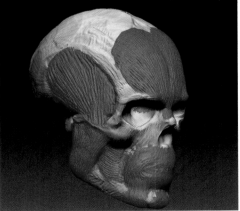

Figure 2.50: Sculpting the frontalis

11. The zygomaticus major and minor connect the cheekbones to the corner of the mouth. They create the plane change from the face to the cheeks. These muscles help in creating the smiling expression.

   Using the Clay brush, add the two-pronged shape here. Notice how it connects to the corners of the mouth. When we add skin, the combined effect of the zygomatic major and minor, buccinator, and triangularis creates an important form on the skin since they all pull that one area (Figure 2.51).

12. Mask out the recesses of the eye sockets. Stepping down subdivision levels (so the effect of the brush is stronger) smooths the faces to pull them closer to the surface (Figure 2.52).

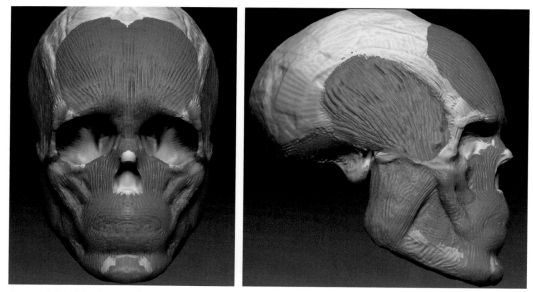

Figure 2.51: The levator labii muscles appear as two triangles coming down either side of the nose. Zygomaticus muscles connect the cheekbones to the corners of the mouth.

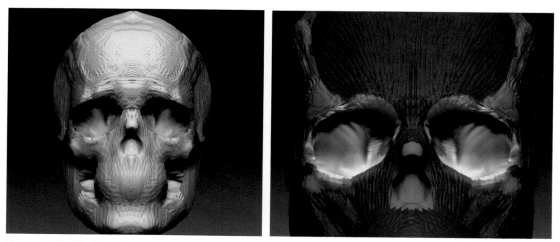

Figure 2.52: Masking the eyes

Adding the Eyes

We'll now create a sphere for the eyeball and add it as a subtool to the current model. The typical human eyeball is about 28 mm. It's best to make sure the sphere fills out the socket with a slight give on each corner. The depth of the eye can be determined by the angle in Figure 2.53. A diagonal drawn between the brow bone and the cheekbone should just touch the corneal bulge of the eyeball. Remember that you can fill the eye subtool with a material so it will display the same value as the other tools.

1. To create the eye, save your current ZTool. Drop it to the canvas by exiting Edit mode by pressing the T key. Press Ctrl+N to clear the canvas. Select the Sphere3D tool and draw it on the canvas. Enter Edit mode and select Make Polymesh 3D from the Tool menu.

2. Now return to the head ZTool and choose Tool → Subtool → Append. From the Append menu, select the sphere to add it into the current tool. It is likely the sphere will be too large for an eye. Using the Transpose tools, scale it down and move it into place, as shown in Figure 2.54.

3. Once the eye is placed, you need to copy and mirror it. To do this, select the Eye subtool by Ctrl+Shift-clicking the ball. Under Tool, select Clone. This makes a new tool based on the position and scale of the current eye. Click Tool → Subtool → Append.

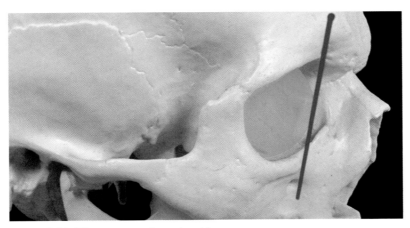

Figure 2.53: The eyes seen from the side

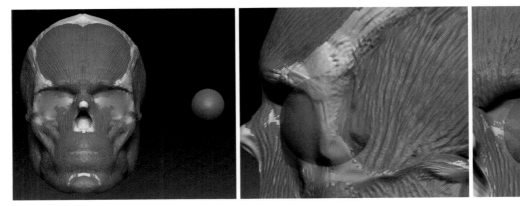

Figure 2.54: Making the eyes

Notice that the eye is in the same place as the other; mirror it to place on the other side. Using the Rake with ZAdd on, create the circular muscle of the Orbicularis oculi. This wraps around the brow and ends on the cheekbone (Figure 2.55).

4. Mask out the shape of the eyelids. Be sure to keep the angle up to the outer edge (Figure 2.56).

5. Invert the mask and using Claytubes with ZSub on, press the inner eyelid into the head. Invert the mask again and, using Move, tug at the edges. Be sure to work from multiple angles to turn the lids around the sphere of the eyeball (Figure 2.57).

6. To add the nose, mask the nasal cavity and invert the mask. Be sure to keep the nasal bone masked out since this is a bony landmark on the skinned face and we don't want to alter its original shape too much from the skull (Figure 2.58).

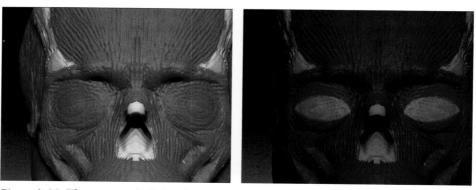

Figure 2.55: The eye muscle Orbicularis oculi   *Figure 2.56: Masking eyelids*

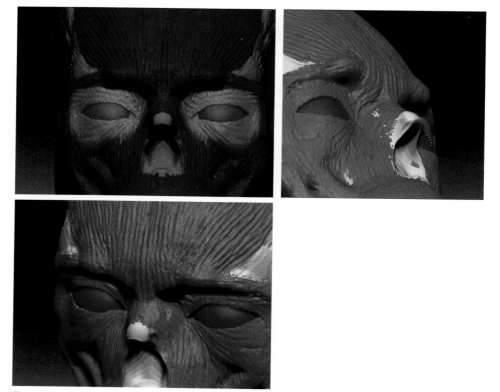

Figure 2.57: Moving eyelids

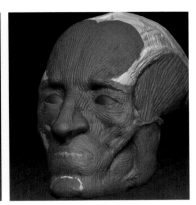

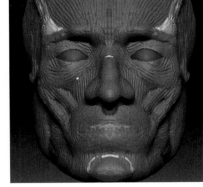

Figure 2.58: Adding the nose   *Figure 2.59: Adding the nostrils*

7. Using Inflate and Claytubes, pull the profile of the nose out and mass out the nostrils (Figure 2.59).
8. Using Rakes with ZAdd on, add the upper lip. Be sensitive to the corners where the zygomatic muscles insert (Figure 2.60).

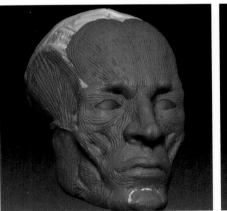
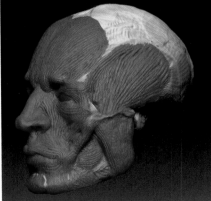

Figure 2.60: Adding the upper lip with a ZAdd rake

9. Keep a gesture to the upper lip that looks somewhat like the letter M. Be sure the upper lip overlaps the lower.

The underside of the chin is filled out with the digastric and mylohyoid muscles. Mask out the jawline and, using Rakes, create these muscles. They are thickest at the neck, tapering and becoming thinner toward the chin, thus creating an important aspect of the profile. These muscles connect to the Adam's apple (Figure 2.61).

Congratulations! You have now added the major muscle forms to the face (Figure 2.62). This is an abbreviated list of facial muscles, but the major forms are there that influence surface details. Now let's move on to transitions and skinning.

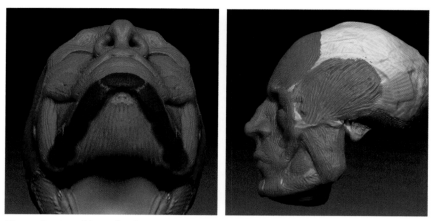

Figure 2.61: Adding the digastric and mylohyoid muscles under the chin

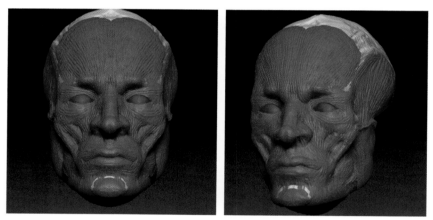

Figure 2.62: Ecorche shots

Sculpting Skin and Fat on the Face

In this section we'll bring it all together by adding the skin and fatty tissue over the bone and muscle sculpted so far. Having the structural elements of the skull and muscles in place makes this is a much simpler process.

Begin by filling the head with the White Cavity material using Color → Fill Object while only M is active and the White Cavity material is selected. Then follow these steps:

1. Using the Claytubes brush with a low ZIntensity setting, begin to refine between the rake marks of the cheeks. The Clay brushes have the nice effect of adding material to the low points first, making this an ideal way to fill out rake marks on a sculpt. There are fat deposits at the cheeks; sometimes these can be thinner in more built individuals showing the line of the masseter muscle as a delineated plane change. Continue up the face, taking care not to disturb the form as much as fill out the recessed areas (Figure 2.63).

2. Using a smaller rake size with ZAdd on, move across the transitions between forms, trying to tie them together. Take care to rake in the direction of the flow of the form (Figure 2.64).

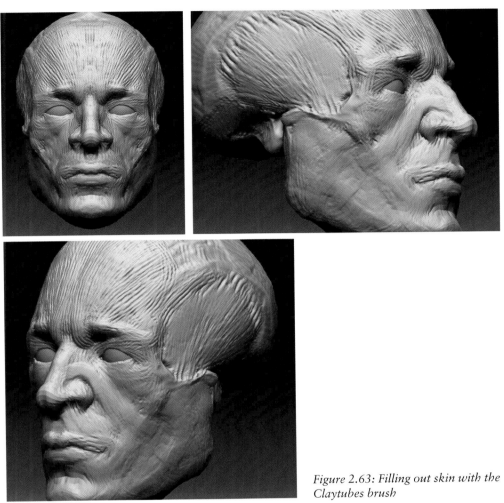

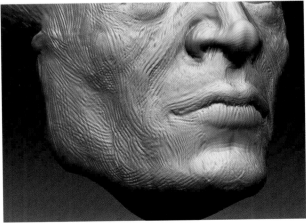

Figure 2.63: Filling out skin with the
Claytubes brush

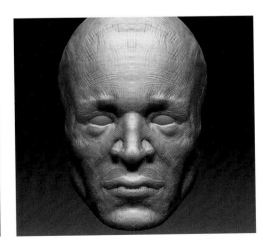

Figure 2.64: Raking with the direction of the form

3. To reduce the roughness of the surface and take down the rake marks while maintaining the form you have created, select the Smooth brush and set the BrushMod slider to −100. Then lower your ZIntensity and smooth out the rakes (Figure 2.65).

4. Mask out the area next to the nose (this is called the nasolabial fold). While most prominent in the old or obese, it is present in all faces and we want to accentuate the plane change here (Figure 2.66).

5. Add the fold in the upper eyelid and the fatty tissue and skin between the outer edge of the eye socket and the eyeball. Mask out the line, and then invert (Figure 2.67).

6. Using the Standard brush with low Draw Size and Intensity settings, gently add the width of the lower lid.

7. Mask the upper lid and mass out the flesh that hangs between the brow and the sphere of the eye, giving it some sense of gravity by pulling on the skin and moving it slightly down at the corner.

8. Add a recess at the lower lid where the sphere of the eyeball curves back into the socket (Figure 2.68).

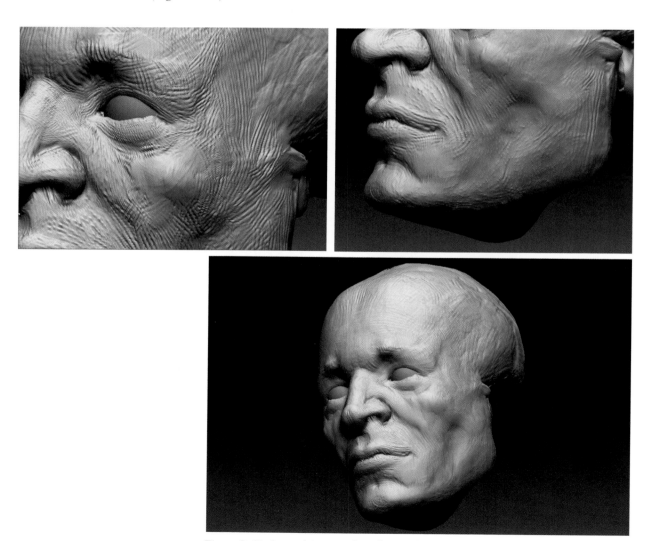

Figure 2.65: Smoothing out the rake marks

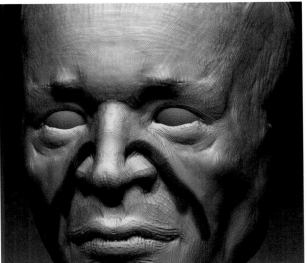

Figure 2.66: Masking out the nasolabial fold

Figure 2.67: Masking the eye wrinkle

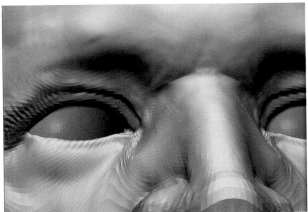

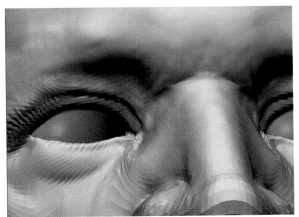

Figure 2.68: The lower lid recess

9. While sculpting the eyes, take care that the outside corner is slightly higher than the inside corner, or *canthus* of the eye. This is an important consideration when dealing with the eyes; placing both corners on the same level would create an unnatural look. See Figure 2.69 for an example of how to place the medial canthus.

10. Hide the eyeballs and mask out the medial canthus (Figure 2.70). Using the Inflate brush, add the small pink tissue in the corner of the eye. It is important to include this node, called the lacrimal caruncle, when sculpting the eye (Figure 2.71).

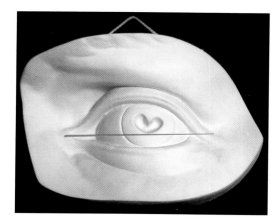

Figure 2.69: This casting from the David by Michelangelo shows how the medial canthus of the eye should be slightly lower than the lateral (outer) corner.

Figure 2.70: The medial canthus

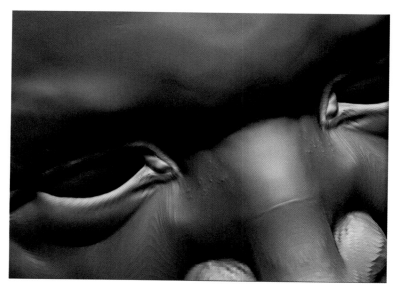

Figure 2.71: Inflating the lacrimal caruncle

Adding the Neck

I left the neck for last to show how it is possible to pull large forms directly out of a highly subdivided mesh. When adding the neck to the head, you can pull the geometry directly from the faces at the base of the head. We will add new forms directly to the existing sculpt by using the geometry that is there.

1. Mask out the underside of the head and invert the mask. Use the Move brush to pull the faces down (Figure 2.72). Be sure to mask up to the digastric and include the mastoid process and occipital region (the back of the skull).

2. Once the area where the neck will connect to the head is masked out, invert this mask by Ctrl-clicking it. This will mask the rest of the head, leaving unmasked the area we painted in (Figure 2.73).

3. Use the Smooth brush set to ZIntensity 100 and BrushMod set to 0 to smooth out the unmasked areas. You want to remove the nuances to the form, thus making a smooth distribution of edges that can be pulled down into the shape of the neck. This may be easier from a lower subdivision level. If the Smooth brush is not responsive, step down a level from the top.

4. Using the Move brush in combination with the Alt key to pull along the normal direction, then start to tug the unmasked faces out from the base of the skull, as shown in Figure 2.74.

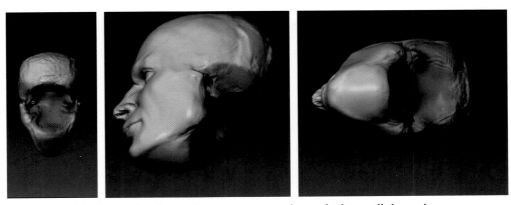

Figure 2.72: Masking under the head to create a space from which to pull the neck

Figure 2.73: The neck mask inverted

Figure 2.74: Pulling the neck out with the Move brush

5. From the side, pull the faces down and back from the head (see Figure 2.75). The head pictured here is at subdivision level 4 so it is easier to grab large groups of faces and move them together. These changes will telegraph through all subdivision levels because of the ZBrush multiresolution editing approach discussed earlier in this chapter.

6. From the back, the neck is very narrow. Using the Move brush, pull the sides out until they are even with the base of the skull. See the example in Figure 2.76.

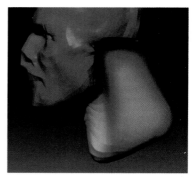

Figure 2.75: Pulling the neck down with the Move brush

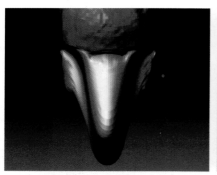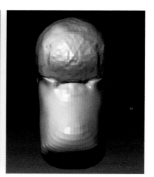

Figure 2.76: Widening the neck

Sculpting the Neck Muscles

Now that the overall shape and gesture of the neck has been established, step back up to a higher subdivision level so we may again use the Clay brushes. When you step back up, because of ZBrush multiresolution editing the details of the mastoid process and the base of the skull are reapplied to the shifted faces. In this case, we don't want to retain the former high-resolution details; instead, we'll sculpt new ones. Using the Smooth brush, remove these remaining details (Figure 2.77). Try to give the neck the shape of a cylinder.

1. Hold down Ctrl to make a mark with the Masking brush on the neck to represent the start and end of the sternomastoid muscles. The sternomastoid originates at the pit of the neck, and its insertion point is behind the ear at the mastoid process. By making a mark for the insertion and origin, we can easily draw the direction and flow of the muscle as it turns around the cylinder shape of the neck. When the shape is masked in, Ctrl-click the background to invert the mask (Figure 2.78).

Muscle Origins and Insertions

Many anatomy books will refer to a muscle's point of origin and insertion. The origin of a muscle can be determined by the direction in which it pulls or the end at which the muscle has the least range of motion. For example, the origin of the sternomastoid is the pit of the neck; the muscle moves the least here. The insertion is at the mastoid process. Here the muscle moves with the head in all directions. You can also remember this by the fact that the muscle pulls down toward the pit of the neck when in flexion.

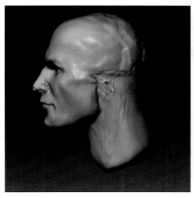
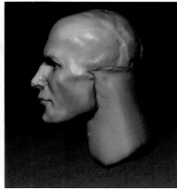

Figure 2.77: Smoothing out remaining neck details

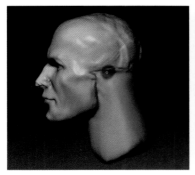

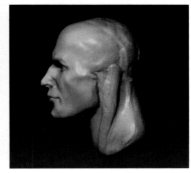

Figure 2.78: Adding the sternomastoid muscle

Figure 2.79: Adding the trapezius muscle

2. Using the Claytubes brush, mass in the muscle form. Try to keep it thicker at the top than the bottom. When it reaches the pit of the neck, the sternomastoid splits into two distinct heads.
3. Invert the mask again to start roughing in the trapezius muscle. The trapezius forms a sheet of muscle over the back of the neck and turns around to attach to the shoulders (Figure 2.79).
4. Using the Rake, stroke across the forms of the sternomastoid and the trapezius. The intention here is to start to tie the two shapes together more. Notice the use of ZAdd rakes in the recess on either side of the sternomastoid. This softens the transition between the muscle and the rest of the neck (Figure 2.80).

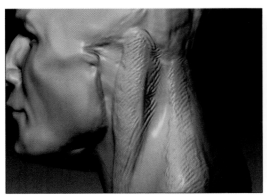

Figure 2.80: Raking across the neck

5. With a ZAdd rake, continue to rough in the trapezius from behind. An important distinction to be aware of is that, from behind, the sternomastoid should be just visible on either side of the neck (Figure 2.81).

6. Rotating around to the front, the neck is raked further and the two heads of the sternomastoid are suggested at the pit of the neck in Figure 2.82. With a combination of raking and smoothing, you can gradually build up the form. By smoothing as you work, you can make the shapes flow into one another in a graceful and subtle manner.

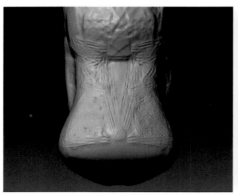
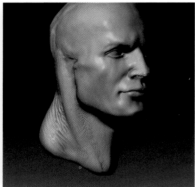

Figure 2.81: Raking the trapezius

Figure 2.82: Refining the sternomastoid

7. Using the Move tool, adjust the shape of the shoulders. Then use the Claytubes brush to fill in the transition between the sternomastoid and the neck a bit more (Figure 2.83).

8. The goal is to change the character of the shadow so that it's less pronounced, thus making the appearance of the sternomastoid less overt. We want to make the muscle appear to be under a layer of skin, not inflated out from its surface.
Figure 2.84 shows the neck after some smoothing and adding for form between the shapes. By crosshatching ZAdd rakes, the transitions can be worked further.

9. Once you've added some clay to the transition with the Rake, use the softSmooth brush we created earlier in this chapter to smooth out this area. This helps push the rakes back into the surface, thus softening the strokes (Figure 2.85).

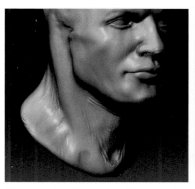
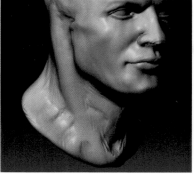
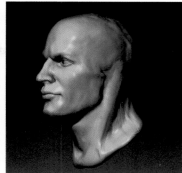

Figure 2.83: Using the Clay brush to refine transitions

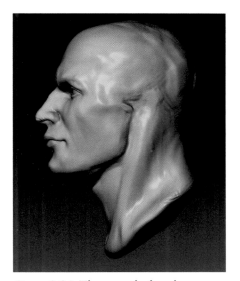

Figure 2.84: The smoothed neck

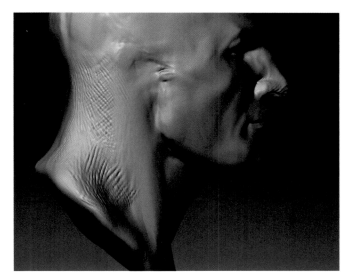

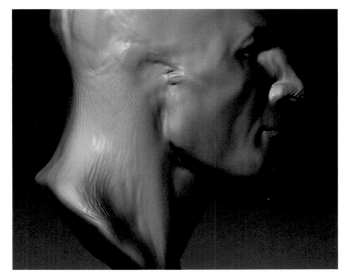

Figure 2.85: Smoothing rakes

Sculpting Ears

We'll now sculpt the ear directly from the side of the head. Since we began with a low poly sphere, we can easily divide the geometry up to millions of polygons. In the case of this mesh, it is currently 2 million polys. The secret to pulling protruding shapes such as ears and noses from a sphere is to ensure the underlying edges are evenly distributed in this area. In cases where the underlying geometry is stretched to the point of artifacting, then the ZBrush tool Reproject Highres Details can be used to correct these areas. We'll use Reproject Highres later in this section.

Complex compound shapes like ears are easier to dissect and re-create if you break them into their individual parts. We'll examine the ear and its anatomy, and through a combination of sculpting and masking, we'll sculpt the ears on the head.

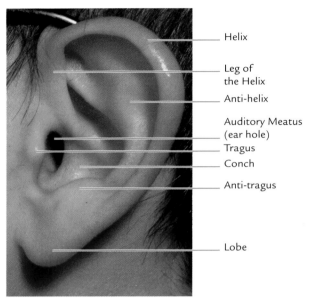

Figure 2.86: Ear with labeled parts

Figure 2.86 shows a human ear with its parts labeled.

1. Using a mask with the Standard brush, sketch in the placement of the auditory meatus again (Figure 2.87). This represents the ear hole and tragus. Finding this first helps place the ear correctly on the head. The ear itself lies just behind the midline of the head. It sits at an angle roughly equal to the angle of the jaw (Figure 2.88). Notice as well that the top of the ear is roughly in line with the brow bone, while the earlobe is in line with the bottom of the nose.

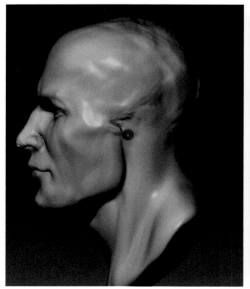

Figure 2.87: The auditory meatus

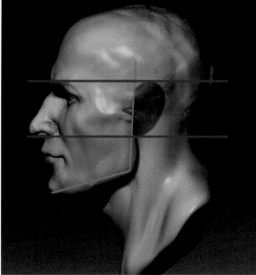

Figure 2.88: The angle of the ear

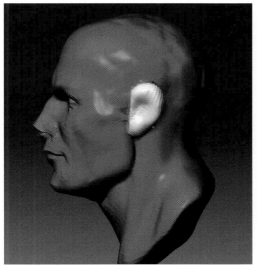

Figure 2.89: Ear mask

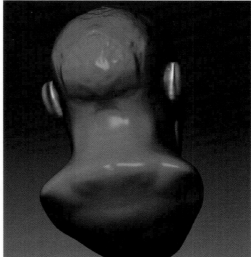

Figure 2.90: Working behind the ear

2. Invert the mask and step down a subdivision level. Using the Claytubes brush, pull the ear out. Take care to make it thicker near the back of the head so that it blends off in a wedge shape to the side of the head (Figure 2.89).

   Masking behind the ear allows you to pull the helix out as well as invert the mask and press the back of the ear in creating a draft behind the ear (see Figure 2.90).

3. Using Ctrl+Shift-click, draw a show marquee around the ear to hide the rest of the face. In Figure 2.91 you can see the ear isolated from the rest of the head. With the mask inverted, use the Standard brush with ZSub on to press the internal faces of the ear to make room for the antihelix and conch of the ear. The masked helix will remain in place.

4. The helix has an extension that dips down and terminates into the conch, or bowl, of the ear. This is called the *leg* of the helix. Mask out the leg of the helix. Invert the mask, and using the Standard brush, sculpt the extension of the helix that sweeps down into the conch of the ear.

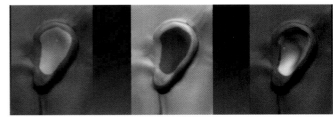

Figure 2.91: Building the basic ear wedge in steps

5. Mask out the shape of the antihelix (Figure 2.92). Invert the mask, and using the Inflate brush, build the general shape of the antihelix inside the ear. Rotate the model around as you work, and be sure not to take any part to a finish yet—just suggest the general shapes. Use the Move brush to pull out the shape of the tragus and deepen the conch of the ear.

6. Using the Inflate and Standard brushes, refine the shape of the antihelix, as shown in Figure 2.93.

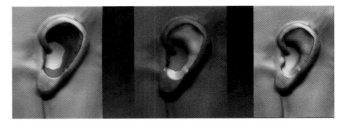

Figure 2.92: The antihelix

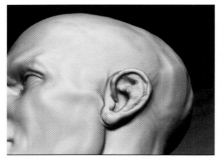

Figure 2.93: Antihelix and tragus

Figure 2.94: You can find the Reproject Higher Subdiv command in the Tool → Geometry menu.

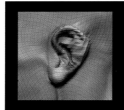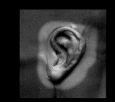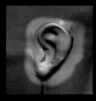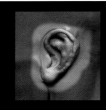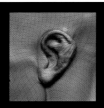

Figure 2.95: Reprojecting higher subdivision levels

7. If you find in the process of editing the ear that the underlying edges are spread apart or flowing off in another direction that interferes with the form you are trying to make, you can easily correct this. ZBrush has a tool called Reproject Higher Subdiv (Figure 2.94).

This tool allows you to let ZBrush relax the edges of your underlying subdivision levels while retaining the higher resolution sculpting you have already applied. This is useful when you are pulling large protruding forms from the mesh—you can reduce artifacts by redistributing the edges in a more efficient manner. To use Reproject Higher Subdiv, first mask out the area you want to correct at the highest subdivision level. Step down a couple of levels and smooth the surface gently with the softSmooth brush or a smooth brush with a low ZIntensity. The idea is to gently relax the edges without destroying all the form.

8. Select Tool → Geometry → Reproject Higher Subdiv, and ZBrush will reproject the detail onto this new subdivision level, retaining your work while taking advantage of the new edge distribution. See Figure 2.95 for these steps in action. Notice how the last wireframe shows edges that are evenly spaced and not spread apart as in the first wire.

9. You can deepen the furrow between the helix and antihelix by masking into this area and inverting the mask. Use the Standard brush with ZSub on to press in, thus creating the necessary draft.

10. Using the Pinch brush with LazyMouse on and BrushMod set to 10, you can finesse the planes between the ear's parts. Adding these touches helps reduce the lumpiness of the ear and gives it that structural cartilaginous quality (Figure 2.96).

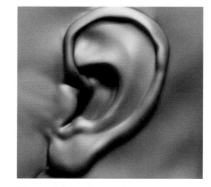

Figure 2.96: The ear in progress

11. After a few more passes with the Pinch brush, the ear is complete. If you have X Symmetry turned on, the changes are mirrored to the other ear as well. While it is easier to create the depth and draft on actual protruding geometry rather than pulling it from the surface of a sphere, it is important to know how much is possible with just very basic geometry. There may be times you want to sculpt an element that has no underlying topology to support it. Instead of letting the topology dictate your design, these shapes can be pulled from the existing surface. Later in this book we'll use ZBrush's topology tools to create an organized mesh from this head. Once the topology is optimized, you can make even more specific edits if you wish to refine the surface further.

This MatCap material, by Ralph Stumf, is available in his Creature Core thread at www.zbrushcentral.com. To use it, simply load it into the Material menu and fill the object by choosing Color → Fill Object (be sure that M is on).

Congratulations! You have now completed a human head sculpt from nothing more than a ZBrush primitive sphere (Figure 2.97). Although this mesh is not animation ready, ZBrush comes with a suite of remeshing tools that will allow you to take all your sculpted details and transfer them to a completely new level 1 mesh that is suitable for animating and rendering in a third-party application. See Chapter 10, where we'll remesh this head into an animation-ready model. In the next chapter, we'll move away from ZBrush primitives and explore sculpting on polygon models.

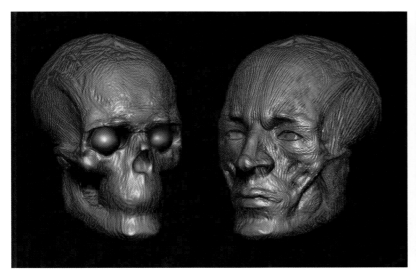 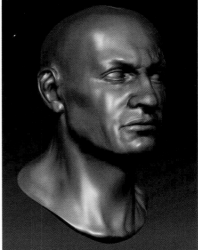

Figure 2.97: The final head

three

CHAPTER

Designing a Character Bust

In the previous two chapters *we have been working with ZBrush primitives to start our sculptures. While sculptures started from ZBrush primitives can be rebuilt into animation ready meshes using the ZBrush topology tools, in some cases you will want to start from an imported mesh instead. This may be a case where you have a generic head or body model, or perhaps an animation-ready mesh is completed and you are using this as a base. For more information on remeshing your finished sculpture to create an entirely new edge layout see Chapter 7.*

In this chapter, we will import a polygon mesh from a third-party modeling package. This will be a relatively simple humanoid head mesh from the Pixologic website. This is from a selection of meshes modeled by Ang Nguyen and made available for free. In this chapter we'll create two character busts. I'll walk you through the steps involved in designing and sculpting the primary and secondary forms; we'll talk detailing in the next chapter when we cover alphas and texture stamps.

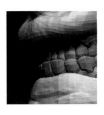

ZBrush and Working with Imported Meshes

In ZBrush, models are 3D meshes that are imported into ZBrush to become ZTools. The difference between ZTools and models is that a model is just a 3D mesh file that contains polygons and UV information. A ZTool is ZBrush's native file format for sculpted objects. A ZTool can contain multiple levels of subdivision, high-resolution sculpting details, texture, and PolyPaint information, as well as alpha maps and layer data. The ZTool format allows you to store far more than just an OBJ file.

Models are imported into the tool palette where they become available with the other ZTools listed there. When importing models into the tool palette, it is important to be sure your mesh is optimized for detailing in ZBrush. If your mesh is ordered and animation ready, or is part of an existing production pipeline, you may not have the freedom to lower the initial polygon count. The edge flows and topology have already been approved for rigging and animation. When loading a model into ZBrush, it is important to understand how ZBrush determines subdivisions levels and where the system limits are.

Physical memory is the most important deciding factor in determining your highest subdivision level, followed closely by processor speed. ZBrush is not concerned with graphics cards, and multiple processors are only useful when moving the model around the screen and sculpting. ZBrush uses the amount of physical RAM installed on the system to determine the highest possible subdivision level attainable. The processor comes into play when you start to rotate and manipulate the sculpture onscreen. A faster processor will allow you to move more polygons with less lag.

Figure 3.1: The Mem preferences

You can find the maximum subdivision level that ZBrush has set for the machine by choosing Preferences → Mem. The MaxPoly-PerMesh slider will show the value in terms of millions. A value of 50 here means that ZBrush will only allow you to subdivide to 50 million polygons (Figure 3.1). As shown in Chapter 1, it is possible to raise this value, but it is not always recommended as it can cause instability. If you raise the MaxPolyPerMesh value slider, be sure to raise the CompactMem slider to 2048 or 4096. This increases the amount of memory ZBrush will use before starting to write temp files to the hard drive, which slows down performance.

The question arises of how to ensure you get the maximum subdivision levels from ZBrush. Often an artist will load a mesh for sculpting only to find that it subdivides to a level that is unsatisfactory to get the level of detail desired. Starting with a lower polygon count can help ensure you reach the highest possible subdivision level. This works because of the algorithm ZBrush uses to subdivide.

ZBrush uses Catmull-Clark subdivision each time the Divide button is clicked. This means for each subdivision level, ZBrush multiplies the total polygon count by 4. So if level 1 is 4,000 faces, level 2 will be 4,000 × 4. That gives you a level 2 poly count of 16,000. If this mesh were divided again, ZBrush would multiply 16,000 by 4, giving you a level 3 polygon count of 64,000. If your initial poly count at level 1 were 17,000, you would reach 1 million faces by three subdivisions. Unless your MaxPolyPerMesh slider were set to something above 4, you would not subdivide again as the fourth subdivision level would be over 4 million.

Underlying topology can become a concern in ZBrush if your edge loops define forms that you choose to change later. There are times where your topology may fight the forms you are trying to make. Because of this, simple block models can be beneficial when working in ZBrush. They offer extremely simple bases that can be moved at the lower subdivision levels easily as well as subdivided up to millions of polygons for fine detailing. Once the sculpture is completed these meshes can easily be retopologized to any mesh resolution you desire. This helps keep the sculpting process separate from polygon modeling and allows you to focus on topology and technical concerns after the design phase is completed. The leg in Figure 3.2 illustrates how much form can be pulled from a simple block model.

Organized meshes are models that have been specially built for animation,. They have edge loops containing major muscle forms and areas of deformation (Figure 3.3). When retopologizing a design sculpt, you will strive

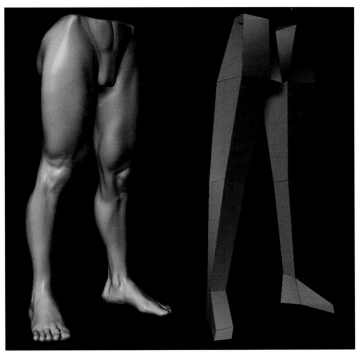

Figure 3.2: A leg sculpted from a box model

to create an organized mesh. It is often the case that organized meshes are built before the sculpting phase. This is valid approach, but I find that it limits the sculpture and can limit the subdivision levels in some cases. Organized meshes work best for animation, while sculpting can benefit from a much simpler mesh.

If you have holes in your base mesh that you want to maintain, for instance a head which is separated from a shirt, you will find smoothing in ZBrush will cause the border edges to shrink. To correct this when you import your base mesh, click Tool→ Geometry Crease button. This will tag the border edge of the geometry and keep it in place while smoothing the rest of the model.

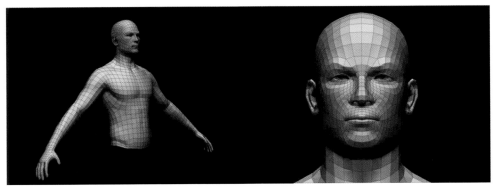

Figure 3.3: A mesh organized for animation (model by Ricardo Ariza).

Another option for creating meshes in ZBrush is ZSpheres. ZSpheres are a mesh generation tool in ZBrush that allow you to quickly generate models using chains of spheres and attractors (Figure 3.4). Chapter 6 will cover ZSpheres in more detail. Although ZSpheres do not offer the same direct control of edge placement that direct polygon modeling does, ZSpheres use certain controls to create form and edge loops. These controls are best suited for rapid form development and not for the creation of organized meshes. ZSpheres allow you to quickly sketch a 3D model.

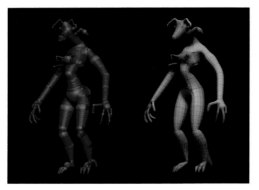

Figure 3.4: A ZSphere model

Optimizing Meshes for ZBrush

In this section we will import a simple mesh to show how a poorly distributed edge layout can create problems with sculpting. For this example I'll use the model goblin in Figure 3.5. Notice the edge distribution on this character. The goblin has a concentration on edges in the face and arms. These areas will subdivide denser than the rest of the body as you subdivide. This may be desirable in some cases, but most of the time it's best to keep an even mesh. Preplanning is key to getting a suitable mesh into ZBrush. If you can avoid topology at the outset and remesh later, I find this is the most versatile approach.

Also notice the stretched faces in his tail (Figure 3.6). Because the faces are tighter in the body and longer in the tail when subdividing, these faces will not divide as densely as other areas, making details here softer and less sharp.

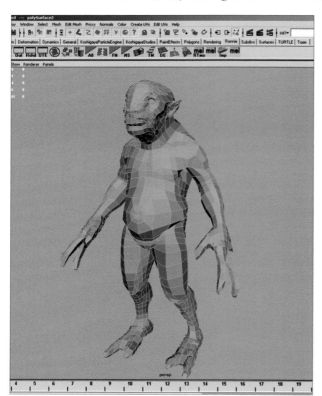

Figure 3.5: A low-poly goblin model

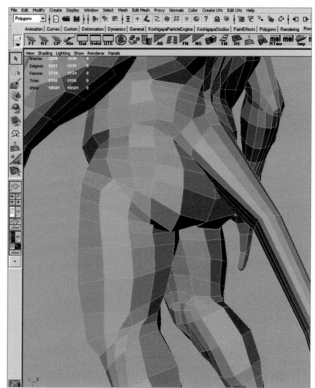

Figure 3.6: Stretched faces in the tail

Figure 3.7 shows the underlying mesh in Frame display. Notice how the areas of tighter edges at the small of the back are denser than the tail (Figure 3.8). If I make a long curved stroke with the Standard brush, you can see the difference between the stroke at the small of the back and the faceted quality at the tail. This is because the edges are not distributed as evenly in this area due to inconsistencies in the base mesh. With higher subdivisions, this problem would be less pronounced, but whenever possible try to keep the edges evenly dispersed across the base mesh (Figure 3.9).

Frame mode (Shift+F) will display the model in polyframe. This shows the current polygroups as well as the edges of the polygons. It allows you to see the edge distribution and flow as you subdivide.

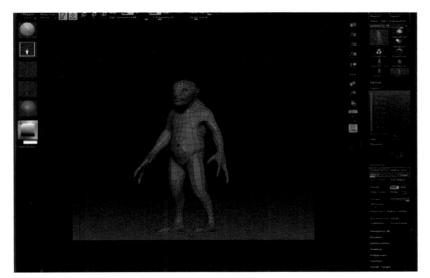

*Figure 3.7:
Goblin mesh
in Frame mode*

Figure 3.8: The stretched faces subdivide less efficiently.

Figure 3.9: Details here are less sharp because of the lower subdivision level in the longer areas.

Now you can see how evenly distributed edges and a low polygon count can help you get the most out of your ZBrush subdivision levels. Unless you have a specific plan for your mesh and a need to bring finished topology into the program at the outset, the best work-flow is to work on a design mesh optimized for ZBrush and then use the ZBrush topology tools to generate a mesh suited to your needs—be they in games or film res models ready for animation.

Common Topology Issues

There are some problems you may encounter when using models that contain irregular topology. ZBrush prefers quad geometry or tris. A quad is a polygon face with only 4 vertices while a tri has only 3 (Figure 3.10). ZBrush will not accept n-gons, that is, a polygon with 5 or more vertices. ZBrush will triangulate these faces before importing.

Another common problem will come in star configurations (Figure 3.11) (also known as extraordinary vertices). These can sometimes pinch while sculpting and be difficult to smooth out. They will also often cause problems when rendering with a displacement map in Maya. This will usually manifest as a pinch or split in the mesh.

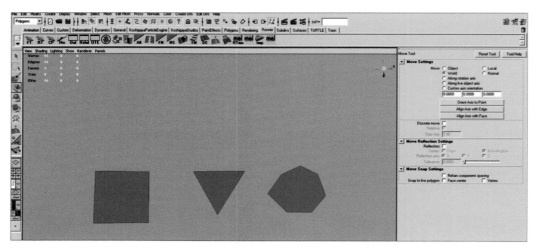

Figure 3.10: The polygon on the left is a quad, the middle is a tri, and the right is an n-gon.

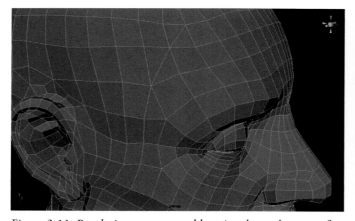 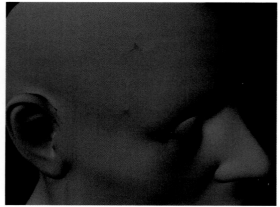

Figure 3.11: Rendering error caused by triangles and star configurations

Increasing Polygon Counts with Local Subdivision

In some cases, you may find that you need to subdivide certain areas more than others. This could be when you are working on a character in costume whose body is not as important as, say, his head and hands. In these instances, it is good to keep your subdivisions in these areas to maximize detail instead of spreading it over the entire model. Another case may be that you have maximized your subdivisions and yet you still need more detail in a certain area of the mesh. A full subdivision level would put you over the max levels, but dividing a portion of the mesh would work. This can be accomplished with local subdivision.

Figure 3.12: Masking the area to subdivide

To locally subdivide a mesh, follow these steps.

1. Load your ZTool into ZBrush, enter Edit mode with the T key, and step up to the highest subdivision level.

2. Mask the area you to which you want to add detail. In this case I am masking the face (Figure 3.12). Invert the mask by Ctrl-clicking on the background (off the model) or by selecting Tool → Masking and clicking the Invert button. When the area you want to subdivide is unmasked, step down to the lowest subdivision level and press Ctrl+D to subdivide.

3. The unmasked area will subdivide. Notice the connecting region in the mesh (Figure 3.13). If you need more subdivision levels, it is a simple process to repeat. By simply Ctrl+Shift-clicking a polygrouped area, you can isolate it from the rest of the mesh mask again, invert the mask, and further subdivide by pressing Ctrl+D again until the area is dense enough for your needs. Figure 3.14 illustrates the process of local subdivision.

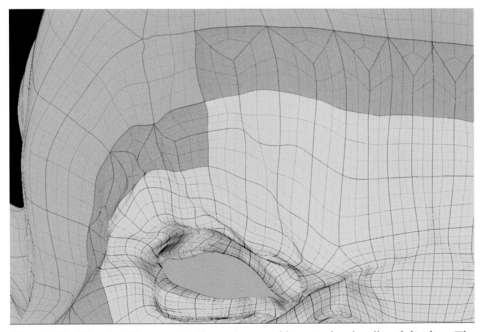

Figure 3.13: ZBrush will automatically retain a quad layout when locally subdividing. The connecting area in red represents the transition between areas of higher density and areas of lower density.

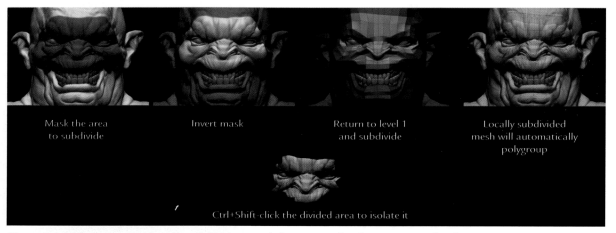

Mask the area to subdivide

Invert mask

Return to level 1 and subdivide

Locally subdivided mesh will automatically polygroup

Ctrl+Shift-click the divided area to isolate it

Figure 3.14: The process to locally subdivide a mesh for greater details concentrated in key areas

This area can now handle much higher levels of detail than other, less important areas of the character. When you locally subdivide the original mesh, the transition area and the high detail area are separately polygrouped to help you work with them.

The Making of "Elite Soldier"

Featured Artist: Fabian Loing

I start a character by analyzing the concepts; I try to understand the character better by gathering as many references as I can possibly find. If your character has folds, then start gathering images that have leather folds in them, and so on. While making the base character here, I did not model any detail whatsoever but my focus was on the general shape.

When the base models are done, I bring all the pieces together, appending them one by one in ZBrush as subtools. Then, I start increasing the subdivision level of each subtool one at a time. The main thing here would still be shape and silhouette. The way I work, I sculpt my entire subtool simultaneously instead of finishing one subtool to the highest detail and move to the next one. That way, I could actually make much better details that flow together.

When I am satisfied with the shape and silhouette, which by now would be in Subdivision 3 in ZBrush, I start thinking about my approach for the detailing. For details such as folds, I start sculpting major folds first. At this point, references will be most important to me because I want to create a detail pass that feels natural and real. For folds, I would use just "simple brushes" with the combination of different Focus Value, Move brush, and Inflate brush a lot. Always start with a low intensity value of any brush you are using. Look for any defining folds and sculpt those in.

continued

After the major folds are in, I then move to the more difficult and time consuming part, the hard body. As you can see, my character actually has a considerable amount of hard-body objects. So, before I detail any of the helmet, backpack, or boots, I have to, again, analyze the concepts. I have to figure out what will be the major details and what will be the smaller and finer detail. I think masking is an absolute must if you want to create a nice and crisp hard-body details. Let's say we are making a belt buckle: I would simply look at the general outer shape of the buckle, create a mask with that buckle shape, and then, before inflating that mask, I would actually smooth out the surface with the Smooth brush and the Flatten brush. When I am done with the masking, I then use Tool → Deformation → Inflate. (Also, I always create a new layer for any new major detail I sculpt in.)

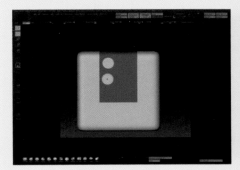

The following image shows the steps I made for masking the boots. I always mask out the bigger areas first before masking the smaller and detail area.

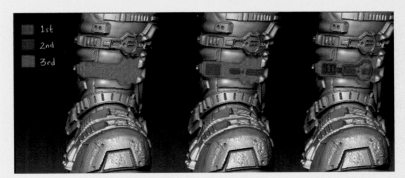

Now, for the base I actually used a lot of real photo references of snow and rocks. After gathering all photos, I would then convert them into alphas in ZBrush, and just drag the alpha just like when you want to mask anything. Only this time, the mask will actually be the image you have taken earlier. Now, turn off the mask, make sure your brush has no mask too, and start sculpting the base; this way, the only geometry being affected is the ones that are unmasked. I use this method for any high-frequency details of the models, including the pants as shown. Always do high-frequency details last.

Importing and Preparing a Mesh for Sculpting

To begin, we'll import the base geometry into ZBrush as a tool. Previously we were selecting ZBrush primitives from the Tool menu. These meshes come preloaded. For the generic head, we need to import it into the program. Remember a model is an OBJ file, which is just a polygon mesh created in a polygon modeling package, it does not carry multiple subdivision levels, layers and other information. ZTools on the other hand are ZBrush models that save polygons, multiple-subdivision levels, sculpted detail, subtools, color and texture information, as well as alphas.

To import the model into ZBrush, choose Tool → Import. This will open a file browser dialog box. Browse to the Chapter 3 folder on the book's DVD and select generichead.obj. This will load the head OBJ file into ZBrush. There will be a new icon in the tool palette representing your imported model under user 3D meshes and 2.5D brushes. By default this new tool is already selected, so you may now draw it on the canvas by left-clicking and dragging into the document window (Figure 3.15).

Enter Edit mode, and you are now ready to sculpt on the model.

Figure 3.15: Drawing the imported tool on the canvas

Before we can sculpt on the tool, it must be immediately placed in Edit mode. If you were to stroke on the canvas again, it would only draw more instances of the mesh on the canvas. As soon as the tool is drawn, enter Edit mode by pressing the T key on your keyboard or by clicking the Edit button at the top of the screen.

Using Polygroups to Organize Your Mesh

When sculpting a character, it is beneficial to have the model organized into easy-to-select parts to facilitate working on the ears or mouth separately. I want to make sure that I can isolate the ears from the head and manipulate the various parts of the ear without affecting the back of the head. The same is true for the lips. Notice that if you try to move the upper lip with the Move brush, often the lower lip will be moved too since it is in close proximity and falls under the falloff of the Move brush. Masking offers similar problems when you're trying to paint a mask on just one lip and not both.

Polygroups allow you to quickly and easily isolate parts of the model for sculpting. Polygroups in ZBrush are simply selections of polygons that are tagged as being part of a group. They are similar to selection sets in Maya. Polygroups are assigned a separate color and can be viewed by entering Frame mode by pressing Shift+F or selecting the Frame button on the Transform panel (Figures 3.16 and 3.17). In Figure 3.17 this stegosaurus has its parts polygrouped into different selections.

Polygroups can help you organize parts of your model into easy-to-access groups. Having polygroups for the character's ears makes it easier to quickly show or hide the ear geometry to mask this geo independently of the head. Any polygroup can be isolated by Ctrl+Shift-clicking the group. This hides all other polygroups. You can invert this selection to show the hidden groups and hide the currently active one by Ctrl+Shift-clicking and dragging a marquee anywhere off the model on the document background. To reveal all groups again, Ctrl+Shift-click anywhere off the model on the document background.

Figure 3.16: Model in Frame mode

Figure 3.17: The Frame button on the Transform panel

You create polygroups by choosing Tool → Polygroups. In the resulting dialog box you will find three options: Auto Groups, UV Groups, and Group Visible. Auto Groups will automatically create polygroups from separate objects in an imported OBJ file—for example, if you imported an OBJ that was a sphere and a box (Figure 3.18), ZBrush loads them as a single tool. You cannot manipulate them independently from each other. Auto Groups will automatically polygroup the two objects since the OBJ file recognizes them as separate objects even though they import as one tool (Figure 3.19).

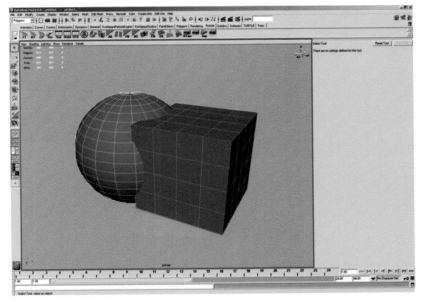

Figure 3.18: Sphere and box OBJ file

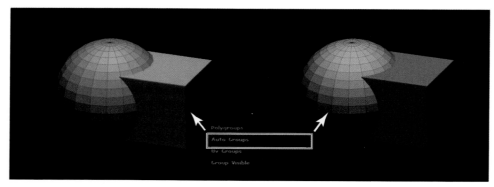

Figure 3.19: Polygrouped sphere and box

UV Groups will create polygroups from faces arranged in the UV Texture space outside 0 to 1. Notice in Figure 3.20 that the UVs of this character are shifted outside 0 to 1. UV Groups will create new polygroups for any faces outside 0 to 1.

Group Visible will polygroup the faces visible in the document window. So if you hide part of the model and then apply Group Visible those visible faces are tagged as a new polygroup. This is the option we will use to group the ears into separate parts. It is important to note that this does not separate these faces from the mesh or change the geometry at all; it is simply a tool for quickly showing and hiding saved selections.

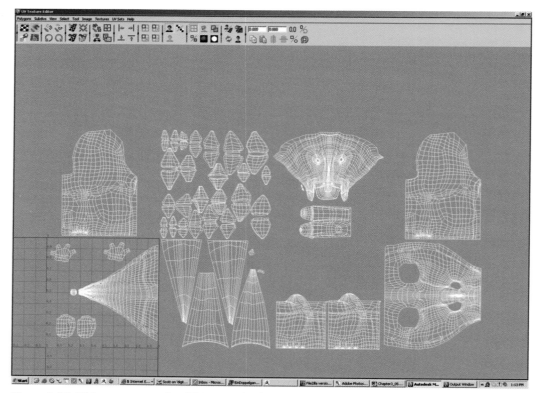

Figure 3.20: This stegosaurus has UVs in multiple regions outside 0 to 1.

It is possible to use the Subtool menu to break apart polygroups into separate subtools. To do this, click Tool → Subtool → Group Split. This will separate the grouped parts into different subtools. For more on subtools, see Chapter 5.

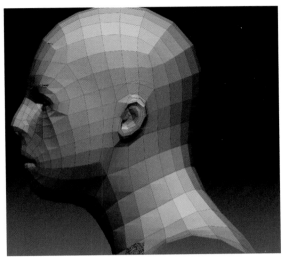

Figure 3.21: *When using the Move brush on an unmasked ear, the ear as well as the faces of the head are changed.*

Polygroups have several functions in ZBrush. The one we will examine here is for organizing a complex mesh into easy-to-isolate parts. Notice that if I use the Move tool on the ear I pull not only the ear faces but the faces on the head behind the ear (Figure 3.21). Masking into a tight area like this can be tricky, not to mention time-consuming, if you have to repeatedly mask the ears each time you want to work around them.

To polygroup the ear, follow these steps:

1. Begin by hiding the faces using Ctrl+Shift-drag to create a hide marquee. Around the head faces, hide until just the ears are visible. Since this head is symmetrical, if you snap to a side view you can hide both sides at once.

2. Once the ears are visible, choose Tool → Polygroups and click Group Visible (Figure 3.22). To make hiding faces easier, you may want to turn on Lasso Select by clicking the Lasso tool button at the left side of the screen ▦ . This allows you to make irregular-shaped selections instead of using only a marquee. When hiding faces with the Show Hide Marquee, it can be easier if you turn on Point Select ▦ . This will cause any face from which you select one vertex to be hidden. Point Select is in the Transform menu (Figure 3.23).

3. The ear is now polygrouped. To see this, Ctrl-drag in the document window to reveal all again. Now press Shift+F to go into Frame mode and you can see the different-colored faces for the two polygroups (Figure 3.24).
   It will be useful to have the ring of faces around the ear separated from the ear and head for more flexibility when working on this area. To accomplish this, hide the faces of the head so that only the ear is visible.

4. Hide the ring of faces around the ear. Once the faces are hidden, you can invert what is visible on screen by Ctrl+Shift-dragging a marquee in the document window. This will show the previously hidden parts. Since the head is grouped separately from the outer ear ring, you can hide the head by Ctrl+Shift-clicking the head mesh. Now only the outer ear ring is visible. Assign this a new polygroup by choosing Tool → Polygroups → Group Visible. Figure 3.25 shows the ear and its individual polygroups.

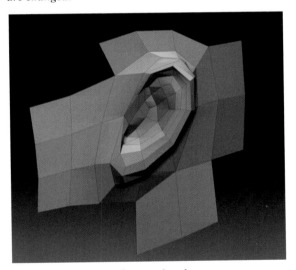

Figure 3.22: *The ear faces isolated*

Figure 3.23: *Point Select*

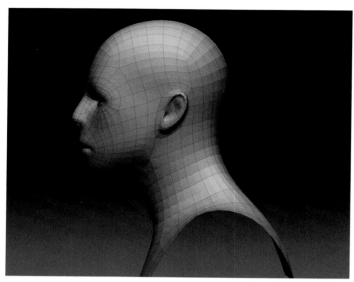

Figure 3.24: Polygrouped ear faces

Now you can easily mask the ear area by hiding the head using Ctrl+Shift-click. Only the head is visible; the ear is now hidden. Ctrl-click-drag a masking marquee to mask these faces (Figure 3.26). Invert the mask by Ctrl-clicking the background to keep the head masked and the ear unmasked.

Figure 3.25: Outer ring polygrouped

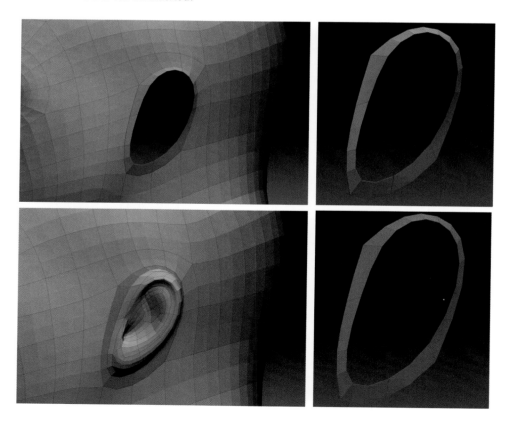

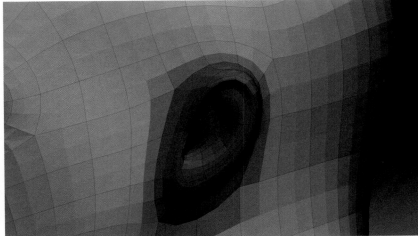

Figure 3.26: Masking with polygroups

By masking the ear, you can sculpt against the back of the ear, or by masking the head, you can easily modify the ear and move it without disturbing the faces of the head (Figure 3.27). This makes the process of sculpting the ears independently of the head much easier, especially since you don't have to constantly re-create a complex mask. Any time you need to mask the head, ear or outer ring, simply hide the rest of the mesh and mask the visible parts.

Using Polygroups to Move the Mouth

The same problems with sculpting the ears also manifest when you're trying to move the lips independently of one another. When trying to mask or move the upper lip, you will often find the lower lip is moved as well due to their proximity to each other. The brushes will simply affect anything underneath their falloff rings that isn't masked. The solution to this is to polygroup the lower lip separately from the rest of the head. This makes it very simple to grab one part of the mouth and quickly manipulate it while sculpting.

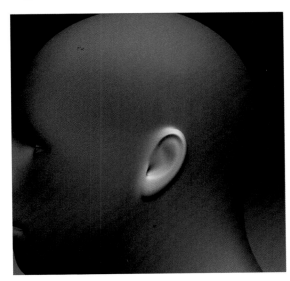

Figure 3.27: Using masking to help manipulate ear shapes

To polygroup the mouth, we will use steps similar to those we used with the ear, but we first need to mask the lips separately from each other. This can be difficult since the lips are so close; masking one lip invariably seems to create a mask on part of the other. We will need to spread the lips open.

1. Store a morph target of your model by selecting Tool → Morph Target and clicking the StoreMT button. This creates a copy of the mesh shape in memory that we can easily return to. We are storing this morph target because we will now stretch the mouth open to facilitate masking the lips. By returning to the stored shape, we can correct any changes made to the mouth while keeping the mask.

2. Select the Smooth brush and smooth the mouth area. This will have the effect of spreading the mouth faces open. You can also get good results using the Inflate brush set to ZSub, as this will push faces apart (Figure 3.28).

This process is somewhat involved, so you would not want to repeat it each time you want to open the mouth. Although the mesh is masked, we can easily create a polygroup; therefore, hiding one half of the mouth is easier.

3. With the lower lip still masked, select Tool → Masking and click the HidePt button . HidePt will hide any unmasked faces. With the lower lip visible, you can now polygroup it separately from the rest of the head (Figure 3.29).

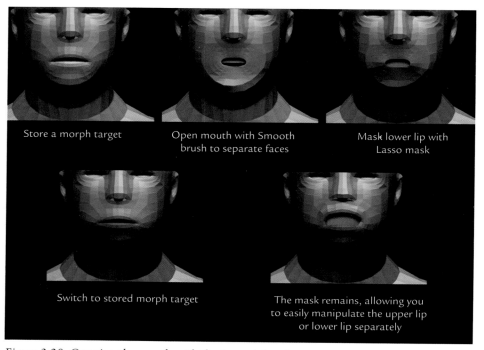

Store a morph target

Open mouth with Smooth brush to separate faces

Mask lower lip with Lasso mask

Switch to stored morph target

The mask remains, allowing you to easily manipulate the upper lip or lower lip separately

Figure 3.28: Opening the mouth with the Smooth brush

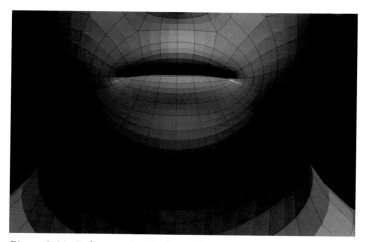

Figure 3.29: Polygrouping the lower lip

Sculpting a Character Bust

In this section, we'll sculpt a character from the generic human head bust (Figure 3.30). This ZTool is prepared with mouth and ear polygroups to facilitate a quick sculpting workflow when dealing with these areas. We'll also add new parts to the head directly using the Insert Mesh function. In the course of this demo, we'll also make use of the Gravity brush modifier as well as Transpose.

Figure 3.30: This character bust was sculpted from the generic human head mesh.

1. Initially we know we want this character to be leaning his head back and grinning. The orientation of the head we want is different than that of the generic head mesh. To accomplish this change, use Transpose to shift the orientation of the head on the shoulders. To do this, snap to a side view and mask the shoulders with a lasso. Switch to Transpose Move by pressing the W key and shift the head back slightly (Figure 3.31). Subdivide the mesh by pressing Ctrl+D, and using the Standard brush, build up the anatomy of the neck, at this stage just suggesting the form and direction of the sternomastoid and clavicle.

2. Now let's take advantage of the ear polygroups to change the ear shape. Ctrl+Shift-click the ear to hide the head. Using the Move brush, adjust the ear shape into a more monstrous form (Figure 3.32).

3. Using the Move brush, stretch the mouth back, starting to suggest a grin. At this stage, you can widen the neck and shoulders to give the character a more muscular look (Figure 3.33).

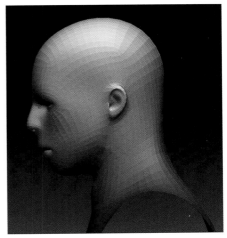

Figure 3.31: The head shifted back with Transpose Move

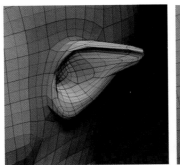
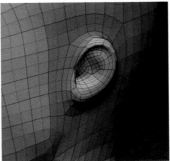

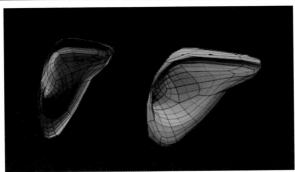

Figure 3.32: Isolating the ear and changing its shape

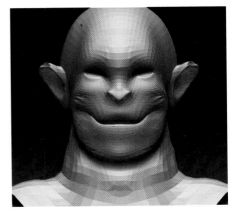

Figure 3.33: Creating the grin and adjusting the shape of the shoulders

4. Taking advantage of the polygrouped mouth, let's open the mouth by masking and moving the shapes (Figure 3.34). At this point let's also add teeth to the model. (The teeth in this example were modeled by Jim McPherson.) Import them into the Tool palette, then append them to the model as a subtool. Using the Transpose Move and Scale options, place the teeth in the head. Notice that the teeth here are upside down—I liked the ferocity that this underbite suggested, so I left them flipped (Figure 3.35). At this stage let's also add polymesh spheres as eyeballs.

5. To sculpt the forms of the ear, add another subdivision level and mask out inside the helix of the ear. Invert the mask and, using the Standard brush set to ZSub, carve away the negative space and start to introduce the ear forms (Figure 3.36). Remember to address the parts of the ear as discussed in Chapter 2.

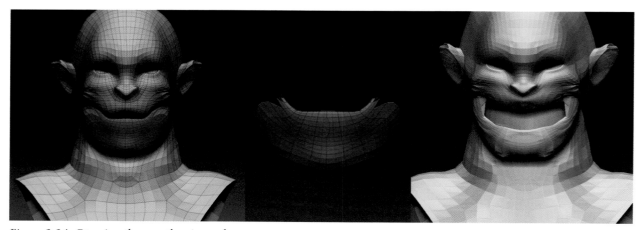

Figure 3.34: Opening the mouth using polygroups

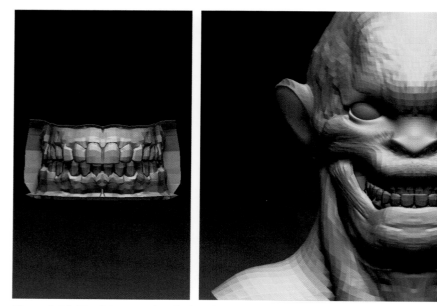

Figure 3.35: Teeth imported and placed

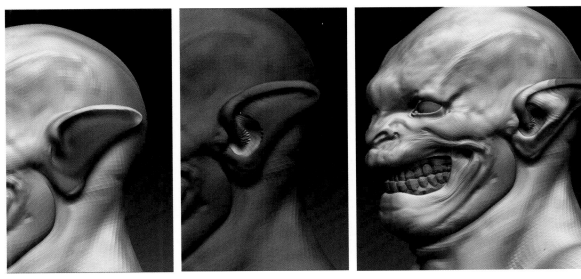

Figure 3.36: Sculpting the forms of the ear

6. Using the Standard brush and alternating between ZAdd and ZSub, carve in the flow of major folds of flesh around the mouth and in the forehead. Take care to make the skin seem compressed at the cheeks by making deep recesses and high puckering rolls to help create the impression that the big mouth is stretching open. We can start to refine the anatomy of the neck, so also use the Interactive Light Utility `InteractiveLight` to move the light around and check the forms under different lighting conditions. Remember that this utility will only work with the standard materials and not the MatCap materials. For this example, I'm using the BasicMaterial.

7. Since this character is intended to be very fat, we want to add fleshiness and folds to the cheeks and under the chin. Using the Elastic brush set to Zadd, start massing out the fat underneath the chin. Elastic is similar to Inflate, but it tries to maintain the forms already sculpted and tends to be less destructive of the area you are sculpting over (Figure 3.37).

Figure 3.37: Adding fat to the neck with the Elastic brush

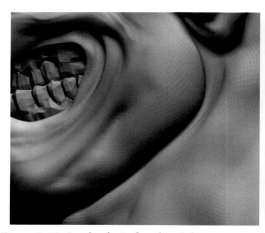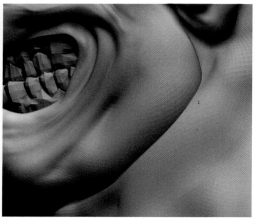

Figure 3.38: Stroke the Inflate brush between two folds to draw them together in compression.

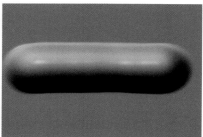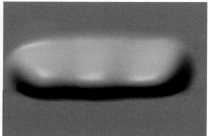

Figure 3.39: This figure illustrates gravity and its effect on form. The left image is the sculpted form; the right represents the silhouette of the shape depicted. By adding more visual weight to the bottom of a form, you can create the impression that gravity is acting on it.

8. Let's make further refinements to the shapes of the face (Figure 3.38). Use the Smooth brush on a low intensity to soften the forms. Create tight puckers between the folds of flesh by using the Inflate brush along the space where two folds meet. This has the effect of creating the look of two folds of skin pressing together.

9. Now use the Gravity modifier on the Elastic brush to add a sense of weight to the skin folds. Gravity is acting on our bodies at all times, but it is most apparent in loose-hanging skin like this character's jowls. Figure 3.39 shows two forms. The form on the left has no sense of gravity, while the one on the right has a sense of weight and drag. By adding more body to the bottom of the fold, it appears that the fatty tissue is being pulled down by gravity. This applies to skin folds, finer wrinkles, and even cloth. The Gravity brush tries to automate this process by adding to the surface in the direction of the Gravity arrow (Figure 3.40). You can use Gravity on any brush by simply raising the Gravity slider value under the main Brush menu (Figure 3.41).

10. The form is nearly finished and the sculpt is showing a strong sense of character (Figure 3.42). Turn off X symmetry by pressing the X hotkey and start to "break" symmetry. Breaking symmetry means adding asymmetrical elements to different sides of the head to combat the perfect 3D look.

Figure 3.40: The Gravity brush modifier

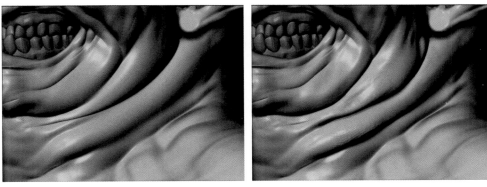

Figure 3.41: Using the Elastic brush with Gravity to add weight to the flesh folds

Figure 3.42: The final form development

Adding Geometry Using Mesh Insert

At this point let's add more geometry to the head. We'll add a pair of curved horns to the head. There are two approaches we can take to add geometry. The one we'll use in this section is called insertMesh. This tool allows you to insert new geometry to an existing ZTool and blend it off, just like adding clay! If the model needs to go into an animation pipeline, the resulting model can be retopologized in ZBrush to create a new ZTool with all the detail but as a single mesh.

1. For the horn let's use a spiral primitive. You can use any imported mesh, but the spiral is close to the shape we want so it is faster to create the horn from a ZBrush primitive. From the main Tool menu select the Spiral3D tool; draw the spiral on the canvas and enter Edit mode by pressing the T key.

2. Under Tool → Initialize, change the following settings to alter the shape of the horn to what we need for this character: Coverage 619, SDisp 3.10, SDivide 9.

3. To insert this horn ZTool into the creature ZTool it must have the same number of subdivisions. This is so ZBrush can divide and lower the meshes together and let you retain your subdivision levels after inserting new geometry. If the two tools had different numbers of levels, ZBrush could not step them back down together had you lowered subD levels. The creature head is currently five subdivision levels. With the Spiral3D tool active, click make-Polymesh3D under the Tool menu 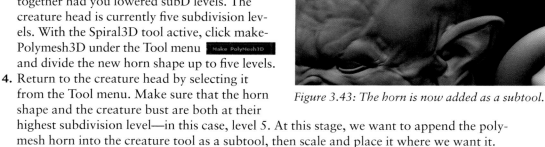 and divide the new horn shape up to five levels.

Figure 3.43: The horn is now added as a subtool.

4. Return to the creature head by selecting it from the Tool menu. Make sure that the horn shape and the creature bust are both at their highest subdivision level—in this case, level 5. At this stage, we want to append the polymesh horn into the creature tool as a subtool, then scale and place it where we want it. Click Tool → Subtool → Append **Append** and select the polymesh horn from the tool list. Be sure to select the PM3D version and not the original ZBrush primitive.

5. This will add the horn as a subtool. Activate the subtool by selecting it from the subtool list (Figure 3.43). Use the Transpose Move Rotate and Scale buttons at the top of the screen to move the horn into place (Figure 3.43). Be sure to sink it slightly into the surface of the head.

6. We now want to clone this subtool so we can insert it into the head as a single mesh. This will allow us to blend it into the skin as a single object, something that is impossible with subtools. Under the main Tool menu, click the Clone button **Clone** . This will create a copy of the current subtool in the Tool menu. This copy will carry all the same scale, position, and rotation as the original. With the horn subtool selected, click Delete under Tool → Subtool. This will delete the subtool horn from the character ZTool. The cloned copy is still in the Tool palette.

7. If you have multiple subtools like eyes and teeth, make sure the head is selected in the Subtool menu. Open Tool → Geometry and click the InsertMesh button. This will bring up the Tool palette.

8. From the Tool palette select the cloned horn that you want to insert into the current ZTool. As long as both tools have the same number of subdivision levels, you can insert the horn and retain all your divisions (Figure 3.44).

Figure 3.44: Once the horn is inserted, it becomes part of the head geometry and you regain all your subdivision levels.

A benefit of using Mesh Insert to add geometry is that it can now be seamlessly sculpted into the other mesh. Using the Clay brush, we'll blend the horn into the character head.

1. Select the Clay brush from the Brush menu. Make sure the brush is set to ZAdd and the BrushMod value is set to 10 or more. Stroke along the edge where the horn intersects the head and the seam will blend away (Figure 3.45). While these two objects are not merged geometrically, simply using the ZBrush Remeshing tools can allow you to make a single ZTool from multiple inserted meshes.

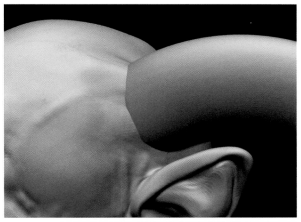

> Using the Smooth brush across a MeshInsert seam can cause the two parts to separate. Instead of using the Smooth brush there, use the Claytubes brush with no alpha. This will have a smoothing effect on the surface while maintaining the blend. Once the seam is smooth, you can switch back to the standard Smooth brush.

2. To add the second horn, simply append the horn back in as a subtool. We'll use Mirror to flip the horn, but this only works on objects with a single subdivision level. While at the highest subdivision level, click Tool → Geometry → Delete Lower to delete the lower SubD levels. With the horn subtool still selected, click Tool → Deformation → Mirror (Figure 3.46) to flip the orientation to the opposite side.

3. Reconstruct the subdivision levels by clicking Tool → Geometry → Reconstruct SubDiv. This button causes ZBrush to re-create each subdivision level. Click ReconstructSubDiv until you have five levels again.

4. Step back to the highest subdivision level and clone this mirrored horn, then delete the subtool. Then follow the same steps as earlier to MeshInsert the mirrored horn into the ZTool (Figure 3.46).

Figure 3.45: The Clay brush can blend away seams between inserted meshes.

Figure 3.46: Use the Mirror function to flip the horn to the other side.

That completes the first character we'll design in this chapter. We have looked at polygrouping, creating a sense of gravity in our sculpture, introducing interactive light, and using MeshInsert. If you would like to see the entire screenshot process involved in creating this character, check the accompanying DVD. In the next section we'll create the character from the cover of this book. We'll use many similar techniques, but we'll add new geometry in a totally different way.

Advanced Techniques: Sculpting the Stingerhead

In this section, we'll look at the steps used to sculpt the Stingerhead character from the cover of this book. I designed the Stingerhead from the same generic head mesh used in this chapter. When adding the long horn on the back of his head, I used a different technique than Insert Mesh; I used a displacement map to transfer detail. This is a valuable workflow in a production pipeline as it allows you to transfer sculpted details between meshes with different topology but similar UVs. Let's take a look at the process used to create the Stingerhead. Please see the DVD for a timelapse sculpting video of this character.

1. Using the Move brush, begin to pull at the mesh. Make sure that X Symmetry is turned on. At this point you are most concerned with the overall silhouette and the form of the creature. Pull at the forms of the back of the head, elongating the mesh to give the character a long spiked back to his head (Figure 3.47).

2. Using Transpose, lengthen the neck. You can use Transpose with masking to rotate and scale parts of a mesh rather than the mesh as a whole (Figure 3.48). Mask out the head, leaving the neck unmasked. Step up to level 3 and press the W key to enter Move mode. To soften the edges of the mask, Ctrl-click the mask a few times. This will feather the edge. Draw a transpose line from the base of the skull to the shoulders. Select the lower ring center and pull to stretch the neck out (Figure 3.49). For more information on Transpose for posing see Chapter 7.

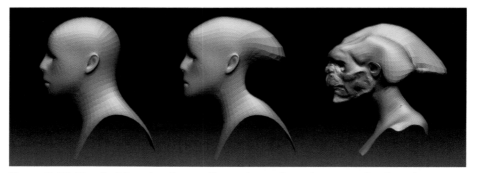

Figure 3.47: Use the Move brush to pull new shapes from the generic head mesh.

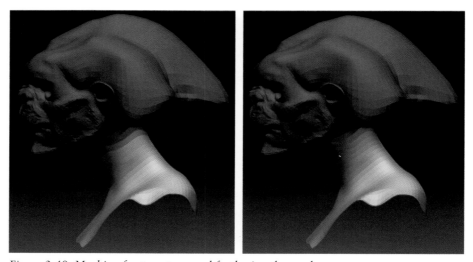

Figure 3.48: Masking for transpose and feathering the mask

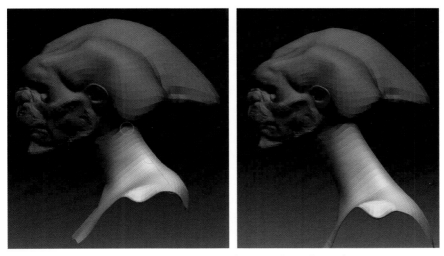

Figure 3.49: The transpose line before and after stretching the neck

3. Begin to rough in the basic forms of the neck and shoulders using a custom brush I call flatInflate. This brush is available to you on the DVD. This is a variation of the Inflate brush that adds form in a flattened gradual build-up. I find it most useful when trying to subtly build up forms over the progress of a sculpture.

This brush was created and saved with the same steps detailed in Chapter 2. By altering the brush Edit curve, I was able to change the manner in which the Inflate brush affects the surface. See Figure 3.50 for a look at the Edit curve composition for the flatInflate brush.

Removing all surface shading and looking at just the silhouette allows you to concentrate on the overall silhouette of the character. The silhouette is a very important aspect of design since it is the first read, meaning the first thing your mind processes when you look at a character. Figure 3.51 shows examples of different character silhouettes and how they affect the read of the character.

Figure 3.50: The flatInflate brush Edit curve

Figure 3.51: Various silhouettes

Figure 3.52: The character bust with the Flat Color material applied

A useful trick when trying to judge the overall proportions of the character is to switch from the current material to the Flat Color material. This will allow you to spot the silhouette of the character quickly as well as sculpt while looking just at the profiles (Figure 3.52). Reducing to the overall outline can help you see when a shape needs to be pushed to help communicate the feeling you are trying to inspire or depict the anatomical form you want to represent.

It is possible to snap to an orthographic view and move the mesh in Flat mode, manipulating just the overall outlines without being distracted by internal details. When you are ready to view the whole mesh again, simply select another material.

4. Using the flatInflate brush from the DVD, block in the clavicles, sternomastoid, and jaw muscles (Figure 3.53). These forms may be overstated now, but as the sculpt progresses they will be smoothed back and into the surface forms.

5. Eyeballs are added to this head just as they were in Chapter 2. Simply create a Sphere3D tool and append it into the current head.

When making a sphere for an eyeball, be sure to click the MakePolymesh3D button to create a polygon sphere. If you don't make the eyeball a polymesh, you won't be able to sculpt on the surface later if you choose to create corneal bulges on the surface of the eye.

---

6. Move and scale it to match a single eye socket. Clone this eyeball and append it back into the mesh. Be sure to clone the eyeball instead of appending the original sphere back into the tool. The reason for this is that the current eye subtool has been placed and scaled correctly. Cloning will copy this sphere's placement and allow you to simply mirror flip the copy when it is appended to the tool. Two identical eyes are now sitting on top of each other in the Subtool menu. Use the Mirror function under Tool → Deformation to flip the sphere to the other side.

7. A long, curved horn down the back of the head will serve our design well. However, this is difficult to do because if we want to pull the form out from the head and curve it down, it may extend the faces too far for even subdivision. This would create issues similar to the tail demonstration at the beginning of this chapter. As we saw in Chapter 2 the Reproject Higher Subdiv button sometimes corrects issues like this.

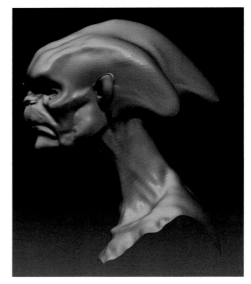

This can be accomplished with Insert Mesh as we saw in the previous demonstration or with a process I call "Displacement Map Detail Transfer." This technique uses a displacement map to transfer sculpting from one ZTool to another with an altered base mesh.

Figure 3.53: Blocking in the forms of the neck

Adding Geometry to an Existing ZTool

ZBrush keeps track of your sculpted detail based on vertex ID. In an OBJ file every vertex or point had a numerical ID assigned to it. This is why you can sculpt in ZBrush without UVs on your mesh. ZBrush is keeping track of your detail based on the IDs of the vertices. The problem arises when you want to add new geometry to a ZBrush tool. If you change the vertex order for any reason the mesh will "explode" when you step up subdivision levels. If you add new geometry you will not be able to re-import the mesh into the ZTool. The solution to this problem is using a method called displacement map detail transfer. Essentially we will create a displacement of our work-in-progress (WIP) mesh export and go to Maya. Add new faces, then re-import the obj to ZBrush and displace the mesh to recapture the lost details.

1. Return to the lowest subdivision level and apply AUV tiling to the mesh. AUV tiles are a ZBrush automatic UV solution and are quick and efficient. For more information on UVs in ZBrush see Chapter 5. With UVs on the mesh we can now create a displacement map to capture the sculpting work we have done so far. Go to Tool → Displacement and set Adaptive mode on and mapRes to 1024; then press Create Displacement Map. At the top of the screen a status bar will run until the map is completed. When the map is done generating it will be loaded into the alpha palette. Click on the alpha icon at the left of the screen and select the displacement map. Export it as a PSD.

2. Now you want to export your level 1 mesh as an OBJ file. This OBJ file we will open in Maya to add new faces and geometry. To export from ZBrush select Tool → Export and save as an OBJ file.

When Exporting OBJ files from ZBrush be sure to turn on MRG under the Tool → Export menu. Mrg will merge your UVs on export rather than keeping each one a separate shell. This setting can be set by default in the Preferences → Import-Export menu.

---

3. Now we have a displacement map that carries the details of your higher subdivision levels and a level 1 OBJ file. Notice how the level 1 mesh is so much different than the original head mesh we started with. This is because of ZBrush's Multi Resolution Editing, or MRE technology. Changes we make to the higher levels telegraph all the way down to the bottom levels.

Now we will move to Maya to add new faces and organize the mesh for re-import to ZBrush. These steps can be followed in most third-party modeling packages. Export level 1 from ZBrush as an OBJ file.

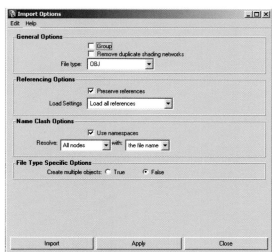

Editing the Mesh in Maya

In this section we will import the mesh into Maya and extrude new faces. We will also UV the new faces and shift them outside 0 to 1 to better facilitate Polygrouping and masking in ZBrush.

1. In Maya go to File → Import and select the option box (Figure 3.54). Set your file type to OBJ and make sure at the bottom of the menu Make Multiple Objects is set to false. This ensures that Maya imports the obj as one object and it also preserves the vertex order. While

Figure 3.54: Maya file import option box

this is not a concern with this tutorial it is a good habit to develop since changing vertex order on meshes can cause big problems in ZBrush. See Chapters 10 and 11 for more information on moving between ZBrush and Maya. Figure 3.55 shows the mesh loaded into Maya.

2. With your mesh loaded into Maya, select the faces at the back of the head you want to extrude (Figure 3.56). Using edit mesh extrude, pull a long horn out of the head and make sure to cut new edge loops so the face are evenly distributed (Figure 3.57). Don't add too much geometry here since denser lower level meshes can cause you to lose subdivision levels.

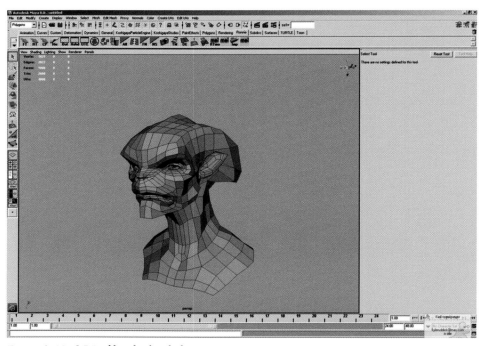

Figure 3.55: OBJ of level 1 loaded in Maya

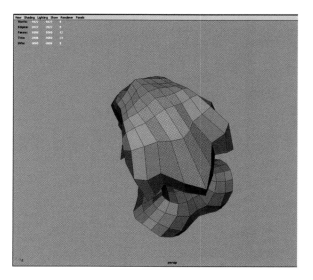

Figure 3.56: Faces selected on head in Maya

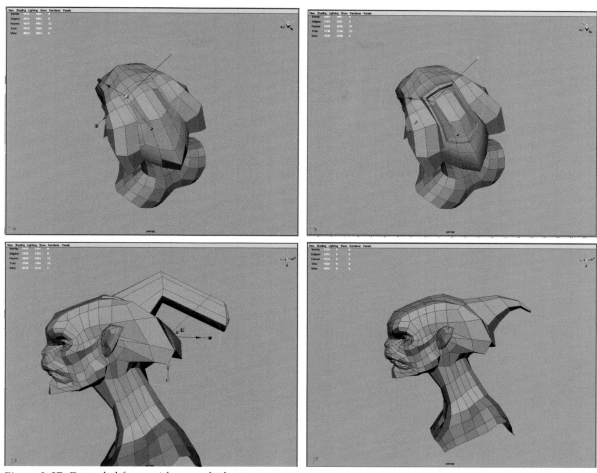

Figure 3.57: Extruded faces with new edgeloops cut

3. Once the faces are extruded, select all the new faces and click Create UVs Automatic Mapping to restore the default settings and apply the mapping (Figure 3.58). These do not need to be the final UVs; we are only using these texture coordinates to shift the UVs for the new geometry and polygroup the mesh later. New UVs can always be imported into ZBrush later. We want to select the UVs for the new geometry and shift them outside to the 0 to 1 UV space. This allows us to use UV grouping in ZBrush to add the new faces to a polygroup and easily mask them. Go to Window → UV Texture Editor (Figure 3.59).

4. Here you will see the AUV tiles and your highlighted automatic mapping on the horn. If these faces are no longer selected simply reselect the new geometry. When the new faces are selected convert the selection to UV with the hotkey Ctrl+F12. With the UVs for the horn selected use the following MEL command to shift

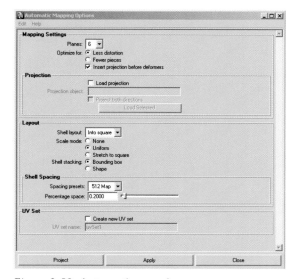

Figure 3.58: Automatic mapping menu

them outside 0 to 1 exactly (Figure 3.60). In the MEL window at the bottom of your screen type:

```
polyEditUV -u 1 -v 0;
```

This will shift the UVs exactly 1 unit in the U direction (across from left to right). (Figure 3.61). By preserving the UVs on the rest of the head we can use the displacement map in ZBrush to reapply details to the mesh. Return to Object mode and select the mesh. You are now ready to export it again as a new OBJ Go to File → Export and export the mesh as an OBJ file, and then return to ZBrush.

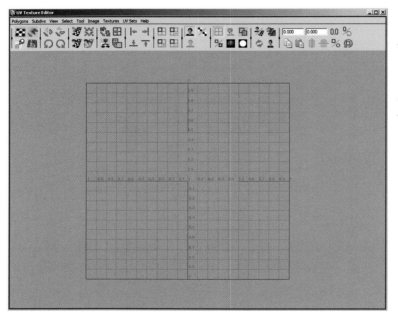

Figure 3.59: UV Texture editor. This grid represents the 0 to 1 texture space. UVs placed outside this unit can be automatically poly-grouped separately in ZBrush.

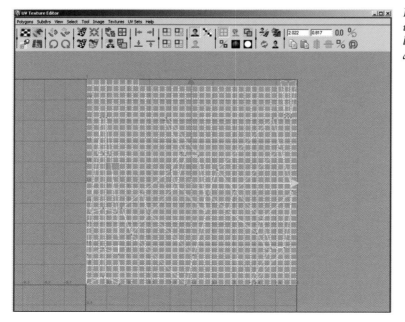

Figure 3.60: UV window with overlapping UVs for all parts

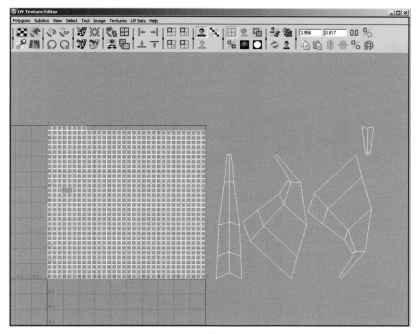

Figure 3.61: The horn UVs have been shifted outside 0 to 1. The AUV tiles are on the left while the UVs for the horn are on the right.

Working Back in ZBrush

Back in ZBrush the original head is still open. If you were to try and import the new topology back into the tool ZBrush would give you an error. Try to import the new mesh while the old ZTool is still in Edit mode. Select Tool → Import and select the new mesh. ZBrush will produce the following error:

```
The current mesh has a different polygon count. You can only import meshes
with the same polygon count to a tool in edit mode...
```

This means that the new mesh has more faces and a different vertex order than the last one. ZBrush would allow us to reimport the mesh if only the UVs had changed; it would update the UVs on the ZTool and preserve all the levels of detail. This is very useful when you want to change UVs on a model after you've finished sculpting, and we will cover this more in a later chapter. Simply UV in Maya and reimport. If you preserved the vertex IDs this would go smoothly.

Adding Details Back to the Imported Mesh

Because there are new faces in this case, merely reimporting is not possible. We will need to transfer details using the displacement map technique.

1. Initialize ZBrush to clear the Tool palette and remove all old maps and tools. Before you do this make sure you have exported the displacement map created earlier. Import the new geometry from Maya and enter Edit mode. Subdivide up to a higher level by pressing Ctrl+D. You want at least as many faces as the original ZTool so you can recapture the details.

Figure 3.62: Store morph target

2. When the mesh is subdivided go to Tool → Polygroups → UV Groups (Figure 3.62). This will polygroup the horn faces separate from the head since those faces are outside 0 to 1. Now we want to store a morph target. Store a morph target with tool → Morph Target → Store Morph Target (Figure 3.63). Morph targets are copies of a current mesh stored in memory. This will allow us to return parts of the model to its original shape after the displacement.

> You can create morph targets by selecting Tool → Morph Target → Store Morph Target. Morph targets are copies of the mesh stored in memory so you can switch between a previous version of the model and an altered version. You can also use the Morph brush to alter parts of the mesh to revert back to the stored version.

3. In the Alpha palette import the displacement map you exported from the earlier model. With the displacement map active in the Alpha palette you can now displace the existing mesh to recapture the details of the original ZTool. Go to Tool → Displacement → and select the Mode button (Figure 3.64). This tells ZBrush to use the current alpha as a displacement map and not a bump map. Set the Intensity slider to 5 and click the Apply Displacement Map button. ZBrush will displace the mesh based on the alpha displacement map. If the effect is too weak, undo by pressing Ctrl+Z and raise the intensity value, then press Apply Displacement Map again. If the effect is too strong, undo and lower this value. See Figure 3.65. You will notice that the horn faces get noise as you displace them; this

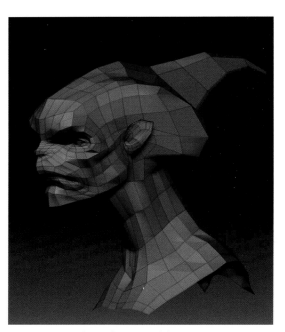

Figure 3.63: The polygrouped horn

is because the map is applying to these new faces as well (Figure 3.66). By storing the morph target any artifacts can be easily removed by using the morph brush (Figure 3.67).

4. Go to Tool → Brush and select the morph brush. The Morph brush blends between the current mesh and the stored Morph target based on the intensity slider value. Ctrl+Shift click the horn to hide the head and set the Morph brush to 100. Brush on the surface to return the horn to its original surface smoothness.

5. If you find small artifacts on the face, you can remove them with the Smooth brush set to an elevation of −80

Figure 3.64: Apply Displace menu

You have now added new geometry to the head and transferred you existing details to the new mesh. You'll find this technique handy if you work several hours on a model only to be asked to add new parts that could mean duplicating all your work. With this technique details can be transferred between meshes with different topologies with no problems. Save this ZTool. Now we will add some more secondary form to the model and continue to refine its character.

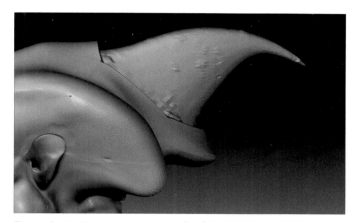

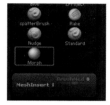

Figure 3.65: Horn noise as a result of the detail transfer between meshes.

Figure 3.66: Morph brush

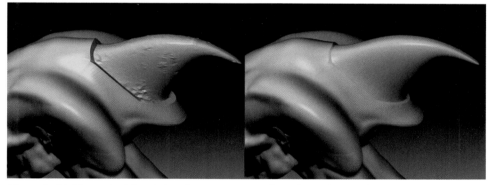

Figure 3.67: Using the Morph brush to remove artifacts from the new horn.

Refining the Character Bust

Next we'll continue to refine the creature head and tie together the shapes we have blocked in. For the majority of this sculpt, we're using the flatInflate, Standard, Move, and Smooth brushes. Since we have reimported the mesh, the ear polygroups are gone. You may want to re-create these before you proceed.

1. Use the Standard brush to create some recesses along the side horn shapes and refine the bone structure of the face. Use the Move brush to create a sweeping curve to the new stinger geometry (Figure 3.68).
2. Using the Move brush, add a gesture to the curve of the horn at the side of the head (Figure 3.69).
3. At this stage the head seems too narrow, so use the Move brush to widen the head. Also raise the crown of the head. Using a combination of the Move and flatInflate brushes, refine the area around the eyes and cheeks, trying to give more of a sense of character to the bust (Figure 3.70).

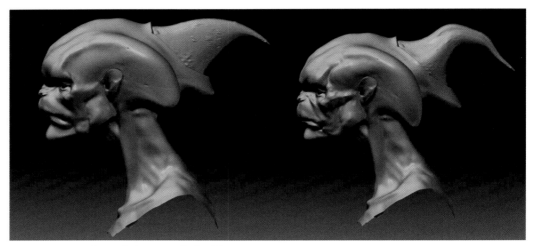

Figure 3.68: Refine side horns and cheekbones.

Figure 3.69: Curve the side horns.

Figure 3.70: Sculpting the forms of the eyelids

4. Using the flatInflate brush, build up the forms of the face. To avoid creating bloated forms, step down a subdivision level, smooth, then step back up to create more subtle shape changes. This has the effect of making the shapes at the higher subdivision level less pronounced because even though you smoothed the forms, the high level remembers the previous shape and tries to reintroduce the form. Move the light often to get a clearer picture of the shapes you are making. (I have a hotkey set for the Interactive Light utility. For more information on setting hotkeys, see Chapter 12.)

Figure 3.71: Smoothing, then stepping up and dialing in transitions

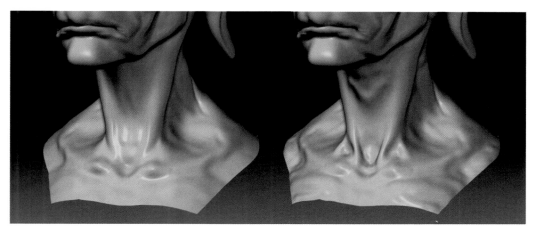

Figure 3.72: Refining the forms of the neck anatomy

5. Insertions and transitions can then be picked out using the Standard brush to accentuate shadows (Figure 3.71). Use this method to refine the forms of the neck, dialing in the origins and insertions of the neck muscles, the collarbones, and the chest (Figure 3.72).

6. Following steps similar to those in Chapter 2, refine the ear using a combination of the flatInflate brush, Smooth, and Move. Use masking to isolate each part of the ear as you work on it. Don't forget to take advantage of the polygroup to isolate the ear from the head.

Figure 3.73 shows the final Stingerhead sculpture before fine detailing. I wanted to focus on form first since no amount of detail will help a sculpture with bad form. It is the primary and secondary shapes, the sense of bone and skin that gives a character life, not the pores and wrinkles. Those details just add even more excitement to an already successful sculpture. We'll return to this head in a later chapter to discuss high-frequency detailing and the methods used to create it.

Figure 3.73: The Stingerhead character bust with primary and secondary forms addressed

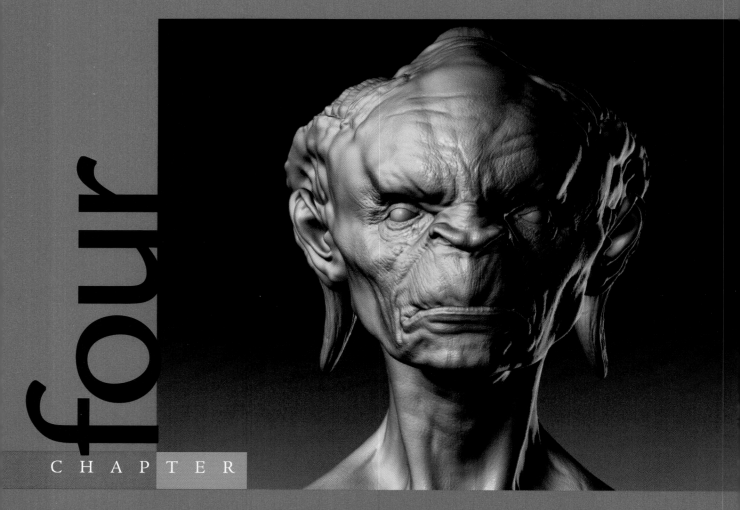

four

ZBrush for Detailing

So far we have been *sculpting characters with a focus on primary and secondary forms—that is, the skeletal anatomy, the muscular anatomy, and the major forms of fat and flesh. The first three projects lack any kind of fine tertiary details. This was intentional because I wanted to illustrate that form is the most important consideration before you start to detail your character. Good form is what makes the sculpture believable, not pores and wrinkles. High-frequency details on top of bad form will do little to help the overall effect of the sculpture.*

Form and Details

Form can be broken down into three categories. The *primary* form represents the largest basic shapes of the character. *Secondary* forms are muscle forms and folds of flesh. *Tertiary* details are things like pores, fine wrinkles, and scale details. For a sculpture to work, the primary and secondary forms are the most important. As we discussed in Chapter 1, a sculpture with form that is resolved will work even without fine details. The tertiary forms are icing on the cake and cannot make a bad sculpture good. Figure 4.1 illustrates these three levels on a single character.

Once you have the form established and the character works without detail (Figure 4.2), you are ready to use ZBrush's alphas to add the fine details for which the program is so well known. This is where the ability to subdivide into millions of polygons starts to shine. Figure 4.3 shows a mummy sculpted by ZBrush artist and sculptor Alex Oliver. Notice how the details in this mummy serve to support the overall character.

In this chapter we'll take our sculptures to the next level by adding fine tertiary details. We'll discuss alphas and strokes. We'll also look at ways of creating your own alphas from existing photography or sculpting them from scratch in ZBrush. Finally, we'll explore the dynamics of wrinkle patterns and how to create natural patterns on the skin.

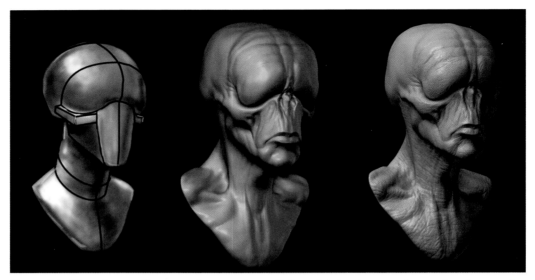

Figure 4.1: These images illustrate what constitutes (left to right) primary and secondary form and tertiary details.

  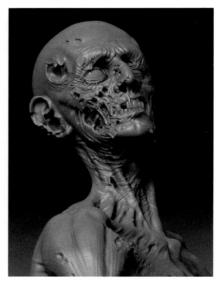

Figure 4.2: The Stingerhead character, pictured on the left with only form addressed and on the right with the addition of tertiary forms. Notice that the sculpture works even without the fine details.

Figure 4.3: This mummy by Alex Oliver shows how a sculpture with good form is well supported by a few fine details.

Alphas

Alphas in ZBrush are grayscale images that serve three major functions: they can be brush shapes, texture stamps, and stencils. You load, export, and manipulate alphas via the Alpha menu located at the top menu bar. There is also an Alpha palette on the side tray on the left

(Figure 4.4). This is an abbreviated Alpha menu since it offers only a few menu options, but it provides easy access to the entire alpha library currently loaded. Combined with various stroke settings, alphas offer a powerful tool for adding high-frequency details to your sculpture.

Figure 4.4: The Alpha palette from the left tray

Alphas are 16-bit grayscale images that serve three purposes in ZBrush: brush shapes, stencils, and texture stamps. You can also use alphas to generate 3D objects by clicking the Make3D button under the Alpha menu.

With alphas you can alter your brush shape to sculpt in high-frequency details like rivets (Figure 4.5) or fine organic details like the withered skin on this creature (Figure 4.6). They may also be used as texture stamps to add pores and scales. Alphas can be used to create stencils to assist in the sculpting or painting process by masking out complex areas of texture. Finally, you can use alphas to quickly create actual 3D geometry that can be inserted into your mesh.

There are two locations where you can find settings that pertain to alphas. On the bar at the left of the screen is the Alpha palette, which contains an abbreviated selection of the main alpha menu options. Here you will find your currently loaded alphas and a few selected options for basic conversions and operations. These menu options are also accessible in the main Alpha menu at the top of the screen; we'll look at the main Alpha menu in depth now (Figure 4.7).

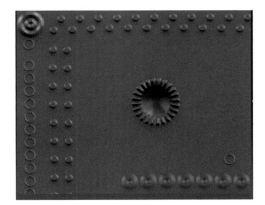

Figure 4.5: Rivets added with a tileable alpha and LazyMouse

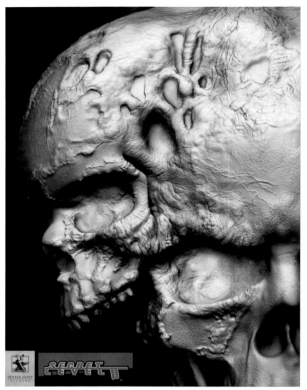

Figure 4.6: The fine details on this skeleton monster were created by using alphas and freehand sculpting. (Image courtesy SecretLevel/Sega and Gentle Giant Studios.)

Figure 4.7: The main Alpha menu

The Alpha menu allows you to import and export images to use as alphas; grab the canvas as an alpha; select already loaded alphas; manipulate the images once they are loaded; and convert the selected alphas to stencils, geometry, or textures. The most common use of alphas is to alter the shape of your currently selected brush. In Figure 4.8, a Freehand stroke is drawn on the model surface with different alphas selected. Notice how the radial alphas create a seamless fluid stroke while the arrow or other alphas with a more directional appearance will follow the stroke, reorienting as you drag. A description of each Alpha menu setting is available in Table 4.1.

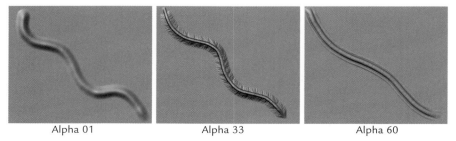

Figure 4.8: A Freehand stroke using various alphas

Table 4.1: The Alpha Menu Options

Menu Option	Description
Blur	Adds a Gaussian blur to the current alpha—useful for counteracting noise
Noise	Adds noise to the current alpha
Max	Specifies the maximize range—similar to Auto Level in Photoshop
MidValue	Sets the midline value of no displacement
Rf	Specifies radial fade
Intensity	Specifies intensity
Contrast	Controls alpha contrast
Alpha Adjust	Allows fine-tuning of alpha values
Flip H	Flips the current alpha horizontally
Flip V	Flips the current alpha vertically
Rotate	Rotates the alpha 90 degrees
Invers	Inverts the alpha
Mres	Sets the resolution of the mesh generated from the alpha when you click the Make 3D button
Mdep	Sets the depth of the mesh generated with Make 3D
Msm	Sets the smoothness of the mesh generated with Make 3D
Dbls	When generating a 3D object from an alpha, specifies double sided
Make 3D	Makes a 3D object from the current alpha
Make Tx	Makes texture from the current alpha
Make St	Make stencil from the current alpha
Make Modified Alpha	Saves a copy of the current alpha with all modifiers baked in
Cc	Clears color information from the canvas when cropping and filling with an alpha
Crop and Fill	Crops the canvas to the current alpha size and fills it with the alpha texture
GrabDoc	Grabs a depth map of the current canvas layer and stores it in the Alpha palette
Alpha Depth Factor	Controls the depth intensity of the alpha when applied to the canvas with Crop and Fill

Alphas can be used as texture stamps in conjunction with the Stroke menu. By changing to a nonradial alpha like Alpha 07, which is a bump alpha, and using the DragRect stroke, you can add surface details as if stamping them directly from the alpha image (Figure 4.9).

ZBrush comes with an alpha library loaded by default. If you have a selection of alphas you want to load, when ZBrush starts simply save them in the ZStartup/Alphas folder of your ZBrush installation. Make sure they are not in a subfolder because ZBrush will load the files only in that directory and not in any subdirectories. ZBrush 3 comes with a selection of the Gnomon Alpha library as well. These can be found in the Gnomon-AlphaLibrary subfolder in the ZBrush3 folder. To load these alphas, copy them into the ZStartup/Alphas folder and restart ZBrush.

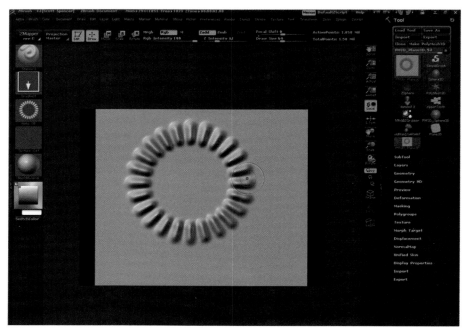

Figure 4.9: DragRect texture stamp process

Alphas and Strokes

The way the currently selected alpha is applied to the surface of your sculpture is controlled by the stroke selection. In this section we'll experiment with various types of alpha and stroke combinations (Figure 4.10).

Understanding the Stroke menu and settings opens up a world of interesting and useful alpha effects. We'll look at the various settings by sculpting on a 3D plane. The Stroke palette is located on the left side of the screen directly under the Brush palette (Figure 4.11). Here you will find the available strokes as well as an abbreviated selection of the options from the main Stroke menu (Figure 4.12).

1. Select the Plane3D tool from the Tool menu. Be sure to make it a polymesh and draw it on the canvas. Enter Edit mode and subdivide the mesh several times. When you are detailing the model, it is important to be at the highest possible subdivision level your system can handle.

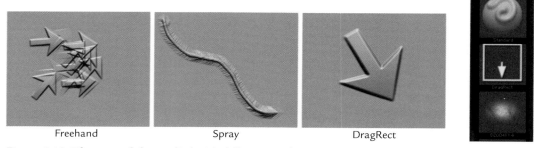

Freehand   Spray   DragRect

Figure 4.10: The same alpha applied with different strokes

Figure 4.11: The Stroke palette located at the left side of the screen

2. From the Brush palette select the Standard brush, and from the Alpha palette at the left side of the screen select Alpha 01. From the Stroke palette just above the Alpha button, select a Freehand stroke.

3. Start to draw strokes on the surface of the plane. Notice how with this brush combination you get a smooth-flowing line. As you stroke an alpha, the image rotates to follow the direction of your stroke. Since Alpha 01 is a radial round alpha with no directionality, this effect is not apparent (Figure 4.13).

4. Change from Alpha 01 to Alpha 33. Notice that this alpha is an arrow shape as opposed to a circular alpha (Figure 4.14). This shape has a definite direction, so the rotation with your stroke should be apparent. Draw a stroke on the plane surface. Note how the arrow is drawn repeatedly over the course of the stroke, reorienting to your direction (it should look like the Spray image back in Figure 4.10). This is how the Freehand stroke works; it draws multiple instances of an alpha along the course of the stroke. If the instances are close enough together and the alpha nondirectional, it looks like a smooth line. There are ways to space out the instances for other effects, as you'll see shortly. If your stroke seems too staggered because your machine is slower or the geometry is extremely dense, you can raise the mouse average setting.

5. Turn on the Roll modifier in the Stroke menu. Activating the Roll button will draw a single instance of the alpha tiled along the stroke. This is useful when you have a tileable alpha to draw on the surface.

6. Click Stroke from the main menu bar at the top of the screen. At the bottom of the Stroke menu you can access the sliders for each stroke. Freehand has only one slider: MouseAverage. By default, this is set to 4. Raising this value smooths the stroke more and adds a slight draw delay; lowering it reduces the delay but can create a stagger in the stroke if your computer's memory is being taxed by numerous subdivision levels.

7. This Freehand stroke behavior can be used to create interesting wrinkle effects. Change your alpha selection to Alpha 58. This alpha consists of several sketched lines running in one direction. Use the Freehand stroke to draw circular patterns on the plane. Notice that the instances of the alpha rotate while you draw, thus creating a realistic crosshatched wrinkle pattern from this very simple alpha. You may need to adjust your ZIntensity if the effect is too strong.

Figure 4.12: The main Stroke menu

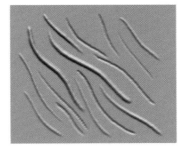

Figure 4.13: Freehand strokes

Figure 4.14: Alpha 33 is a directional pattern.

Now that you understand the Freehand stroke, let's try a different one. Create a new 3D plane or undo your strokes from the previous section. We'll now look at the DragRect stroke. DragRect is great for applying alphas as stamps to include surface detail.

1. Select the DragRect stroke from the Stroke menu and Alpha 07 from the Alpha palette. Alpha 07 is a bumpy alpha (Figure 4.15).

2. Click and drag on the plane. This will draw an instance of the alpha. You can rotate while you draw by moving the mouse to the left and right, allowing you to scale and rotate the alpha to fit as you like.

3. Continue to add strokes to the surface. Notice how quickly an area can be textured with surface details using this stroke. You can also easily vary the scale and orientation (Figure 4.16).

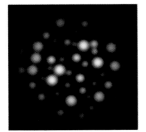

Figure 4.15: Alpha 07

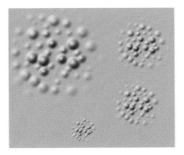

Figure 4.16: DragRect instances of Alpha 07 on a plane

Figure 4.17: Replay Last button

A useful trick when adding alpha texture is to use the Replay Last command under the Stroke menu (Figure 4.17); this will repeat the last stroke, which is helpful when trying to detail skin. When stamping a texture with an alpha, it can be easy to make the texture too strong, causing you to have to undo and reapply. Using Replay Last in conjunction with the DragRect stroke can help you create more subtle surface details by gradually building strokes at a low ZIntensity setting. In the following section, we will apply an alpha to a 3D plane using multiple instances of replay last.

1. Create a new plane3D on which to draw or undo your previous strokes.
2. Make sure the DragRect stroke and Alpha 07 are still selected.
3. Set your ZIntensity to 60 and draw an instance of the alpha on the surface of the plane. It will be overstated at this stage. The point is to get the size and placement where you want it. Once the stroke is complete, undo and lower your ZIntensity at the top of the screen to 4.
4. Under the Stroke menu at the top of the screen, click the Replay Last button, or press Ctrl+1. This will repeat the last DragRect stroke but use the new ZIntensity settings. You can repeat the Replay Last several times, watching the texture build up softly on the surface. Replay Last works with any stroke on the canvas. If you were to move your model by clicking and dragging in the document window and then use Replay Last, the mesh would continue to rotate on the screen.

The Stroke Menu

Now that we've looked at the Freehand and DragRect strokes, let's explore the Stroke menu overall. All strokes have a set of modifiers that can be accessed either through the Stroke palette on the left of the screen or in the main Stroke menu at the top of the screen. Notice that the Stroke palette is broken into two sections. The top section are strokes that can be used in 3D sculpting as well as 2.5D, while the bottom section contains 2.5D-only strokes. Table 4.2 lists the various 3D strokes and their subsettings.

Table 4.2: The Stroke Menu Options

Stroke	Description
Dots	Places continuous instances of the alpha on the canvas.
DragRect	Creates one instance of the alpha with the ability to rotate and scale the stroke.
Freehand	Similar to the dot stroke, except it creates extra instances between each dot, giving the impression of a smooth stroke.
Color Spray	Applies random instances of the alpha. When painting RGB, it modulates the selected color based on the two selected colors in the active and secondary swatches.
Spray	Same as colorized spray, except the stroke modifies the intensity of the selected color unless the color modifier slider is set to 0.
DragDot	Applies one instance of the current alpha. Allows you to click-drag to place. Rotation and scale is not available. Brush size is used to determine the size of the alpha.

Some strokes, like Line, Conic, and Radial, are available in only 2.5 D mode. The two strokes you use most commonly when sculpting are Freehand and DragRect; the other more specialized strokes can come in handy for hard surface or mechanical modeling, or texture painting (as in the case of the Spray stroke).

Using LazyMouse to Texture Large Areas

The freehand stroke creates a smooth line by drawing many instances of the selected alpha close together over the course of the stroke. The Dot stroke is essentially a freehand stroke with more space between each instance of the alpha. It is possible to increase this distance between the steps using LazyMouse. This is useful when you're trying to apply high-frequency concentrated details across a large surface area. An example of this is stamping a repeating texture, such as skin pores over a head. With the pore alpha loaded; select the Dots stroke, turn on LazyMouse, and set the LazyRadius and LazySmooth sliders to 0. Raise the LazySteps slider to about 1.25.Apply the stroke to the surface. The texture will apply in concentrated single stamps along the direction of the stroke. Using this technique, you can quickly and easily cover a large surface area with fine texture.

Alphas as Stencils

While alphas may serve as brush shapes or texture stamps, they may also be used as stencils. In ZBrush, stencils function much in the same way as they do in the real world. A stencil is a piece of cardboard with a shape cut out. Typically you will spray paint through the cardboard. Some areas are blocked while the openings allow paint through. This allows you to paint complex shapes quickly. Stencils in ZBrush function the same way, but they may be used for painting or for sculpting. Stencils become complex movable masks that can be interactively placed and rotated on the surface as well as tiled and wrapped to the shape beneath

Figure 4.18: Make St button

them. In this demonstration we'll use a ZBrush alpha as a stencil:

1. Open the demo head from the ZBrush3/ZTools folder. Draw it on the canvas and enter Edit mode. From the Alpha menu at the top of the screen, select Alpha 59.

2. In the main Alpha menu, click the button marked Make St. This will make a stencil from the current alpha (Figure 4.18).

3. The document window will now be light gray with a red box in the center. Inside this box is the Alpha 59 (Figure 4.19). This is the stencil. Press the spacebar to bring up the coin operator, which allows you to move, rotate, and scale the alpha in relation to the ZTool. Left-clicking and dragging in each quadrant will execute that action (Figure 4.20). For example, move the alpha over the forehead of the ZTool. You can still move and rotate the ZTool with the standard mouse movements. Press the spacebar and click in the quadrant marked Move. Drag the mouse to place the alpha.

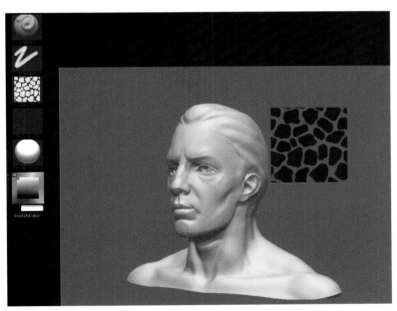

Figure 4.19: Alpha 59 as an active stencil. I pressed the spacebar in this shot so the coin operator is visible (at the bottom right).

Figure 4.20: The coin operator: left-clicking and dragging in each quadrant will perform the labeled action.

4. To scale the alpha, press the spacebar and click in the bottom section marked Move. Notice the top section is marked Mov Rot; this will move your alpha along the surface, rotating it to the surface normal. Do not use this option.

5. To scale the alpha down, click in the right section marked Scale. Notice that there are two other smaller sections here marked H and Z. H will allow you to scale in horizontal; V scales in vertical. The stencil should now be placed as shown in Figure 4.21. When rotating and scaling a stencil, note that the action occurs around the spot where the coin operator is. So if you want to scale a stencil from the left side, move to the left side, press the spacebar to bring up the coin operator, and scale.

6. The alpha is now placed and ready for use. In the Alpha palette at the left of the screen, change to Alpha 01. Since Alpha 59 has been converted to a stencil, you can select any other alpha to sculpt through it. Sculpt some strokes through the stencil. Notice how the white areas block your stroke (Figure 4.22).

If you are accustomed to using the right-click menu to access your brush settings, be aware it is disabled when in Stencil mode. Instead, use the brush control sliders at the top of the screen or the hotkeys: S for Draw Size, I for RGB intensity, and U for Z Intensity.

---

7. Move the stencil and continue to sculpt. Try to rotate and scale the alpha as well.

You may notice that the stencil sits just above the surface of your model. It does not conform to the shape beneath it, so sculpting across areas like the nose or cheeks can be tricky. It is possible to make the stencil conform to the shape beneath it. For this and other more advanced stencil options, we'll look at the Stencil menu.

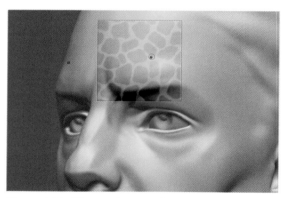

Figure 4.21: Placing the stencil

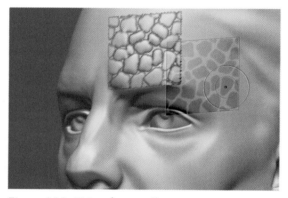

Figure 4.22: Using the stencil

The Stencil Menu

From the top of the screen, select the Stencil menu (Figure 4.23). Use the radial button to tear this menu off to the side tray on the left. This menu is the control hub for how stencils behave and display. The first button is marked StencilOn. This is the on/off switch for the stencil. The Invr button will invert the stencil, flipping the black and white values.

Beneath these first two buttons are the remainder of the Stencil options. The Alpha Repeat slider will tile the current stencil. Set this to 6 to see how a seamless scale texture is created. This is because Alpha 59 itself is a seamlessly tileable alpha (Figure 4.24). We'll cover how to make your own tileable alphas later in this chapter.

The buttons marked Stretch Actual Horiz and Vert will fit the current stencil to the canvas. Stretch will stretch the stencil to fit; Vert will fit it vertically. See Figure 4.25 for an example of these buttons in action. When these buttons are on, Interactive will turn off. Interactive will reactivate as soon as you invoke the coin operator to go back into interactive placement mode.

Wrap mode is one of the most useful stencil modifiers. Wrap mode will project the stencil so that it conforms to the shape of the underlying mesh. Figure 4.26 shows the stencil in Wrap mode. Notice how it conforms to the shape of the nose and eye socket instead of just sitting above it. You can further define how tightly the stencil wraps to the underling detail by using the Res and Smooth sliders.

The final selection of buttons in the interface deals with the way in which the stencil is displayed. Sometimes the stencil can be distracting when sculpting. You can turn off Show to keep the stencil active, but it will not be visible unless you have pressed the spacebar to change its position. You can use the R, G, and B buttons to change the color of the masked area when using a stencil in Show mode. The Elv button displays the alpha in Elevation mode. This creates an elevation map display of the stencil as opposed to the masked view (Figure 4.27).

Figure 4.23: The Stencil menu

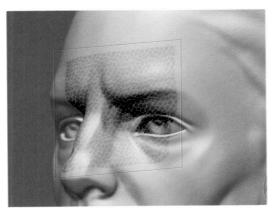

Figure 4.24: Alpha Repeat set to 6

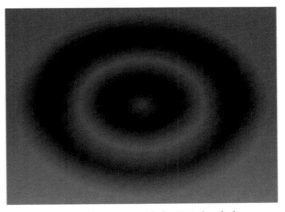

Figure 4.25: In this image Alpha17 is loaded as a stencil and Stretch is on. The stencil stretches to the proportions of the canvas.

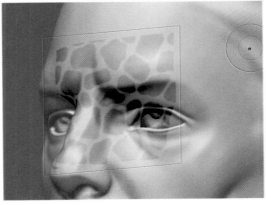

Figure 4.21: Placing the stencil

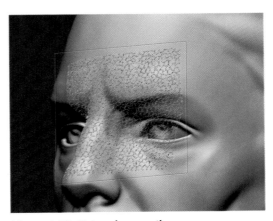

Figure 4.22: Using the stencil

Stencils do not have to be created only from alphas. When you Ctrl+Shift-drag a show marquee in the document window, releasing Shift first will create a stencil from the selection. Try this with Lasso mode on. You can also use ZAppLink to create stencils.

ZAppLink Stencils

Stencils for complex mechanical shapes are easy with ZMapper. By defining a custom selection in Photoshop, you can generate a stencil back in ZBrush. Use the following steps for this process.

1. Create a Cube 3D primitive from the Tool menu. Click Make Polymesh 3D and draw the tool on the canvas. Enter Edit mode and subdivide as high as possible.

2. Center the cube in the document window and press the Ctrl+Shift+S to call ZAppLink. Deselect all the check boxes in the ZAppLink window that appears and click Drop Now. ZAppLink will open Photoshop and load a copy of your ZBrush document (Figure 4.28).

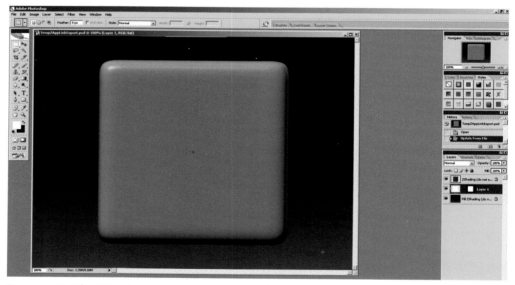

Figure 4.28: The ZBrush document transferred to Photoshop with ZAppLink

3. Create a selection in Photoshop, and save it by choosing Selection → Save Selection. Name the selection **stencil** (Figure 4.29).

4. Save the Photoshop document and return to ZBrush. When you return to ZBrush, click the OK (Unchanged) button, and your stencil will automatically load and apply to the model (Figure 4.30).

You may now sculpt through the stencil to create hard-edged details. By repeating this process with multiple selections, you can build complex shapes quickly and easily (Figure 4.31).

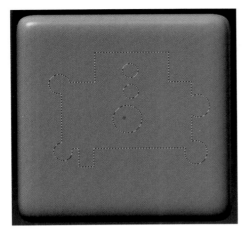

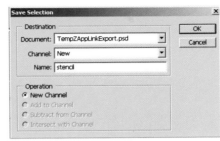

Figure 4.29: Create a selection in Photoshop and save it as stencil.

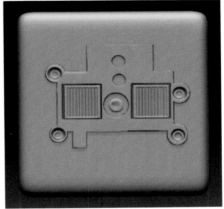

Figure 4.30: The stencil applied in ZBrush   *Figure 4.31: Mechanical details built from ZAppLink stencils*

Importing Images to Use as Alphas

Any image may be loaded into ZBrush and used as an alpha. The file formats ZBrush supports for import are PSD, BMP, and 16-bit TIFF (single-channel grayscale). To import an alpha, open the main Alpha menu at the top of the screen and click the Import button. Browse to the file you want to load.

> There is no shortage of great texture reference that can be used as alphas: on the Internet, in books, even around you. Try taking photographs of plants and fruits for use as texture stamps. For the best all-around skin alpha set, I recommend checking ZBrushCentral. Rick "Monstermaker" Baker made some of his skin alphas available in his Old Man thread. This is a fantastic selection of pore, wrinkle, and bump alphas.

When a photograph is loaded into the Alpha menu, it is automatically converted to 16-bit grayscale. In the Alpha menu beneath the active Alpha boxes there are several sliders that will allow you to postprocess the alpha and make various alterations to the image. With these modifiers, you can maximize the range (similar to autoleveling in Photoshop) by crunching the levels, thus giving you the maximum displacement between black and white. You can also use the Blur slider to slightly blur your image, removing artifacts from JPEG compression or other noise. See Tables 4.1 and 4.2 earlier in this chapter for a description of what each of these menu options does.

In this section we'll import an image of skin detail and use it as an alpha (Figure 4.32).

1. From the DVD, load `skinswatch.psd` into the Alpha menu by clicking Import.
2. This is a skin detail from a photograph. To optimize it for use in ZBrush, click the Max button in the Alpha menu. This will maximize the value range to help get better details. You will also want to raise the Rf slider to 10 to add a faded border. This prevents the alpha from leaving a square artifact when used.
3. From the Tool menu select the Sphere3D tool. Click MakePolymesh3D and draw the sphere on the canvas. Enter Edit mode and divide the sphere as high as possible on your system.
4. Select the Standard brush, set ZIntensity to 12, select the DragRect stroke and the SkinSwatch alpha. Drag the alpha on the surface. Figure 4.33 shows the sphere with the custom pore alpha applied.
5. The image file has a bit of noise from both JPEG compression as well as high contrast lighting. You can reduce this with the blur slider. Raise Blur to a value of 2 and redraw the stroke. Try adjusting the other sliders such as Contrast and Noise.

Figure 4.32: This image of skin texture can be applied directly to your model as an alpha texture stamp.

Figure 4.33: The custom SkinSwatch alpha applied to a sphere with a DragRect stroke

Baking Changes to the New Alpha

It is important to understand that changes made with these sliders are applied as a process to the imported alpha. If you want to save the alpha with these changes applied, you must "bake" them into a new instance of the alpha. To save a modified version of the alpha, follow these steps:

1. With your alpha active in the Alpha palette, set the modifiers you want to adjust and save. This can include turning on the Max button, adding a Blur, and adjusting the Rf slider.
2. When the Alpha is to your liking, click the Make Modified Alpha button in the Alpha menu. This will create a new alpha in the palette that has the modifier settings "baked" in.

3. Select this new alpha and in the main Alpha menu click the Export button. This will save a copy of the currently selected alpha as the default PSD file type. Save the alpha in the `ZStartup/Alphas` folder if you want it to load by default each time ZBrush starts.

Your Alpha Library

To have ZBrush load your favorite alphas by default, simply copy them into the `Pixologic/ZBrush3/ZStartup/Alphas` folder. The alphas cannot be in a subfolder; they must be in the root `Alphas` folder. Any images in this location that are readable in ZBrush will be loaded at startup into the User Alphas section of the Alpha palette.

Sculpting Alphas in ZBrush

There may be occasions when you'll need a specific kind of surface texture that is unavailable in photo reference or perhaps you'll have two alphas you want to combine into a single alpha. In these cases, you can use ZBrush's 2.5D canvas to sculpt the texture you want by hand and then capture the sculpted detail to a grayscale alpha.

To use the brush document window to sculpt your own alpha, follow these steps:

1. First resize your document to 300 × 300 pixels. From the Document menu, click the Pro button to disable Constrain Proportions. Click in the Length slider to activate it, and enter **300**. Repeat the same process for the Width slider. Now click the Resize button to create a new canvas that is 300 pixels square. Alphas need to be square so as not to distort when redrawn with the sculpting brushes. If you intend the alpha to be used only as a stencil, it can be any proportion.

2. You now need a surface on which to sculpt the alpha. Since the alpha is derived from depth information you want to select a flat surface on which to sculpt. From the Tool menu, select the Plane3D icon. Click MakePolymesh3D and draw the plane on the canvas. Enter Edit mode and divide the plane as high as possible by pressing Ctrl+D or choosing Tool → Geometry and clicking the Divide button. You want as many subdivisions as possible to support the fine details we'll sculpt in the next step. Note that the material selection will have no effect on the alpha created in this step—your surface material can be anything you prefer. In this case, I used White Cavity.

3. Scale the 3D plane up to fill the canvas window. Now select the Standard brush and Alpha 01. From the Stroke menu, select Freehand. Begin to sketch in a wrinkle pattern on the 3D plane. In Figure 4.34 I have sculpted a crosshatched wrinkle pattern suitable for high-frequency skin texturing.

Figure 4.34: Sculpting a wrinkle pattern

4. When you have completed the sculpt, select the Alpha menu at the top of the screen. Scroll to the bottom of the menu and click the GrabDoc button. This button grabs a snapshot of the ZBrush canvas depth information. Remember that ZBrush's canvas is depth enabled, so the 3D plane will be read as white (no displacement) while your strokes will be captured as shades of gray.

If you had used ZAdd instead of ZSub, the alpha would be white on black. This is important to note. If you had used a combination of both ZAdd and ZSub, ZBrush would record the depth of the plane as 50% gray. This is because it's compensating for pushing out as well as in. This is an acceptable way of making an alpha. However, you will have to use a radial fade; otherwise each alpha stroke will have a visible border when used on a model. This can be remedied by adding a radial fade with the Rf slider under the main Alpha menu.

---

5. The canvas snapshot is now loaded in the Alpha palette. Since it captures black strokes on white (ZBrush sees subtraction as shades of gray beneath 50% gray), you need to invert the alpha. Under the main Alpha menu, click the Invr button. We'll now reapply it to the canvas. Undo your previous strokes or create a new Plane3D so you have a clean surface on which to sculpt.

6. With the Standard brush selected, pick the DragRect stroke and your new alpha. Click and drag on the plane surface to watch your alpha draw. As you now know, any surface texture that you can sculpt can be captured as an alpha. To save your custom alpha, from the main Alpha menu click the Export button. Save the alpha as a PSD file.

Details and Layers

As you start adding details to your sculptures, you may want to isolate your detail passes on separate layers. With details isolated in layers, you can turn the details off and experiment with new variations. You can also adjust the layer intensity and fade the surface details if they are too strong. In this section we'll add two layers to the demo head and adjust their intensities.

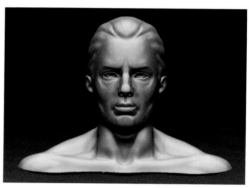

Figure 4.35: The demo head loaded and in Edit mode

1. Load the demo head ZTool from the default ZBrush ZTools folder (Pixologic/ZBrush3/ZTools). Subdivide to the highest subdivision level (Figure 4.35). When you make a new layer, make sure you create your layer at the highest subdivision level. You can create as many layers as you like and add details to each. The details will be separated on each layer, and you can independently adjust their settings or turn them off entirely.

Figure 4.36: Create a new layer and call it sculpting.

2. To create a new layer, open the Layer menu under the main Tool menu. Click the New button to create a new layer. With the layer selected, click the Rename button and name this layer **sculpting** (Figure 4.36).

3. Step down a few subdivision levels and use the Move brush to change the shape of the head (Figure 4.37). Even though the changes are made at a different subdivision level, they are stored in the sculpting layer. You can only change a layer's settings while you are on the same subdivision level where you created it. That is why the layer name will be inactive until you return to the highest level.

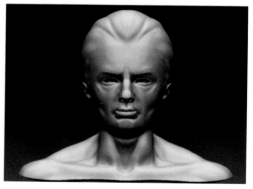

Figure 4.37: Change the shape of the head on the sculpting layer.

4. When you have finished, return to the highest subdivision level to create a new layer. Name this layer **details**. Make sure the details layer is active. The active layer is the one with the white rectangle around the name (Figure 4.38).
5. You are now on the details layer. Select an alpha and create some texture on the model's surface (Figure 4.39).

We have created two layers and added different elements to each. Let's now look at changing layer settings such as Intensity and Visibility.

1. If you are not already there, return to the highest subdivision level. Under Tool → Layers, select details by clicking its name in the list. Click in the Intensity slider and set this value to 0.5. Notice how these details become softer (Figure 4.40). Select sculpting and set the Intensity value to 1.5. This increases the strength of the sculpting layer. Notice that even those changes made at the lower subdivision levels can be adjusted with the layer intensity.
2. You can turn off layers entirely by clicking the eye icon in the Layer menu. Figure 4.41 shows the effect turning off the sculpting layer while keeping the details layer on.

Figure 4.38: The Layer menu. The active layer is the one with the rectangle around the name. In this image the details layer is active.

Figure 4.39: The demo head with sculpting and detailing applied in separate layers

Figure 4.40: Setting the details layer's intensity to 0.5 (left) softens the effect of that layer. Setting the sculpting layer's intensity to 1.5 (right) increases the strength of the layer.

Layers are a useful tool when you're organizing your character sculpting. You can even use them to store different facial expressions. Figure 4.42 shows a character with the mouth open in one layer and closed in another. By changing the layer intensity, you can adjust the amount that the mouth is open. This is the same as a blend-shape modifier in Maya.

The Layer menu under Tool is different from the main Layer menu. The Tool → Layer menu is for sculpting details on a ZTool and storing the details in a layer. These are saved with your ZTool file. The Layer menu is only used in 2.5D illustration and cannot be saved with a ZTool. Consider these more akin to Photoshop layers that happen to also have depth control.

Figure 4.41: The sculpting layer off and the details layer on

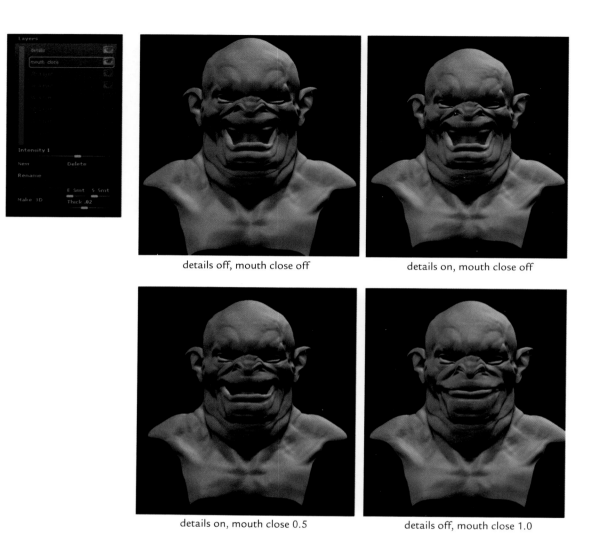

Figure 4.42: This character has details as well as facial poses stored in layers.

Detailing the Stingerhead with Alphas and Stencils

Now that we have covered the various applications of alphas in ZBrush, we'll apply what we have learned to a character head. We'll also look at some design considerations when sculpting skin texture. We'll use the creature from Chapter 3 to demonstrate skin detailing with alphas. You can follow along with your own ZTool or load the Stingerhead ZTool available on the DVD.

1. Load the Stingerhead model from the previous chapter; this file is also available on the DVD. Step up to the highest subdivision level of the ZTool. Remember that you will always get the best results when detailing at the highest subdivision levels. If the subdivision level is set too low, your fine strokes will have a jagged, faceted appearance when on the surface.

2. Create a new layer for the wrinkle details. Choose Tool →
   Layers and click New. Rename this layer **wrinkles**. While at
   the highest subdivision level, also store a morph target. To
   do so, choose Tool → Morph Target and click the StoreMT
   button (Figure 4.43). This stores a copy of the mesh as it
   looks at the highest subdivision level. This will allow you to
   use some techniques for blending details later in this section.

*Figure 4.43: Storing
a morph target*

By storing a morph target of the highest subdivision level, you can use the Morph brush
when you are on the highest level to blend between the current model and the stored
shape. This brush can be used as a blender, helping you to feather texture or erase it
completely without disturbing the form. If you only used layers, the texture could only
be faded as a whole; the Morph brush allows you to stroke over areas you would like to
fade out, retaining the detail in other areas.

---

3. Select the Simple brush and Alpha 43 and a Freehand stroke. Lower your Draw Size
   and ZIntensity to 12. Using short, sketchy strokes, rough in an overall wrinkle map
   for the entire head. This pass will give you an idea of how the wrinkles will flow and
   where they will be most concentrated. Figure 4.44 shows this initial wrinkle map pass.
   In the first image, I have painted color with the stroke to more clearly define the direction and gesture of the lines. I never consider this initial pass to be final; in fact, many
   of these strokes will be covered up by subsequent passes of texture and smoothing. The
   point here is to plan out the face as a whole instead of starting in one area and working
   around the head bit by bit. This helps keep everything unified.

*Figure 4.44: The wrinkle map pass. The strokes in the first image are colorized to help illus-
trate the flow of the lines.*

4. Load the alphas from the Gnomon Alpha library. Remain on the Standard brush but
   change to a DragRect stroke. Selecting the Leathery Skin alphas, stamp in more areas
   of texture; take care to vary the scale and placement as well as the alpha selections
   (Figure 4.45).
5. Continue to manually adjust the patterns applied by the texture stamp, resculpting
   where necessary and blending the textures into one another. Notice the crosshatched
   waffle pattern at the cheek in Figure 4.46 where the wrinkles from the eye meet and
   cross those on the cheek.

Figure 4.45: Adding the Leathery Skin texture with alphas

Figure 4.46: Resculpting the stamped texture. Notice the crosshatched texture at the cheek.

6. In these first stages of texturing, you can smooth the work back into the surface so that it is still slightly visible and then continue to build up over this smoothed layer. Use the Smooth brush set to ZIntensity 15 and Brush-Mod to –100. This will only smooth the details while retaining the larger forms. Don't smooth the detail away entirely; just push it back so it is barely visible. This approach helps introduce a level of randomness to the final product (Figure 4.47).

Figure 4.47: Smoothing back the skin texture before the next pass of detail

Using Stencils for the Eye Wrinkles

To add the wrinkles around the eyes, we can use a stencil. A stencil will allow you to select an image of eye wrinkles and place it directly on the model where you want that texture applied. Then you can sculpt through the stencil with any brush and only the area defined by the stencil will be affected.

1. Included in the Gnomon Alpha library you will find an alpha in the LeatherySkin folder called LeatherySkin67 (Figure 4.48). If it is not already loaded, import this alpha now in the Alpha menu. Click the Make St button under the Alpha menu.

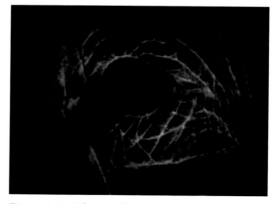

Figure 4.48: The LeatherySkin67 alpha

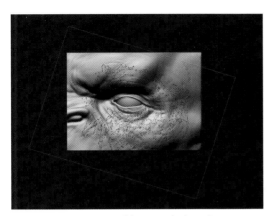

Figure 4.49: Eye wrinkle stencil placed

Figure 4.50: The eye wrinkles sculpted in

2. Under the Stencil menu turn on Wrap mode. Place the stencil over the eye area. Rotate and scale it to the correct placement (Figure 4.49).

3. Once the stencil is placed, turn off Show under the Stencil menu to make your sculpting easier to see. I find it difficult to work with the Stencil visible; turning off Show keeps the stencil active but only shows it when the spacebar is pressed.

4. Change to Alpha 1 and keep the DragRect stroke on. Set the ZIntensity to 5. Draw a stroke on the model. The stroke will be very light because of the low ZIntensity. Use the Replay Last command under the Stroke menu to gradually build up the detail. The stroke will repeat and increment the depth of the eye wrinkles (Figure 4.50). You can continue to replay the last stroke to build up the wrinkles to an appropriate depth. Ctrl+1 is the hotkey for the Repeat Last operation.

Whenever you are using alphas as texture stamps, be sure to go back over the detail freehand sculpting. This helps tie the texture together with other areas of the face and avoids a "stamped" look. Here I have feathered the wrinkles at the corner of the eye and added a sense of direction and flow that follows the secondary forms of the head in this area.

Wrinkle Dynamics

When you're sculpting skin details like pores and wrinkles, keep in mind certain aspects of how these tertiary forms tend to flow on the skin. The skin has a tendency to wrinkle in the opposite direction of the muscle fibers beneath. Take the mouth area, for instance. As you may recall from Chapter 2, the mouth muscle, the Orbicularis oris, runs around the mouth in a circular pattern (Figure 4.51). The primary wrinkles around the mouth should radiate out and transverse the direction of the mouth muscles (Figure 4.52).

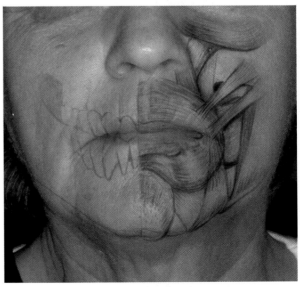

Figure 4.51: The Orbicularis oris muscle around the mouth. Wrinkles in this area tend to run against the direction of this muscle; as a result, they radiate out from the mouth.

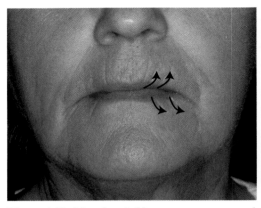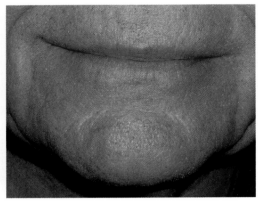

Figure 4.52: Mouth wrinkles run transverse to the muscle fibers

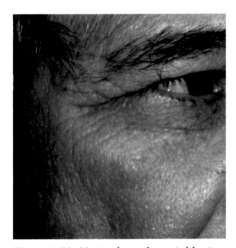

Figure 4.53: Notice how the wrinkles in this image are composed of several broken, sketchy lines. Also notice how some are more visible than others. This disparity in heaviness is known as line weight.

Wrinkles also have a tendency to be broken, sketchy lines and not straight grooves carved into the skin (Figure 4.53). Be careful not to make the wrinkles too deep or too regular. Crosshatch them with secondary wrinkles that run in the opposite direction. When crosshatching wrinkles, give consideration to line weight (Figure 4.54).

Line weight is a design term. It refers to the relative heaviness of one line when compared to another. In Figure 4.55 are two lines: notice how line A is darker and thicker than Line B. Because of this it can be said to have a heavier weight. Lines with heavier weight seem to advance in front of thinner lines. They also tend to command more attention and seem more important. In a design sense, the heavier line has more visual impact.

When detailing your characters, let some wrinkles have more line weight than others (Figure 4.56). This helps add variety and realism to the surface. The manner in which the skin wrinkles can also reveal a lot about a character. If there are prominent frown lines, a character appears to be angry. Skin wrinkles can be considered more than just a polishing pass on the character. Use them as a design tool and guide the eye around the face. See Figure 4.57 for an example of how wrinkle patterns can be used as a design element.

Figure 4.54: Crosshatching the mouth wrinkles

Figure 4.55: Line weight comparison

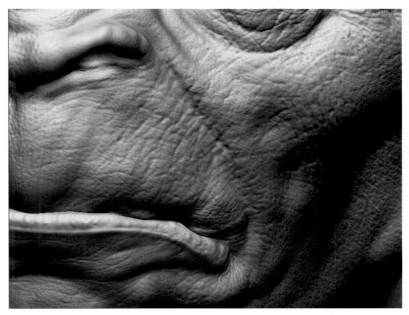

Figure 4.56: Crosshatched wrinkles with varied line weight. Notice the wrinkles that radiate from the mouth have a heavier weight than those that crosshatch them.

Figure 4.57: Wrinkles can help guide the eye around the face and have a logical flow that is determined by the character, underlying anatomy, and aesthetic choice.

Adding Pore Detail

Skin pores can vary in size shape and density. The pores at the nasolabial folds beside the nose tend to be more oblong than those on the forehead, which can be finer and more densely packed. Figure 4.58 shows different sections of pores isolated from the same subject. Notice how much difference exists between areas. Be sensitive to the variations in skin texture rather than just applying the same scale pore alpha over the entire head.

Figure 4.58: A selection of skin pores. Notice how pores change shape over the course of the face.

To stamp in the pore textures, follow these steps:

1. Import `pores.tif` from the DVD. Select the Simple brush with a Freehand stroke and Pore alpha. Under the Stroke menu turn on LazyMouse. Set LazyStep to .71 and LazyRadius to 1 (Figure 4.59).

Figure 4.59: Stroke settings

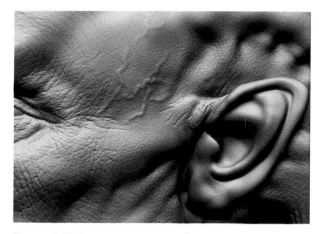

Figure 4.60: Pore texture stamped in

2. Create a new layer by selecting Tool → Layers and clicking the New button. Click the Rename button and name the layer **pores**. Draw a stroke on the surface with ZSub on. These brush settings will scatter the pore texture stamp by increasing the steps in the stroke (Figure 4.60). You can then go in with the DragRect stroke and individual pore texture stamps to vary the shape and size in different areas of the face.

3. When detailing the neck area it is good to add some gooseflesh bumps. Figure 4.61 shows a detail of the neck bumps. This little detail can help add a lot of realism to your characters. The neck typically has tiny raised bumps that can be created with the same pore alpha—simply change to ZAdd (Figure 4.62).

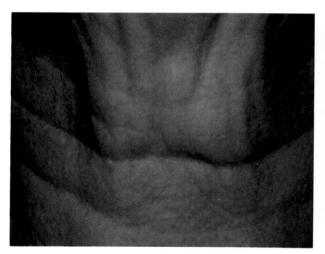

Figure 4.61: The neck typically has several small raised bumps.

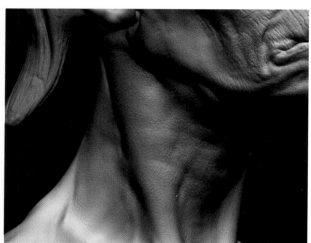

Figure 4.62: Neck bumps

Projection Master for Detailing

For the back horn we'll use the Projection Master script. ZBrush has many useful 2.5D illustration tools for use on the canvas. On the DVD you will find a bonus section from Chapter 1 that details many of these tools.

Projection Master allows you to temporarily drop the model to the canvas and sculpt or paint in 2.5D mode. You may then pick up the model and the work is projected into the high-res mesh. Sculpting done in Projection Master actually displaces the geometry of the surface just like viewport sculpting. The only difference is that Projection Master allows you to use the 2.5D tools. Projection Master is also useful for making fluid strokes at extremely high subdivision levels when your regular strokes may stutter or be too slow even with Lazy-Mouse. While it is still useful, Projection Master is starting to become replaced by entirely viewport-based sculpting. I am covering it here in the interest of competition, but many of the same effects we are building on the horn can be achieved with the Slash brush in the viewport.

We'll use one of the 2.5D brushes on the horn called the Deco brush. The Deco brush creates long, smooth-tapering strokes that are ideal for creating the striations in the surface of the horn. Rotate and orient the horn to be centered on screen. Use the Shift key to snap it to a side view. This will allow us to project the detail from the next stem through to the other side (Figure 4.63).

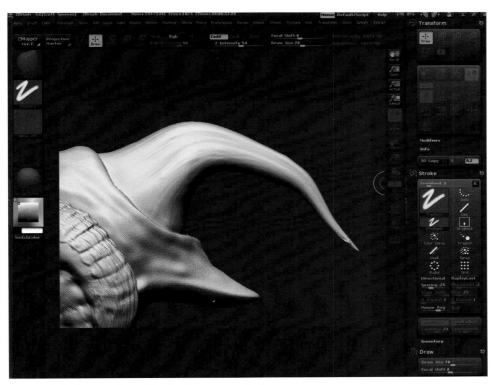

Figure 4.63: Horn oriented in the document window

Start Projection Master by pressing the Projection Master button in the upper left of the screen or by pressing the G hotkey. In the Projection Master window, since we'll be sculpting and not painting, turn on Deformation and turn Color off. Turn on Fade and Double Sided (Figure 4.64). Double Sided mode will project the details from the side you are working on through to the opposite side. This might give unexpected or undesired results if you are not snapped to an orthographic view.

Select the Deco brush. Turn off RBG and turn on ZSub. Turn off the texture on the left side of the

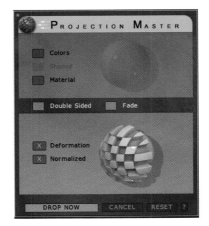

Figure 4.64: The Projection Master menu

screen. Lower your Draw Size and sketch lines on the horn (Figure 4.65). Deco brush strokes are long and calligraphic.

Select the Blur brush. Turn on ZAdd and soften the strokes. When using the Blur brush, be careful not to stroke across the edge. If you blur with ZAdd on, it can create artifacts across the edge when you're picking up from Projection Master (Figure 4.66). If this happens, switch to the Morph brush and stroke out the artifacts.

When you are finished in Projection Master, pick up the model by clicking the Projection Master button again or pressing G. The Projection Master window will appear again, but his time the button will ask you to pick up now. Make sure Double Sided is on and click the Pickup Now button (Figure 4.67). The details will now be applied to the ZTool on both sides. You can rotate and drop again to continue detailing. Be sure to turn off Double Sided if you are on an area that is not symmetrical.

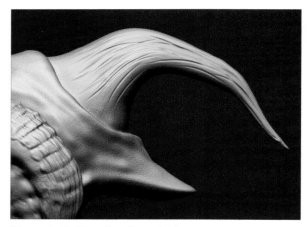

Figure 4.65: Deco brush on the horn

Figure 4.66: Edge artifacts

Figure 4.67: Projection Master pickup

Adjusting the Detail Intensity

By isolating detail passes into layers and storing a morph target, we have given ourselves several ways to adjust the intensity of the sculpting we just did.

If you find that the details layer is too strong, you can soften it by adjusting the layer intensity. From the main Tool menu, open Layers and click in the Intensity slider on the details layer. Set this to 0.5 and notice how the details are softened overall. Raising this value above 1 can make the details appear even stronger (Figure 4.68). Experiment with the Intensity sliders on both your layers. Layers can be turned off entirely by clicking the eye icon.

When adding details to your character, you'll find it beneficial to have a morph target stored. The morph target we stored at the beginning of this section will allow you to soften details or remove artifacts. Using the Morph brush can be similar to lowering the intensity of your layer, with the benefit that you can soften just areas and not the entire details layer (Figure 4.68).

Select the Morph brush from the Brush menu. Set the ZIntensity to 5 and stroke on the surface. Notice how this pushes details back. Now set the brush to 100% and see how it can erase details entirely.

Figure 4.69 shows the final detailed Stingerhead character. To achieve details this sharp, you must be able to subdivide well above 1 million polygons on your system. As we saw in Chapter 3, this is often just a matter of dealing with an optimal base mesh. In situations where system resources will not allow you to divide high enough, there is an alternative, which we'll look at in the next section.

Figure 4.68: Selectively softening details with the Morph brush. This head has the base stored as a morph target. Using the Morph brush with varied intensities, you can blend the texture back to 0.

Head with neutral morph target stored

Morph brush, ZIntensity 0.5

Morph brush, ZIntensity 50

Figure 4.69: The final detailed Stingerhead character (green material back-ground by ZBrush artist Erklaerbar)

The Bump Viewer Material

Depending on your system resources, you may not be able to divide as high as you would like to achieve a fine skin texture. In this case you can use a ZBrush material to paint a bump map instead. Bump maps give the illusion of fine detail by perturbing the surface normal at render time. This does not affect the geometry but does create the impression of fine details. This is an ideal solution when you're faced with diminished system resources and an inability to divide high enough to create a fine detail pass. Often bump maps are used in a production pipeline to carry fine details when putting them directly into the displacement map would be expensive in terms of render time and little if any actual gain in quality would be visible.

The Bump Viewer material is available under the Standard Materials menu. The material reads a grayscale color value and displays it as a bump or recess. Using this material, we can paint on the model in grayscale but see our strokes as if we were sculpting. Because of this, I will refer to *painting* in this section even though we are seeing sculpted strokes. Understand that ZBrush is interpreting a grayscale value and showing you a bump or valley. In reality we are applying grayscale color values as we work with this material. On the DVD, you will also find a video demonstrating the bump viewer material in use.

The Bump Viewer material will work with PolyPaint, but if you are unable to divide to a high level, the results will not be satisfactory. A better solution in this case is to use UV texturing. Follow these steps to use the Bump Viewer material with Projection Master:

1. Open the main Material menu and select the BumpViewerMaterial.
2. Load your ZTool you wish to detail or load the `fishguy.ztl` from the DVD. Draw the tool on the canvas and enter Edit mode. At the lowest subdivision level, create UVs by selecting Tool→ Texture → AUV. If you already have UVs assigned, you can skip this step.
3. Open the System menu by clicking Tool → Color → SysPalette. This opens the system color picker. You want to select 50% gray for your base texture. Select the RGB value 128 128 128. This value is read by ZBrush as neutral and consequently there's no displacement. When we paint on this material with shades of white and black, it will render as a bump for white and a recess for black.
4. With 50% gray as the active color, create a new texture by choosing Texture → New. Make sure your resolution is set to 4096×4096.
5. Make sure the Bump Viewer material is the active material. Under the Transform menu, turn off the Quick button to disable Quick Render mode. This mode can create artifacts in the bump display.

You are now ready to start detailing. Figure 4.70 shows the character in the viewport with the Bump Viewer material assigned. Since we'll be painting in UV space, we need to use Projection Master. Because we are projection painting, we'll only be able to work from a single view at a time.

1. Orient the model to the front view. Turn off Perspective mode by clicking the Persp button under the Draw menu. Drop to the canvas using Projection Master by pressing the G hotkey. In the Projection Master window, make sure Color is on and all other options are not checked. Click Drop Now. Figure 4.71 shows the face oriented to the viewplane and the character dropped to the canvas ready for texturing.

Figure 4.70: The character ZTool with the Bump Viewer material applied

Figure 4.71: The character dropped to the canvas in Projection Master

2. The model is now temporarily dropped to the canvas. From the Tool menu select the Simple brush. Turn off ZAdd and turn on RGB. Select a Freehand stroke and Alpha 42. From the color picker, choose black. We'll use RGB intensity to control how strong our stroke appears instead of ZIntensity.

3. Start sketching in your texture for the front view. If you want to fade or erase strokes, simply select the same 50% gray value and paint over your previous strokes.

4. When you are ready to apply the strokes and pick up the model again, press G. Make sure Color is the only option on and click Pickup Now.

If you want to drag alphas onto the surface and rotate them while you place the texture, select the Directional brush. Turn on RGB and turn off ZAdd. Also turn off Texture. Select the alpha you want to use and a DragRect stroke. This brush behaves like the standard sculpting brushes when it comes to dragging and rotating alphas.

---

5. This will bake the strokes you just made with the Simple brush into the UV texture. Figure 4.72 shows the strokes baked into the texture map of the character head and displaying as a bump map. The map tries to display on all subtools, which is why you see the bump detail on the eyes as well. This is not a problem since the bump map will be exported and applied separately in another application. The eyes will not be affected. You may now rotate to another view and drop again, then continue to detail.

6. When you have finished detailing, the bump map can be exported for use in another application. From the Texture menu, click Export and save the bump map as a PSD file.

As you work I recommend not finishing any view but keep picking up and rotating around the model. This will help keep the texture unified and help you bring the whole character to a finish at one time. Figure 4.73 fades between the Bump Viewer material on the left and the Flat Color shader on the right so you can see the color map under the material. Notice that the surface is not sculpted at all; the color values are being interpreted by the material to display bump detail.

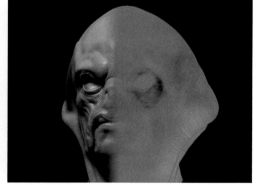

Figure 4.72: The first texture pass displaying as a bump map on the character head. Since we are painting on UV space, the texture will try to display on all subtools, which is why you see the artifacts on the eyes.

Figure 4.73: The first figure shows the character with a texture displayed as a bump map. The second image shows the same character with a Flat Color material applied so you can see how the color map is driving the perceived texture.

Another Take on Detailing

This section was contributed by featured artist Jim McPherson.

In detailing a ZBrush character, it's important to arrange the details into a system. Too often we see the same detailing at the same intensity all over the entire model. Variation in the detail is important. But not just variation for its own sake—variation with a logic.

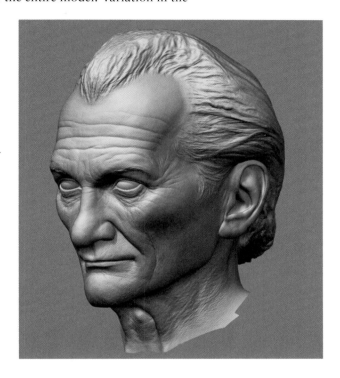

A cheek would have more detail than an ear. A forehead would have a different texture than a neck. Continuing this concept, a sculptor can divide a head into quadrants, with an appropriate texture in each area. Transitions between the quadrants become important. How does one kind of detail blend into another in a pleasing and believable way?

The forms the detail is applied to is more important than the quality of the detail. The details often follow the direction of the wrinkles. The pores and small lines will compress in a similar manner as the wrinkles themselves.

An important concept is that the details are actually forms themselves. Just as you would sculpt a well-defined nose, you should sculpt the detail with the same care. Are some areas flatter? Are other areas more crisply defined? Perhaps the shapes of the eye wrinkles are like tiny plateaus. What direction does the wrinkle cut in at? Does a wrinkle have more weight on one side? Pores and bumps can follow a direction but also a spacing pattern.

A study of life casts can help make you more sensitive to the details of skin and organic form. Or you could carefully study your own face or the faces of others.

An additional important concept to consider is that, although most people do not sculpt, they have a strong awareness and observation of details. They perhaps would have an opinion of what kind of textures that are pleasing and what type are ugly. Therefore you must consider if your texturing is complementary and appropriate to the character you are creating. For instance, does the detail make a heroic character look a bit ugly? Does the detailing call too much attention away from the expression of the face?

If you carefully consider the detailing, you could start to develop more original ideas. Could a frightening creature have a flowing scale pattern? The following is a rough mesh layout just quickly roughed out in Maya:

The next image is a higher level. I've drawn in the crests on the deltoid but haven't smoothed them in yet; I've started to block in the scales on the head. I've just indicated the spacing on the tendons on the hand. This is where you can work out the spacing, or transition between small to big scales.

I try to lay out the patterns of the scales at this point: the directions of the flow, and small-to-large relationships. You can do lots of erasing and reworking at this point. You are now trying to design the scales, a judge whether they are complementary to your character. It's not just outlining the scales. I think of them as flattened forms. The outlining can strengthen the forms.

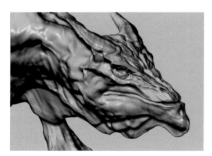  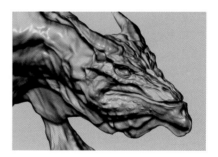

I've done similar steps on the neck. I also use the Move tool to pull the directional spikes:

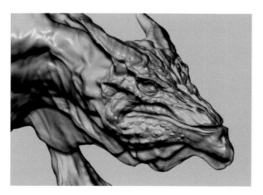 

I applied the same techniques on the arm, with some scales just outlined in on the chest. I roughed in some hand scales. In the following image, there's a lot more small scale drawing in the areas between the big scales. I used the DragRect stroke to pull Alphas 07 and 08 over the figure to give some high-frequency breakup. I also placed horns and teeth.

I like to paint as I sculpt. It's a nice luxury you get in ZBrush. The next image is only three colors:

- Yellow Ochre base
- Lighter Yellow Ochre for the underside of the body with cavities masked
- Black with some yellow for the scales on the top of the body, with cavity masking

The back end is unmodified cavity masking. On the front part I filled in some of the scales more in black. And I added some light color in the cavities around the shoulder:

I'm doing more pinching on the tops of the scales and in the cavities. Also I'm trying to refine the directional flow. I decided to go for smaller scales around the mouth and started using alphas, and cavity masking to draw in directional wrinkles between the scales:

I finished up with more pinching and drawing lines around the scales. Here's the posed version:

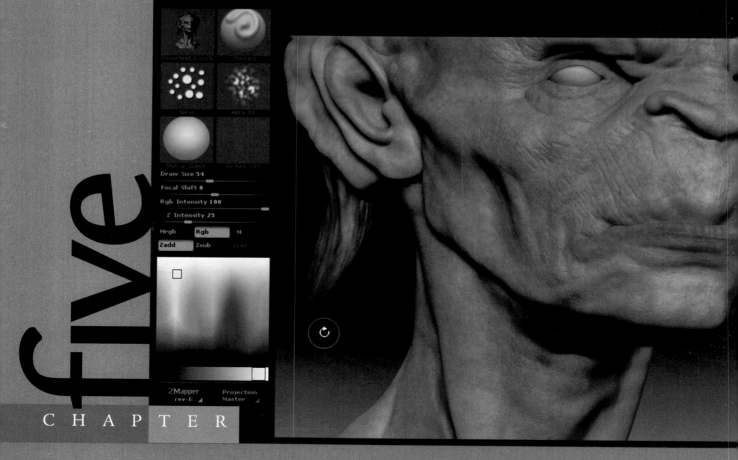

Texture Painting

In this chapter *we'll look at creating color maps in ZBrush. This is accomplished with a combination of hand-painting textures and projecting texture elements from photography onto the mesh or onto a UV texture map. When painting textures in ZBrush, you can take one of two approaches: UV projection or PolyPainting.*

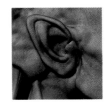

UV projection requires that a mesh have texture coordinates from either ZBrush or an external application. These texture coordinates are called UVs. UVs represent a method for the computer to unwrap a 3D object into a 2D plane so a texture can be applied without distorting. PolyPaint, on the other hand is a Pixologic technology that requires no UV coordinates to function. This can be a huge timesaver as it allows the artist to sculpt, paint, and complete a character in ZBrush without stopping to set up UVs. Once the PolyPaint is completed, the work can be easily transferred into a UV map for rendering in an external application. Both approaches have their strengths, which we'll examine in this chapter.

UVs in ZBrush

UV are the coordinates that allow the computer to unwrap a 3D object into a 2D plane for texture application. A good analogy is to think of unstitching a soccer ball and laying it out flat (Figure 5.1); this is a spherical object that has been unfolded into a flat plane. In Figure 5.2 you can see a 3D model of a head and the accompanying UV Texture coordinates. There are several methods of generating UVs using ZBrush's built in automatic mapping tools or laying out UVs by hand in third-party applications such as Maya or Headus UV.

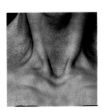

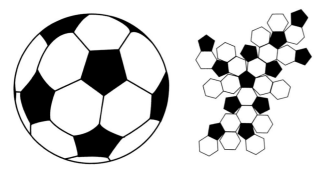

Figure 5.1:
Unwrapped
soccer ball

UVs help determine the amount of pixel space on a map that is devoted to an area. In the UV layout in Figure 5.3, the head and hands get 25% of the map space while the rest of the body gets 75%. Hand-laying UVs also allows you to determine what parts get the most pixels and importance while smaller objects or areas get less pixel space. In automatic mapping like Automatic UV (AUV) tiles, the texture space is divided evenly over the whole object. This ensures there is no wasted texture space, but it also gives all areas of the character equal resolution, which is not always desirable.

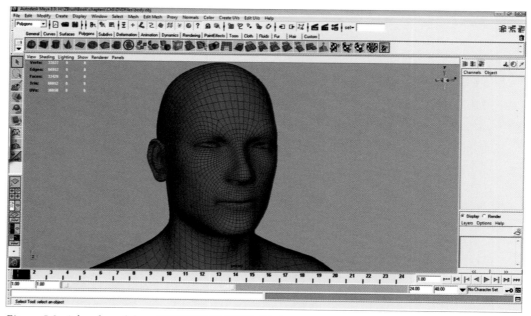

Figure 5.2: A head model
and corresponding hand
laid UVs (model by
Ricardo Ariza)

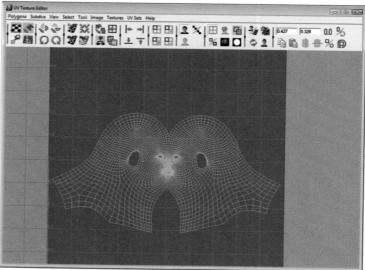

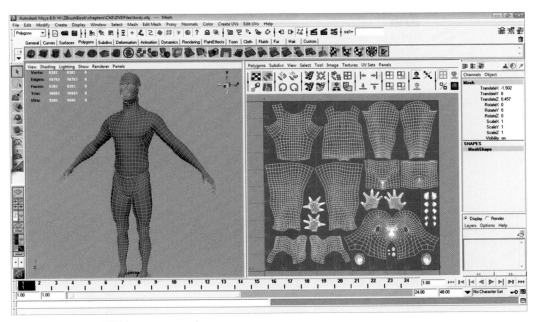

Figure 5.3: 75/25 UV layout example

Automatic mapping has the benefit of speed and, in the case of ZBrush's automatic mapping solutions, efficiency, but they also carry drawbacks. Figure 5.4 shows hand-laid UVs are easily human readable. You could open this map in Photoshop and find the seams and the nose. The same map on AUV tiles is unreadable to anything but a machine and impossible to fully edit in Photoshop (Figure 5.5).

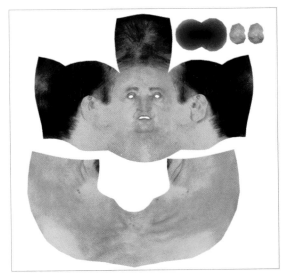

Figure 5.4: Hand-laid texture map (map by Ricardo Ariza)

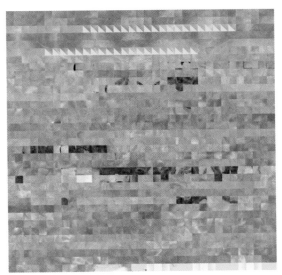

Figure 5.5: AUV texture map

ZBrush comes with several UV mapping methods. The two we'll discuss here are AUV and GUV tiles. AUV tiles are the most efficient— they assign the entire UV space to a character. They are not human readable.

Group UV (GUV) tiles are slightly more readable but not as efficient. When faced with a choice between the two, always opt for AUV tiles (Figure 5.6).

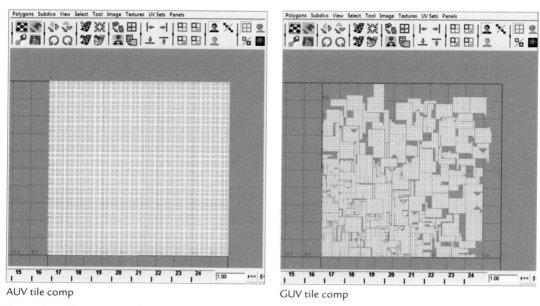

AUV tile comp   GUV tile comp

Figure 5.6: The same mesh with AUV and GUV tiles; notice how there is no wasted texture space in an AUV tile map comp.

Importing and viewing UVs

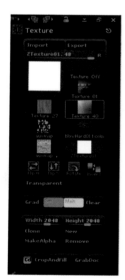

ZBrush sculpting and painting (when using PolyPaint) are UV independent. This means that you could take a character from sculpture through to PolyPainting all before ever laying out UVs. If you then decide to transfer the color to a UV map, you could add UVs in ZBrush or import them into the ZTool. You could also swap UVs with the current set by simply importing a new model with UVs applied. The process of importing and swapping UVs is covered in depth in Chapter 10.

To view your UV corrdinates in ZBrush you can use the Morph UV function included in ZMapper. Zmapper is a normal mapping tool for ZBrush but it has many other useful functions. For a description of its use for viewing UVs see Chapter 11.

The Texture Menus

When working with textures and UVs in ZBrush, be aware that there are two separate Texture menus. There is the main Texture menu accessed from the top toolbar (Figure 5.7). This menu allows you to create new textures, rotate and flip existing maps, import and save maps, as well as providing several other tools for working with file textures. See Table 5.1 for an explanation of each menu option. This menu

Figure 5.7: The main Texture menu

functions similarly to the Brush, Tool, and Alpha menus in that there is a palette for the currently loaded textures as well as several modifiers. The Texture palette itself is accessible on the left of the UI (Figure 5.7).

Table 5.1: The Texture Menu

Menu Option	Function
Import/Export	Imports and exports texture files.
Flip H	Flips the currently selected texture horizontally.
Flip V	Flips the currently selected texture vertically.
Rotate	Rotates the currently selected texture 90 degrees clockwise.
Invers	Inverts the currently selected texture.
Grad	Creates a gradient texture with the color boxes to the right.
Width	The width value in pixels for the next texture created with the New button.
Height	The height value in pixels for the next texture created with the New button.
Clone	Creates a copy of the currently selected texture and places it in the Texture palette.
New	Creates a new texture with the height and width values set in the sliders as well as the currently selected color in the color picker.
MakeAlpha	Creates an Alpha from the currently selected texture. Alphas are 16 bit while textures are 8 bit. This will convert the texture to 16 bit and strip all color information.
Remove	Deletes the current texture from the Texture palette.
CropandFill	Crops and fills the document window with the currently selected texture.
GrabDoc	Grabs the document color information and loads it in the Texture palette.

Figure 5.8: The Tool → Texture menu

The second menu is located under the main Tool menu. This is the Texture submenu (Figure 5.8). This menu contains options for working with UV coordinates, switching between UVs and PolyPainting mode, as well as transferring color information from Poly-Paint to a UV map (and vice versa). See Table 5.2 for an explanation of each menu option.

Table 5.2: The Tool → Texture Menu

Menu Option	Function
Colorize	Enables PolyPaint mode
Grd	Creates a gradient blend between PolyPaint colors—default is on
EnableUV	Enables the generation and manipulation of UV coordinates
Disable UV	Deletes the UVs from the currently active ZTool
Txr>Col	Converts the current texture map to PolyPaint
Col>Txr	Converts the PolyPaint to a texture map
Uv>Txr	Reads the color-coded UV groups and converts them to a texture
Uv Check	Creates a new texture map in which any overlapping UVs are color-code red
Vertex>Txr	Compares vertex order and polygon order
UVc	Applies cylindrical UV mapping

continues

Table 5.2: The Tool → Texture Menu *(contiued)*

Menu Option	Function
UVp	Applies planar UV mapping
UVs	Applies spherical UV mapping
UVTile	Tiles the current texture on all faces
GUVTiles	Applies Group UV tile mapping
AUVTiles	Applies Automatic UV tile mapping
AUVRatio	Controls the ratio of polygon size to texture area assigned
HRepeat	Repeats the texture horizontally
VRepeat	Repeats the texture vertically
AdjU	Adjust the texture in the U direction
AdjV	Adjust the texture in the V direction
ApplyAdj	Applies the adjustments from the above sliders
FSBorder	Sets the width for Fix Seam
FixSeam	Redraws the UV seams to reduce artifacts on the UV border

UV Projection Texture Method

When you texture with UV projection, it requires that the model be temporarily dropped on the canvas in 2.5D mode. You may paint or project from only one view at a time. This is because the computer looks at the color information you have applied to the model and projects it into the UV texture coordinates' corresponding regions. In this section we'll be discussing Projection Master, but be aware that these same techniques can also be applied to PolyPainting.

Projection Master allows you to convert the current canvas view of your model into Pixols. This process is called "dropping" the model to the canvas. This will allow you to use the 2.5D illustration and sculpting tools on a 3D model that is temporarily frozen in a single view and converted to Pixols. When you have finished working on the view, Projection Master will pick up the model from the current view and project the Pixol painting strokes to the model. If you were sculpting, the detail would be projected into the current mesh; if you were painting, the color strokes would be projected into the UV texture map or onto the PolyPaint surface. Projection Master does this by sampling the RGB, Material, and Depth values for each Pixol on the canvas and transferring that information to the corresponding pixels on the color map or polygons on the 3D surface.

Normally in Projection Master you rotate so that the area you want to work on is directly facing you, dropping the model with the Projection Master button, painting or sculpting, then picking up again. This process is repeated as much as needed by rotating small increments around the surface.

Start Projection Master by clicking its button in the upper left of the screen ▨ or by pressing the G key. The Projection Master window (Figure 5.9) has several options:

Color Specifies that the color information you paint in Projection Master will be applied to the model when it is picked up. The option Shaded will "bake" the current surface shading into the model as well as the color information. Material will bake in the material settings. These options apply to PolyPaint or UV projection.

Double Sided Projects your painting or sculpting through to the other side of the model. This is best used on a symmetrical object when you have snapped to an orthographic side view. Remember that Shift-dragging in the document window while a tool is in Edit mode will snap it to the closest orthographic view.

Fade When Fade is turned on, any texture or color painted on the model will fade as the surface turns away from the surface normal. The effect is similar to spraying an airbrush directly at a surface; any areas that curve away get a lighter coat than those facing you. With Fade off, all surfaces get a solid coverage of the texture or color.

Deformation Applies any sculpting strokes to the mesh. These are projected into the mesh at pickup and deform the actual geometry. For deformation to function, there must be enough resolution in the number of polygons to support the level of detail you are attempting to achieve.

Figure 5.9: Projection Master window

Normalized Takes into account the normal of the surface when projecting sculpted details. When Nomalized is off, all sculpting is projected directly back in ZBrush with no attention given to the curvature of the underlying surface.

With the model now dropped to the canvas, you may use any of the 2.5D brushes available under the tool menu. The difference here is that since you used Projection Master to "drop" the model, you can pick it up again and apply the changes you made. To pick up from Projection Master, use the G hotkey and click the Pickup Now button.

It is important to understand that Projection Master techniques used for UV projection are also applicable to PolyPaint. The only difference is the way the color information is interpreted by the computer once the model is picked up from Projection Master. Projection Master is by no means limited to only UV projection painting. By its nature, however, it will always require that you temporarily drop the model to the canvas.

Image Planes in ZBrush

By using a ZScript called ImagePlane3 reference images may be imported directly into the ZBrush workspace for use as a guide while sculpting or as a texturing tool. Included on the DVD is ImagePlane3. Install the script in your ZStartup/ZPlugs directory and launch ZBrush.

Included on the DVD is a video demonstrating a texturing process using Projection Master and the ImagePlane3 script. Although Projection Master is a useful aspect of ZBrush, it is quickly becoming secondary to PolyPainting and ZAppLink as the preferred texturing solutions.

Featured Artist: The Art of Magdalena Dadela

Canadian artist Magdalena Dadela is a character artist at Ubisoft Cinematics in Montreal. She is known for her engaging and realistic character models and traditional styled digital sculpture and anatomy studies.

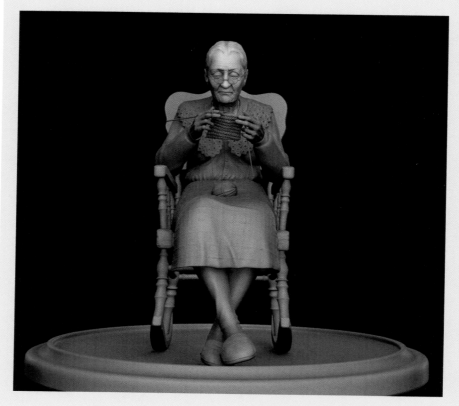

What Is PolyPainting?

PolyPainting is an approach to texturing that lets you color a model by applying a single RGB value to each polygon vertex. This allows you to texture without the need for UV coordinates. By applying color directly to vertices, you also avoid the need to drop the model to the canvas while painting. All texturing can be done in Edit mode, and you can freely rotate around the model.

Because the color is applied to each vertex, this means the resolution of the resulting texture is directly linked to the number of subdivision levels in the mesh. This means that a model of several million polygons can have a sharp, clear texture while a lower resolution level will have a softer texture with less detail.

PolyPainting cannot by itself be exported. To create a map for use in a third-party renderer like mental ray, you need to bake the PolyPainting into a UV texture map. Luckily, this is a simple process covered later in this chapter. The resolution of the color map is again linked to the resolution levels of the model. If you want the equivalent of a 4096×4096 map, you will need 16 million polygons of subdivision.

If you plan on rendering your character in another application, you must eventually use a UV texture map. This can be created from your PolyPainted texture (as we discuss later in this chapter), or you could start with a UV map. Figure 5.10 shows a character painted with PolyPaint but rendered in Maya.

Figure 5.10: Alien rendered in mental ray (image by Andrew Baker)

Painting a Creature Skin

Now that you understand the two methods of painting texture in ZBrush, let's explore color theory. This section focuses on painting a creature skin from scratch, but there is often more to painting than just laying down colors in a random pattern hoping for a good result. By understanding some basic color theory, you can make educated decisions on what color to select and where to place it on your character, thus painting extremely realistic skin textures quickly. For this paint scheme, we'll use a limited palette. Table 5.3 shows the colors that we'll use to paint this particular skin tone.

Table 5.3: Hues Used in the Paint Job

Color	Name	R	G	B
●	Red	255	2	2
●	Yellow	255	255	128
●	Blue	0	128	255
●	Warm brown	64	0	0
●	Cool brown	72	63	53
●	Gray	100	123	122
●	Olive	134	129	89

Color Theory

Color theory constitutes a book unto itself, but some of the most important things to note are in this section.

The color we see can be organized into a color wheel, which consists of the Primary, Secondary, and Tertiary colors. Primary colors consist of red, yellow and blue. These colors cannot be created by mixing any other colors. The secondary colors are created by mixing two primary colors: red and blue make purple, yellow and blue make green. Tertiary colors are created by mixing a primary and secondary color like blue-green or yellow orange. By understanding a few color concepts you can make educated decisions about what colors to put down on a character when painting a skin.

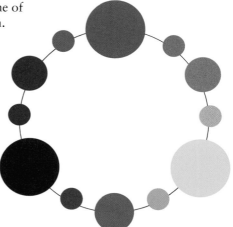

Figure 5.11 The Color Wheel

Temperature

Temperature refers to the relative warmness or coolness of a color. Red is "warm" compared to blue. A color can be warm or cool depending on what is mixed with it; red, for instance, becomes warm when mixed with yellow, or becomes cool when mixed with blue.

Hues that move toward the red area of the color wheel are said to be "warmer" than those toward the blue, or "cool," side. By placing two colors near each other with different temperatures, you create what is known as *temperature contrast*.

In practical terms, try painting a cool color into recessed areas and a warm color on raised areas. This contrast helps to emphasize the form as well as create visual interest.

Saturation

Saturation is the relative intensity of a color. You can reduce a color's saturation by moving the color picker toward gray. This is called *neutralizing* the color and helps create a muted color (Figure 5.12).

Figure 5.12: Neutralizing a color

Optical Mixing

You can see that the color selections in Table 5.3 are a limited palette, especially when compared to the look of the final painted skin. The power of these few color choices comes from the phenomenon of optical mixing. Optical mixing refers to a method of creating a secondary color by placing its two primary components close together. This can be seen in the Pointillist paintings, where tiny dots of color are used to create the entire painting. For example, with stripes of yellow and blue placed close together, the hues combine in the eye to cause the viewer to see green (Figure 5.13). To see this at work in a more practical setting see Figure 5.14. The same approach can be seen in painting where a stroke of one color is dragged across another color. The two colors seen in such a way give the impression of a third color.

Figure 5.13: Optical mixing

Temperature Zones of the Face

Portrait painters have known for centuries that the face can be broken into *temperature regions*—areas that have a defined relative warmth or coolness. This is due to the translucency of the skin and the quality of the tissues, as well

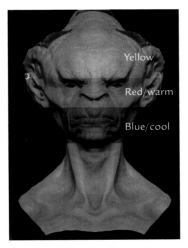

Figure 5.15: Zone theory

as the relative closeness of muscle and bone to the surface. In Figure 5.15, I have broken down the relative temperature relationships between the regions of the face of the character we'll paint later in this chapter. In general, on a light-skinned individual the brow takes on a yellow or golden cast, while the cheeks, nose, and ears are warm, red hues. The mouth and jawline are cooler blues. In men, this is even more pronounced than in women because of the beard line and the presence of hair in the follicles under the skin.

Figure 5.14: Optical mixing seen in a painting by Ryan Kingslein

Airbrush Techniques

The technique we'll use to paint this creature skin is based on airbrush paint techniques from the practical makeup effects world. An airbrush sprays paint on a surface in an adjustable fine mist. Changes to the brush can cause paint to be applied in broken-up, spotty patterns. This kind of paint application is ideal for optical mixing and for giving the skin a realistic look. Look at a close-up photograph of a face and notice how it contains many colors and temperature variations. It is not a single flat hue.

Figures 5.16 and 5.17 illustrate this technique applied to practical creature effects. Just as ZBrush allows us to sculpt with real-world style tools and techniques, it also allows us to paint this way as well. Using an airbrush tool in ZBrush helps us apply some of the same techniques and approaches used to paint prosthetics and animatronic creature skins.

Figure 5.16: This creature mask was painted with several broken-up colors and squiggly lines called mottling. (Creature by Lone Wolf Effects / Bill Johnson)

Figure 5.17: These characters were painted with many of the exact same techniques we'll discuss in this chapter. (Painting by Javier Soto—Balrog Collectable prop Head courtesy of Gentle Giant Studios—special thanks to Weta Workshop)

Making a Custom Spray Brush

We'll use a custom brush for this tutorial. This brush is designed to behave in a manner similar to an airbrush. By using a spray stroke and a paint spatter alpha, we can apply color in broken patterns similar to the airbrush described in the previous section. This ability of ZBrush to mimic real-world tools helps us utilize traditional techniques to achieve great results in a digital medium. To create your airbrush, follow these steps:

1. Select the Standard brush from the Brush palette. Make sure that ZAdd, ZSub, MRGB, and M are off and RGB is on.

2. Open the Stroke menu from the top of the screen. Dock the Stroke menu to the right of the screen and click the Radial button. Select a spray stroke. Be careful to select Spray and not Colorized Spray. Scroll down in the Stroke menu to the options (Figure 5.18). Turn Color and Flow down to 0. If Color is above 1, it will modulate the intensity of the color you have selected, which can cause problems when you're trying to establish color temperatures.

Figure 5.19: Sample stroke from the Spray brush

The spray brush you just created will put down color in a broken, random pattern similar to those created by an airbrush. See Figure 5.19 for a sample of the brush stroke.

3. You can save this brush as a preset by clicking on the main Brush menu and selecting Save As. Save the brush in your BrushPresets folder at \Program Files\Pixologic\ZBrush3\ZStartup\BrushPresets. With the brush saved here, it will always load with ZBrush, thus giving you easy access to this custom brush variant. Another option is to save the brush as a macro. For more information on creating macros, see Chapter 12.

Figure 5.18: Spray stroke settings

Blocking in Temperature Zones of the Face

Using the information we now have about color temperature, we'll begin to block in those areas on the ZTool. Use the custom spray brush and be sure to keep your paint job overstated and vibrant at this stage. This will be the lowest layer of many layers of color, so the

brighter it is now, the better it will look when under several more layers of color. This entire painting process is shown in a video on the book's DVD.

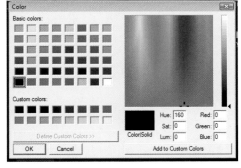

1. Begin by establishing an overall base color for the head. Click Tool → Texture and turn on Colorize. Click the Disable UV button to delete the UVs from the current model. This will free up system resources since ZBrush will not have to track UVs while you Poly-Paint. UVs can always be reimported later. This enables PolyPainting. We

Figure 5.20: Color menu and SysPalette

want to select a base color on which to paint. White is a poor base color as it makes all other colors look too bright. It is easier to paint on a hue that represents the final look we are striving for. Open the main Color menu and click the SysPalette button (Figure 5.20). From the color picker select a light peach hue something near RGB 251 228 198. This is a good base for a lighter skin tone.

2. With the color value selected, make sure RGB is on for your current brush. Choose Color → Fill Object. This will fill the object with the base tone selected.

3. The next stage is to spray in the warm regions of the face. Give the head an overall light pass of red, concentrating it in the cheeks, nose, and neck (Figure 5.21). Also touch the ears with red. Ears have a tendency to be warm (Figure 5.22). When painting, adjust the RGB intensity slider. For most of the painting, I keep the slider around 25. You want to keep the colors somewhat transparent so that they will mix better as they are applied over one another.

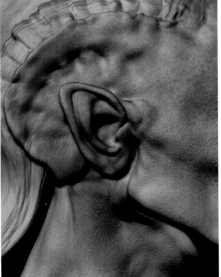

Figure 5.21: The warm regions of the face *Figure 5.22: Detail on the neck and ears*

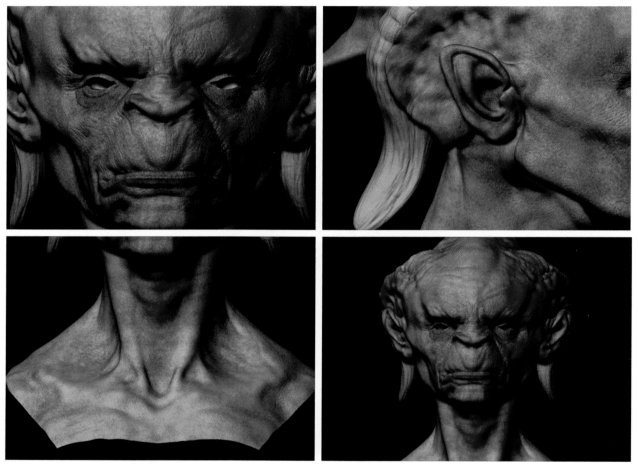

Figure 5.23: The cool regions of the face

4. After this pass of warm hues, select blue RGB 1 128 255, and use the same spatter brush block in the cool regions of the face (Figure 5.23). The area around the mouth, chin, and jawline has a tendency to be cooler. Spray blue in these areas as well as the eye sockets (Figure 5.24). Also use the blue in the recessed regions, such as the neck and recesses of the ears.

5. The next color pass is yellow. Select yellow RGB value 255 255 128, and apply it to those areas of the skin that are thinner, and areas where the bone is closest to the surface, such as the forehead, temporal ridge, chin, and clavicles. Notice how the yellow takes on a green cast in the areas where it meets the blue (Figure 5.25). Use the yellow sparingly.

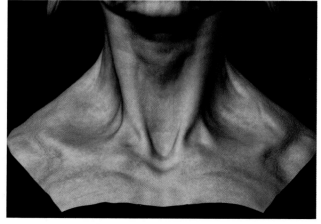

Figure 5.24: Cool hues in the recesses of the neck, eye sockets, and ears comp

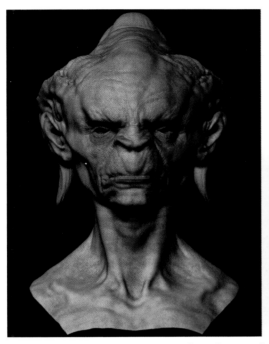

Figure 5.25: Yellow regions. Note the yellow on the chin going green.

Mottling Pass

Now that we have laid out the temperature regions of the face, we can move on to what is called the *mottling* pass. This is sometimes called the noodling pass. The point of this color pass is to break up the previous layers with little squiggly lines to help simulate the fibers and tissues of the deep skin layers.

The mottling pass is an overall coverage of tiny, broken-up squiggly lines. These will look strange now, but when the next step covers the entire head with a light version of the flesh tone, it will break up the saturation of different areas of the face and help create a sense of depth and translucency to the skin.

> Be aware that these early stages of the paint scheme will look overstated and odd. This is intentional; the next passes of color will partially obscure these layers. The more over-stated the under-painting is, the better it will show through the subsequent layers. For example, some classical painters even started portraits with a green under-painting. This green tone would be visible in the shadows after all the skin tones were applied, thus creating a lush shadow and a sense of temperature contrast between the light and dark areas.

Begin by selecting a freehand stroke and alpha 01. Lower your draw size and select white as your color. Begin to make small, tight figure-8 patterns on the skin. Try to be as random as possible, keeping the patterns tight (Figure 5.26). You can vary the patterning around the eyes and lips, making those areas tighter, and make the patterning wider on the head and temples. Experience will dictate how different patterns appear once the painting is completed.

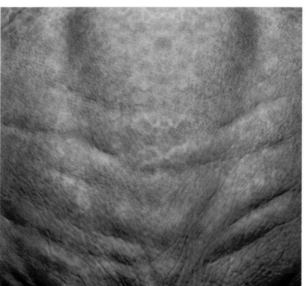

Figure 5.26: Squiggles

I recommend doing as much of this as possible freehand, but you may choose the vein alpha 22 and a dragRect stroke to fill in large areas like the neck and back of the head (Figure 5.27).

Once this mottling pass is completed, your character should look like Figure 5.28.

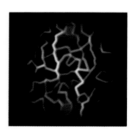

Figure 5.27: Vein alpha

Figure 5.28: The mottling pass

Base Color Washes

At this stage you want to unify the colors from the previous steps with a light coating of the base color. This is called a *wash*, after a traditional painting technique where a color is diluted to make it more transparent. This is also a good point to change to a MatCap skin material. We didn't use a skin material before now so we could get a clearer picture of the primary colors and their intensity as we painted. We may now more easily judge the overall effect with a translucent material.

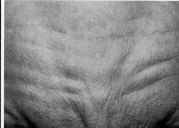

Figure 5.29: *Skin mist in close-up comp duo and full view*

1. Select the Spatter brush. Select the base color again. There should be an area on the head with the base color exposed. The easiest way to select it again is to click and drag from the active color box to a point on the model. The current color will be sampled from this point.

2. Spray this base color over the character with a low opacity and RGB intensity of about 10 (Figure 5.29).

3. Select Skin04 from the MatCap material menu. Click the Material menu from the main menu and click Modifiers. From the rollout options, lower Opacity to around 70 (Figure 5.30). The skin will suddenly take on a much more realistic translucent property (Figure 5.31). This is ideal for the next fine-tuning steps.

Temperature Adjustment

At this stage you will want to adjust the color temperature of certain areas by spraying lighter spatter passes of warm and cool colors. The previous stage of coating the head with a pass of the light flesh color both unified the paint scheme and muted the overall temperature modulations. At this stage we'll also do some shading with cool browns. This will help accentuate the forms of the head.

1. Selecting Red and using the Spray brush, add more red to the area around the horns. This skin should look ruddy and raw since the horns are pressing through the skin. Add this red to the tips of the ears to increase the warmth of these areas. Spray red into the lip and mouth area and the corners of the nostrils (Figure 5.32).

Figure 5.30: *Settings for Skin 04 MatCap material*

Figure 5.31: *With skin material applied*

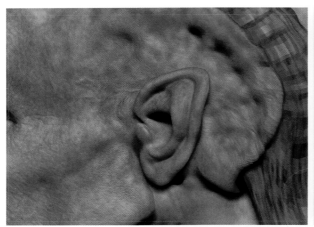

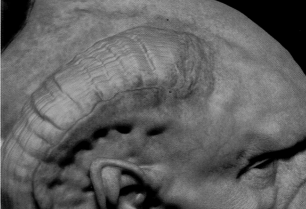

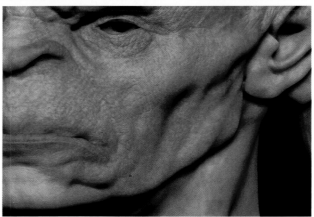

Figure 5.32: Ruddiness around ears, nose, and horns

2. Switch to RGB 0 128 255 primary blue. Lower the RGB Intensity value to around 9 and spray over the lips, confining the spray pattern to the lips themselves, trying not to overpaint onto the surrounding skin. Take this opportunity to spray blue again into the eye sockets and hollows of the ears (Figure 5.33).

3. Switch back to Alpha 01 and a freehand stroke. Turn down the draw size to 5, and with blue still selected, create a light veining pattern at the temples. This will help give the impression of blood vessels beneath the flesh (Figure 5.34).

4. At this point the paint scheme is ready for contouring. Contouring consists of light shading around the major forms to help define them and bring the structure out. Select a cool brown, in this case RGB 72 63 53, and lower the RGB Intensity so the color is very faint. Select the Spray brush and lightly shade around major forms like the collarbones and scapula (Figure 5.35). Spray this color under the cheekbones and in the hollows of the eyes.

5. The final stage is to paint a slightly darker version of the base color into the recesses of the wrinkles. To do this we'll use cavity masking. Click Tool → Masking from the main menu and press the Mask By Cavity button ▪Mask By Cavity▪ (Figure 5.36). If you decide to mask the recesses as opposed to the high points, simply click the Invert button under the Tool → Masking menu to reverse the mask.

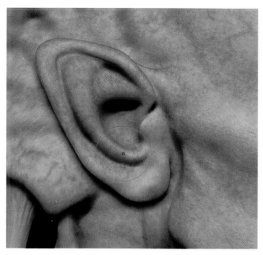

Figure 5.33: *Spraying blue into the ear hollows*

Figure 5.34: *Blue squiggles at temples*

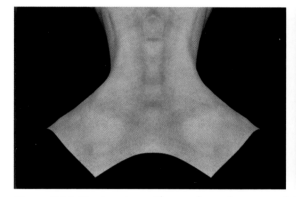

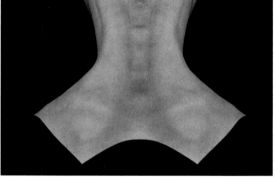

Figure 5.35: *Contouring with a cool gray hue around the forms*

Figure 5.36: *Recesses masked*

6. Click and drag from the active color swatch to the character head. This will select the underlying color. Open the system palette and neutralize the color by reducing its saturation, which you can do by dragging the slider down toward gray (Figure 5.37). It creates a chromatic gray or a gray with some sense of color. Using hues like this helps keep the color palette of the character skin more natural and slightly muted.

7. The head is cavity masked although the masking is not visible. Using the Spray brush with RGB Intensity low, spray into the deep recesses. The cavity masking will protect the raised portions from being colored.

Figure 5.37: Neutralizing the base color by adjusting the slider

Projection Master for the Stinger

For the stinger we'll use Projection Master. This is because using Projection Master allows us to use the 2.5D brushes which are usually only used on the canvas and not on a 3D model. Projection Master allows us to temporarily drop to the canvas and treat the model as a 2.5D illustration. In this case we'll use the Deco brush. The Deco brush creates long, tapered calligraphic strokes as you saw in Chapter 4 (Figure 5.38). In this case we'll use it for color and not sculpting.

1. Since we'll be painting only on the horn, let's mask the skin area we don't want to paint. Select the Lasso tool on the right side of the screen. Using Ctrl+Shift-click, draw a hide marquee around the head ending just short of the stinger.

2. Drop down a few subdivision levels and hide the faces up to the horn. Enter Frame mode to easily see the faces. Turn on Point Select. Hide the faces (Figure 5.39). Mask the stinger and Ctrl+Shift-click the background to show the rest of the head again. Invert the mask by Ctrl-clicking and step back up the subdivision levels. If you still have the polygroups from the sculpting phase of this character, use them to isolate the horn from the head and mask the skin. If your mask appears too light, make sure the RGB slider is set to 100. If this value is lower, the mask will be faint to invisible.

3. Orient the character head so the stinger takes up as much of the document window

Figure 5.38: A Deco brush stroke

as possible. You can zoom out from the stinger using the Zoom button on the right side of the screen ; this will allow you to see the entire canvas. Orient the stinger as shown in Figure 5.40.

4. Drop the ZTool with Projection Master by clicking the PM button or pressing the G hotkey. The canvas is now in 2.5D mode.

5. From the Tool palette select the Simple brush. Turn off ZAdd so only RGB is on. Select a cool white (RGB 240 241 244) and paint the stinger with this base color. Next, select a cool dark brown (RGB 72 63 53) and paint around the base and tip of the horn.

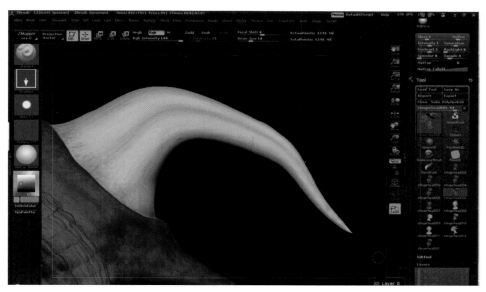

Figure 5.39: Hiding the faces up to the horn

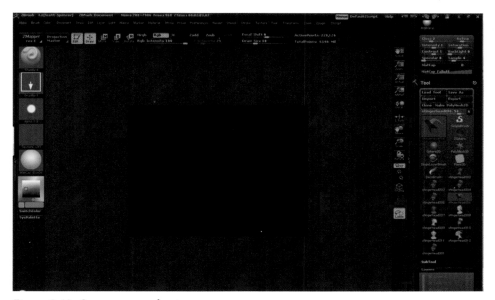

Figure 5.40: Canvas zoomed out

When switching between colors, you may find it helpful to use the V hotkey. Pressing V will swap between the active and secondary color swatches.

6. From the Tool palette select the Deco brush. Turn off the texture in the Texture palette. Turn down the draw size, and with the same brown selected, draw some strokes down the length of the stinger.
7. Select the base color again and drag strokes of the lighter color into the bark stripes at the top and base of the horn (Figure 5.41).
8. Select the Blur brush from the Tool palette. Make sure RGB is on and stroke over the deco strokes. This will soften the strokes and blur them slightly (Figure 5.42).
9. Select the Simple brush and Alpha 01, then lower the draw size to 10. Select a cool brown and paint a light squiggly pattern (Figure 5.43). This squiggly pattern is inspired by photo references I have seen of bison horns that feature this light patterning in the grain of the bone. This is pushed back with the blur brush and a light intensity pass of the original cool white.

Figure 5.41: Brown on the tip and base of horn and Deco strokes on the stinger; then, white strokes dragged into the dark

Figure 5.42: Blurred strokes

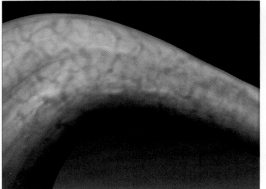

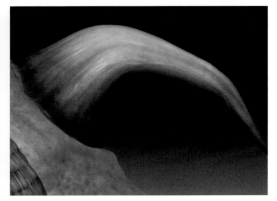

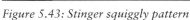

Figure 5.43: Stinger squiggly pattern

10. Continue by misting the original cool white back over the horn with a very low intensity. Also add a touch of yellow and blur again. Pick up the ZTool from Projection Master by pressing the PM button or the G hotkey. Make sure that Double Sided is on; this will create a slight stretching at the top and bottom of the horn. To fix this, simply reorient and drop again to paint the top and bottom of the stinger. Be sure to turn off Double Sided when working on these areas so that your texture does not project through, thus damaging the work on the other side.

You have now completed painting the creature skin and stinger using PolyPaint freehand techniques as well as Projection Master and 2.5D brushes. In the next section, we'll address the side horns of this creature with a slightly different approach.

ZAppLink

ZAppLink is a free plug-in for ZBrush available from Pixologic.com. It is a free add-on to the program and allows you to seamlessly integrate ZBrush's painting tools with Photoshop. This program will allow you to use all your favorite Photoshop brushes and filters in conjunction with ZBrush.

Install ZAppLink by following the instructions included with the download. To see the plug-in, select Document from the main menu. To launch the program, click

Figure 5.44: ZAppLink menu in Document

the ZAppLink button. In the section called ZAppLink Properties (Figure 5.44), click the ZAppLink Properties to open this menu, click the name to unroll the menu and access the options.

The ZAppLink Properties window contains the options for storing views of your model. Views allow you to store a model's position on canvas so you can use layers in Photoshop. We'll cover views later in this section. For now let's look at ZAppLink as a connection to Photoshop. Load the character model from the previous section. Draw the Stingerhead on the canvas and enter Edit mode. Orient so the horns are visible from the top, as shown in Figure 5.45. Mask the horn area and invert so the horns are now unmasked. Load ZAppLink by pressing Ctrl+Shift+S. Photoshop will now open (or the program you have on your system that opens PSD files).

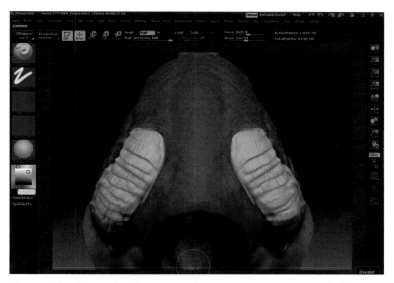

Figure 5.45: Unmasked horns seen from top view orientation before opening ZAppLink

1. Since we only want to color the horn, mask out the rest of the head. The simplest way to do this is to mask the horns and then invert. Orient the head on the canvas so the top view of a horn fills the screen. Once the head is placed, you will load ZAppLink by pressing Ctrl+Shift+S or by opening the document window and pressing the ZAppLink button. This will load the ZAppLink window (Figure 5.46).

Figure 5.46: The ZAppLink window

2. Click the Drop Now button and Photoshop will load with the ZBrush document as an open image (Figure 5.47).

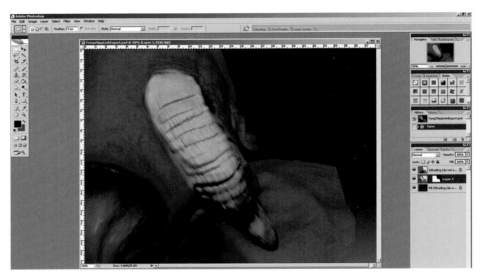

Figure 5.47: Canvas in Photoshop

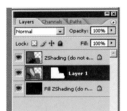

Figure 5.48: Anatomy of a ZAppLink document layer system

The ZAppLink document contains three layers (Figure 5.48):
- The top represents the shading from ZBrush and should not be altered. You can turn this one and off to see the color information with no shading information.
- The second layer is the ZBrush document window image with a layer mask. This layer mask simply cuts off any overpaint that is not directly on the model.
- The third layer is simply a background. When editing, you can change layer 2 or add new layers, but you must collapse your changes into layer 2, always preserving the layer mask when asked. You must have the original three layers before returning to ZBrush.

3. Open an image of a horn in Photoshop, copy and paste it over the ZAppLink image of the document window. Erase the edges of the image so it blends off (Figure 5.49).

4. When you have completed editing in Photoshop. collapse your new layers down to layer 2. Before collapsing to layer 2, Photoshop will ask if you want to preserve the layer mask; select Preserve. Be sure not to click Apply. Now save your document and return to ZBrush.

5. You will see a ZAppLink prompt asking if you want to reenter ZBrush or return to the external editor. Select Re-enter ZBrush and, on the following menu, select Pickup Now. The photo reference that was placed in Photoshop will now bake into the PolyPaint of the model. You can rotate to the other horn and repeat the process. ZAppLink is not limited to simply projecting photo references. You may also use the entire suite of Photoshop painting tools.

6. By continuing to rotate around the head, dropping and projecting a reference in ZAppLink, you can build up a base texture. Continue to adjust the color of the horns in PolyPaint and sample colors directly from the canvas using the projected photo reference as a guide.

For more examples of using ZAppLink, please see the video files on the DVD.

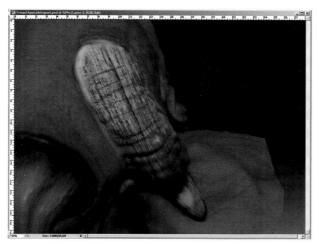

Figure 5.49: Erase edges of the photo to create a softer blend.

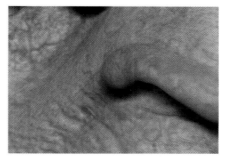

Figure 5.50: A selection of details that help push the realism of the head include spider veins around the nose and eyes.

Let's make some final tweaks to take the paint job one step further. Try using cavity masking (Tool → Masking → Mask By Cavity) and paint a cool brown with a very light intensity into the recesses and skin details. On this character, I selected a purple hue and added some tiny veins around the nostrils, eyelids, and horns (Figure 5.50).

That completes painting the creature skin. By combining Projection Master, ZAppLink, and Poly-Painting techniques, you have painted a detailed character from scratch (Figure 5.51). In the next section we'll discuss how to bake this PolyPainted texture into a UV map so this character can be rendered outside ZBrush.

Baking PolyPaint to UV Texture Space

Once you have completed your PolyPaint, you will at some point want to bake it into a UV map if you plan on rendering outside of ZBrush (Figure 5.52). This simple process is outlined in the following steps:

1. Load the PolyPainted ZTool.
2. Step up to the highest subdivision level. With the texture selected in the Texture palette and displaying on the model, open the Tool menu, click Texture, and press the Tx>Col button. This will convert the current texture to PolyPaint data. If you turn off the texture in the Texture palette, you will see that the color still displays on the surface since the data is in PolyPaint form.

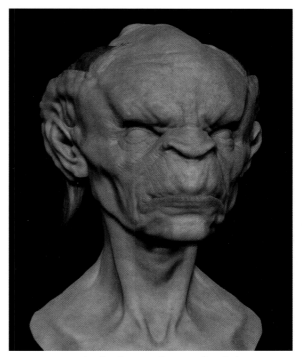

Figure 5.51: The final painted Stingerhead character in ZBrush

3. Step down to level 1. From the Tool menu click the Import button and import the UVed model into the existing Ztool.. Importing a model with new UVs into an existing ZTool is covered in Chapter 10.

4. Create a new texture at the desired resolution in the main Texture menu.

5. Under Tool → Texture, click the Col>Tx button to convert the Poly-Paint to UV texture information.

This process also allows you to transfer textures from one UV set to another by converting a UV texture map to PolyPaint, which you do by clicking the TX>Col button. This workflow is used extensively in my own production pipeline to allow UV changes after a texture has been created.

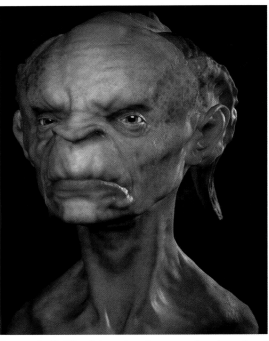

Figure 5.52: The Stingerhead exported and rendered in Maya

ZAppLink Views

ZAppLink allows you to store a Ztool's position on the canvas for later recall. To do this, you must store views under the Document → ZAppLink Properties menu. To store a view, position the model facing the canvas in the center of the screen. Open the main document window and click the ZAppLink Properties menu to open it. Click the Front button to store this view. Rotate to the side and press the Right button to store the right-side view. Notice that ZBrush will automatically store the opposite view for you; in the top view, for instance, the bottom view is automatically stored. If you need to clear a view, click the Clear button. If you need to save the views file for later use, click Save Views.

Now when you open ZAppLink, all the views will export as a single document (Figure 5.53). To work on a single view at a time, Alt-click the layer you want to work on to hide all other layers. Then turn on the visibility for the shading layer directly above it. When done, save your image and return to ZBrush. When you return to ZBrush, any changes made to any of the layers will update on the corresponding side of the ZTool. Click Accept for each view to keep the texturing information; otherwise, click Cancel.

Although this concludes this chapter on painting in ZBrush, there are many more topics and approaches to cover. I encourage you to check the video tutorials on the DVD for more information on texturing in ZBrush.

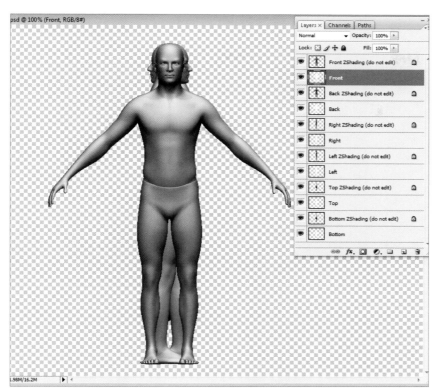

Figure 5.53: ZAppLink layers in Photoshop

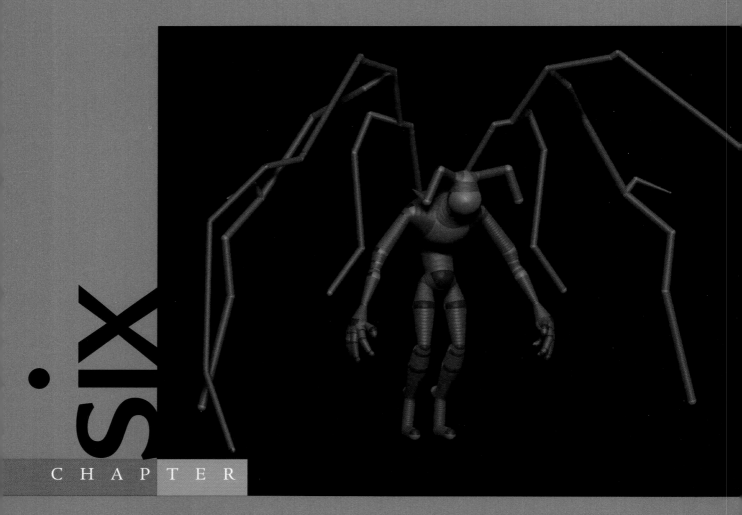

six

ZSpheres

In this chapter, *we'll look at ZBrush's polygon model–generating tool, ZSpheres. ZSpheres are powerful tools for quickly creating base meshes with speed and accuracy, much in the same way you might bend a wire armature upon which to sculpt. You don't have to painstakingly select and extrude polygon components like faces and edges—instead, you can use ZSpheres, which are based on a chain system of spheres where each link contains certain resolution information that allows you to create accurate topology when used correctly (Figure 6.1). ZSpheres have the added benefit that their topology is extremely well suited to the ZBrush topology masking tools as well as Transpose.*

Given these benefits, it is only fair to mention a possible drawback of ZSphere modeling: you do not have the same control over edge placement as you do in traditional polygon modeling. This drawback is nullified, however, when you approach using ZSpheres as a method of building an armature and then use the topology tools to establish a proper layout when your sculpt is completed.

In this chapter, we'll build a biped body with full hands and feet entirely from ZSpheres. It is my hope that you will gain a level of understanding of ZSphere modeling that will allow you to quickly generate base meshes of any variety.

Introducing ZSpheres

ZSpheres are accessed like any other tool in ZBrush: from the Tool menu. The ZSphere icon ⬤ is located under the Startup 3D Meshes section of the Tool menu (Figure 6.2). Clicking the ZSphere icon will allow you to draw a ZSphere on the canvas.

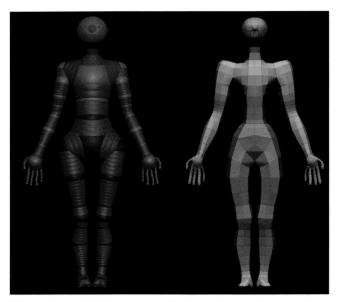

Figure 6.1: A ZSphere body and the resulting polygon mesh

Figure 6.2: You access ZSpheres via the Tool menu under Startup 3D Meshes.

When a ZSphere is drawn on the canvas, you must enter Edit mode as with any other ZTool. This establishes this first sphere as the root of your ZSphere chain. Any other spheres you draw will have to connect to this first sphere. As you work, you can move this sphere but you can never delete it—you can delete other ZSpheres at will, however. The chain created with a ZSphere will be converted to an adaptive skin to make a polygon mesh. An *adaptive skin* is a mesh generated by skinning a ZSphere chain based on the properties set for the spheres. We'll cover adaptive skins later in this chapter, but for now think of them as a polygon sock stretched over the ZSphere chain you created (Figure 6.3).

While in Edit mode you may tumble and navigate as with any other mesh in Edit mode by clicking outside the surface of the sphere on the background of the document window. If you try to click the surface of the sphere, you will notice that drawing on the ZSphere will draw another sphere on its surface, connecting it via a chain of concentric rings called joints (Figure 6.4). You will also notice that ZSpheres are two-toned with red and dark red. This is to help you spot twisting in the chain that will result in bad topology. We'll cover that topic later in this chapter, in the section "Moving, Scaling and Rotating ZSpheres and Chains."

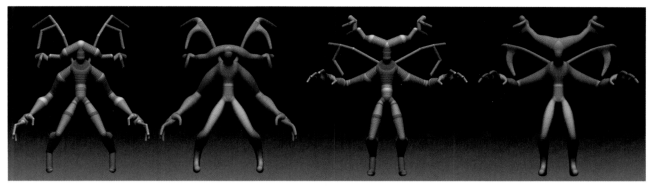

Figure 6.3: Adaptive skins behave like polygon socks stretched over the ZSphere chain you created. When you alter the chain, the sock stretches and adjusts to those changes.

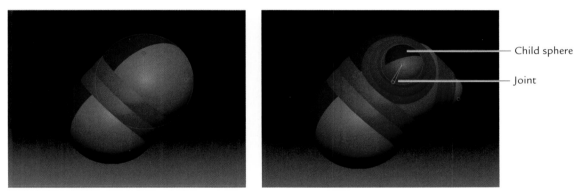

— Child sphere

— Joint

Figure 6.4: Drawing a ZSphere on the root will create a child with a connecting joint.

While drawing ZSphere chains, keep your Draw Size set to 1. This prevents you from accidentally selecting another ZSphere because it falls under your draw radius. It is also helpful to keep X Symmetry on, even when you're working on the center pillar of the body, because it assists in centering the ZSpheres (as you'll see shortly).

Drawing a Simple ZSphere Chain

When you mouse over the ZSphere chain, notice that the ZSphere directly under the cursor is contained in a red circle. This visually cues you that this is the sphere you will be drawing a child to at that point. Let's quickly create a chain of ZSpheres to illustrate this process:

1. Select the ZSphere tool from the Tool menu and draw it on a clear canvas. Enter Edit mode by pressing the T hotkey. Shift-rotate-snap the sphere to an orthographic view so that the division between red and dark red is on the center line, as in Figure 6.5.

2. Turn on X Symmetry by pressing the X key and mouse over the ZSphere. When the two green dots become one, that means you are on the sphere's center line. Hold down Shift and click to create a new sphere the exact same size as the root.

Holding down Shift when clicking a ZSphere will create a child sphere the exact same size as the parent.

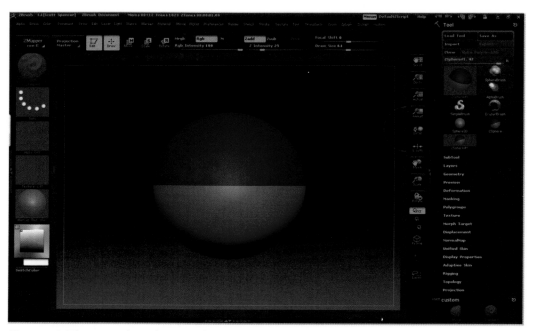

Figure 6.5: The root sphere drawn and snapped to orientation

3. In Figure 6.6 I have rotated off center so you can see the chain as it is drawn so far. There are two spheres; the lower one is the original root while the upper one is the child just created. At this stage, press the A key on the keyboard. This activates Preview Adaptive Skin. This allows you to see a preview of the polygon mesh the current ZSphere chain will generate. Notice that the root sphere creates a hole (Figure 6.7). This is because a root needs two children to form a closed mesh. For our demo this is not important, but it will become a concern when we move on to the biped. Press A again to return to ZSphere view.

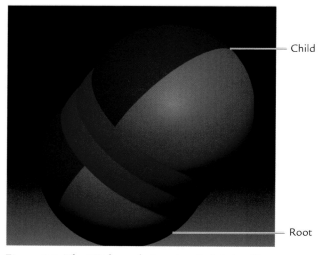

Child

Root

Figure 6.6: The ZSphere chain rotated slightly off center to illustrate the layout at this stage

Double Sided was turned on in this image to help show the hole in the mesh. Double Sided is located under Tool → Display Properties (click the Double button **Double**).

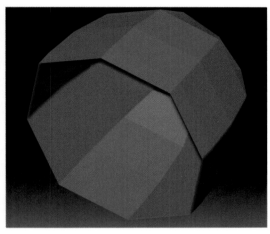

Figure 6.7: Adaptive Skin Preview shows the mesh that will be generated from this sphere layout. Notice the hole at the bottom caused by a root sphere with only one child.

4. Back in ZSphere view mode, mouse over the child ZSphere you just drew. Drag on the surface to draw a new sphere. Since X Symmetry is on, ZBrush will create spheres on either side of the current sphere.
5. Exit Draw mode and enter Move mode by clicking the Move button at the top of the screen 🔲 or pressing the W hotkey. Shift-rotate-snap to an orthographic front view of the chain and click one of the two children just drawn. Drag with mouse to move them off from the center (Figure 6.8). Press the A key to preview the effect this has on the mesh.

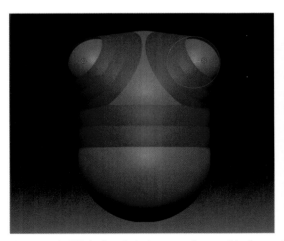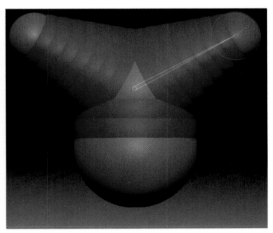

Figure 6.8: With the chain in an orthographic front view, move the two children away from the center line.

6. Notice that the edges stretch between the two child spheres and their parent. To add a new edge loop in this area, simply click the space between them; ZBrush will automatically create a new sphere (Figure 6.9). To delete a ZSphere, simply Alt-click it and it will disappear. This operation is not possible for the root sphere as it cannot be deleted.

7. To scale a ZSphere, enter Scale mode by pressing the E hotkey or clicking the Scale button at the top of the screen. Click the sphere and drag, and it will scale up and down (Figure 6.10).

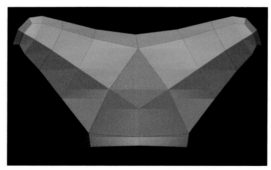

Figure 6.9: Adding new edge loops is as simple as inserting a ZSphere between two others.

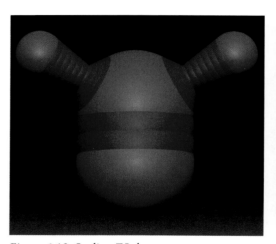

Figure 6.10: Scaling ZSpheres

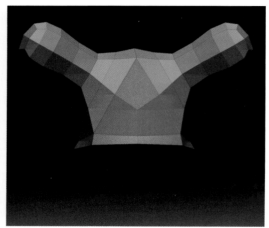

Notice that these transform operations (move, scale, and rotate) can be applied to a single sphere, but if you click the joint between them, the effect will be applied to the entire chain beneath that child. This works for moving, scaling, and rotating, but be careful when rotating ZSpheres as you can cause twisting in the mesh, as you'll see in the next section.

Moving, Scaling, and Rotating ZSpheres and Chains

You've already seen that the transform operations can be applied to individual ZSpheres as well as entire chains. In Figure 6.11, I have rotated the whole arm by selecting Rotate and clicking in the joint between the shoulder and elbow. This action rotates the entire chain beneath the shoulder. Moving and scaling have the same effect. Remember that if you click the sphere it will affect just that sphere, but if you click the joint it will affect the entire chain beneath the bone.

In Figure 6.12 I have rotated just the shoulder sphere and not the joint. It appears fine until you activate Preview Mesh and you can see the faces are twisted. To correct this problem, Alt-drag the sphere, and the individual spheres in the chain will rotate together, thus reorienting and correcting the twist. You may have to experiment with different directions and previews to get it right.

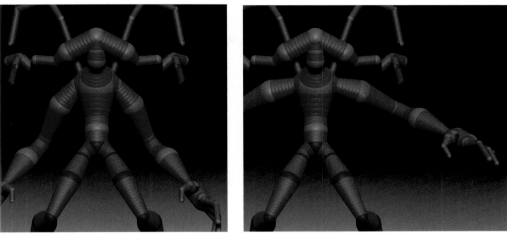

Figure 6.11: Rotate an entire sphere chain by clicking the connecting joint.

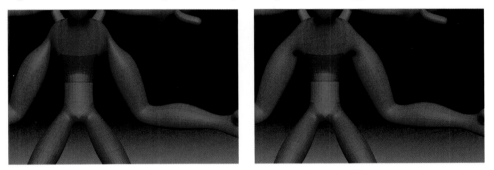

Figure 6.12: Rotating a sphere alone can create a twist in the mesh. To correct the rotations of ZSpheres, select Rotate and Alt-drag to reorient the chain.

You can spot rotation errors in the sphere model by seeing if the ZSphere color codes are consistent. Remember that ZSpheres are red and dark red, so you can visually spot the orientation. In Figure 6.13, notice the orientations don't match, so the resulting mesh is twisted. When corrected, the mesh is fine.

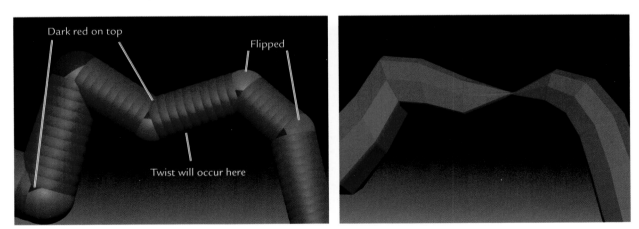

Figure 6.13: When spheres are not consistent in their orientation, a mesh twist will occur.

Building a ZSphere Biped

We are now ready to apply our knowledge of the theory behind ZSpheres and some of their basic controls to creating a biped character. Follow the steps in this section to build a humanoid armature and generate a polygon mesh as a base for sculpting. For a video of this process, see the DVD.

Don't be too concerned with generating a highly accurate silhouette or intricate edge loops at this stage. The point of this exercise is to create a general base on which to sculpt. With the ZBrush topology tools, you can generate any kind of base mesh you like after the sculpting is done.

1. Initialize ZBrush to clear any previous tools from the palette and the canvas. From the Tool menu select the ZSphere tool and draw the root sphere on the canvas. Press the T key to enter Edit mode. Open the main Transform menu and click the Activate Symmetry button, and then enable X and Y Symmetry (Figure 6.14). This will create four circles for your cursor. When all four become one, you know you are dead center on the root sphere. Shift-click to create the first child. If you see only two dots, that means you are looking at the side, so rotate to view the top of the sphere.

Figure 6.14: Activate X and Y Symmetry under the Transform menu.

2. Rotate to the other side of the root sphere and repeat the process of creating a child. The resulting chain should look like Figure 6.15. Notice how the orientation of the ZSpheres flips on either side of the center root sphere. This is normal. Press the A key to turn on Preview Adaptive Skin. Your skin should look like a capsule, as in Figure 6.16.

3. This "capsule" will form the torso of your biped. Now you need to add arms and legs. Rotate to a side view and turn off Y Symmetry; be sure to keep X symmetry on. Draw a ZSphere at the shoulder by click-dragging on the side of the top sphere. This will create a child linked to the top, as shown in Figure 6.17. Repeat this process on the bottom sphere to create the hip spheres. Remember that your cursor will turn green when you reach the center line of a ZSphere. Try to draw new spheres when the cursor is green to get the best result from the mesh.

As you create a ZSphere model, be sure to press A often as you work—checking the adaptive skin preview is the best way to catch mistakes early and save time and effort.

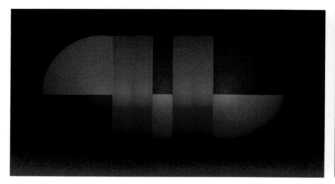

Figure 6.15: The initial ZSphere chain

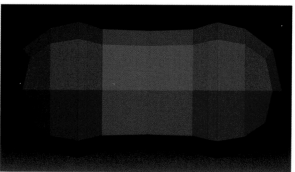

Figure 6.16: The adaptive skin from this mesh should look like a capsule.

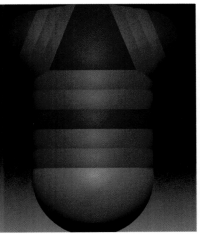

Figure 6.17: Creating the shoulder and hip ZSpheres

Figure 6.18: Making the head and neck

4. It's time to add a neck and head. Rotate to the top view and draw a new ZSphere between the shoulder spheres. Shift-click twice to make a chain of three spheres the same size (Figure 6.18). This process creates a simple head mesh. For a more advanced technique with eye and mouth edge loops as well as ear geometry, see the section "Adding Edge Loops to the Head" later in this chapter.

5. To add the arms, draw a ZSphere child from the shoulder ZSphere. Switch to Move mode (press the W key) and pull the sphere out from the sides. This sphere will be the wrist joint. Repeat the process for the legs (Figure 6.19).

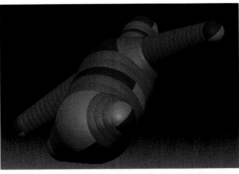

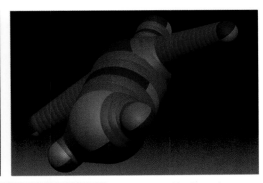

Figure 6.19: Creating the legs

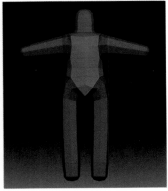

6. You now have a very rough block of the figure. Let's now insert ZSpheres for the joints at the elbows and knees to further refine the gesture and proportion. Make sure you are in Draw mode by pressing the Q key or clicking the Draw button at the top of the screen ⊞ . Click between the shoulder and wrist spheres to add the elbow joints. Repeat this process for the legs. Your ZSpheres should look like Figure 6.20.

7. Switch to Move mode and begin to adjust the gesture of the figure. Look for the natural bend in the elbows and knees. At this stage, you can also lengthen the torso and pull the neck forward (Figure 6.21). Scale the spheres of the head up by scaling the neck bone. You can add a sphere in the abdomen and scale it down as well as rotate the torso back slightly to add a bend to the spine. The ZSphere chain so far is pictured in Figure 6.21.

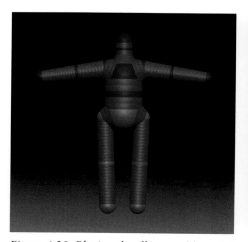
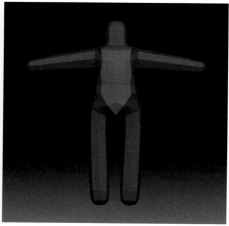

Figure 6.20: Placing the elbow and knee joints

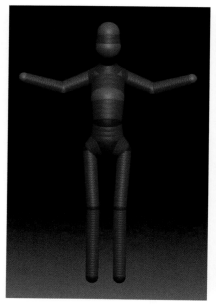
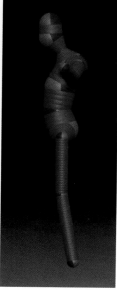

Figure 6.21: The edits to the ZSphere chain create a stronger gesture and adjust proportion.

At this stage, you could move on to hands or add a few more ZSpheres to increase resolution and reinforce the curves of the figure. Usually I prefer to keep ZSphere chains as simple as possible, but adding these next few spheres to establish the rhythms of the body can be helpful. If you choose to skip these spheres, that's fine—the same curves can be introduced in the sculpting phase.

1. Add a new ZSphere between the knee and hip spheres. Scale it up slightly and move it forward to give the thigh its characteristic curve.

2. Let's use the same approach for adding curvature to the back of the calf. Move the sphere back after scaling so the front of the shin is straight while the back is curved (Figure 6.22). You can improve the transition between the calf and knee by making it a sharper turn. To do so, add another ZSphere between the knee sphere and the calf sphere (Figure 6.23).

3. Add a sphere between the shoulders and elbow to serve as the mass of the upper arm (Figure 6.24). Also add a sphere on the upper arm close to the elbow to shape the join and make the arm appear less like a curved tube (Figure 6.25).

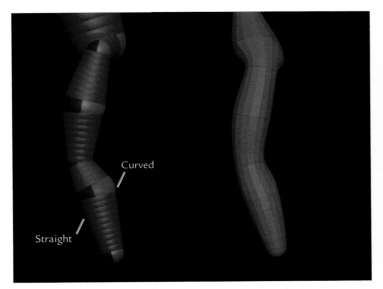

Figure 6.22: Adding a ZSphere to give a more natural curve to the calf

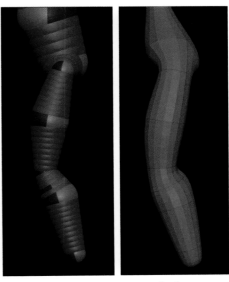

Figure 6.23: You can improve the knee joint by adding one more sphere between the knee and calf.

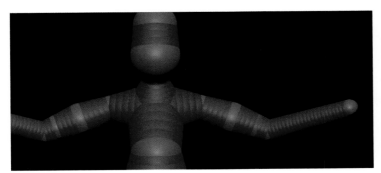

Figure 6.24: Using ZSpheres to refine the shape of the upper arm

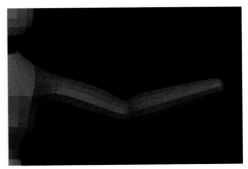

Figure 6.25: Sharpen the transition from the upper arm to the elbow with an extra ZSphere.

4. Add a sphere just below the elbow; this will serve as the forearm mass. The elbow transition can be further sharpened by adding another sphere between the forearm sphere just created and the elbow sphere (Figure 6.26).

That completes the body for the figure. Your ZSphere chain and mesh should look like the one shown in Figure 6.27.

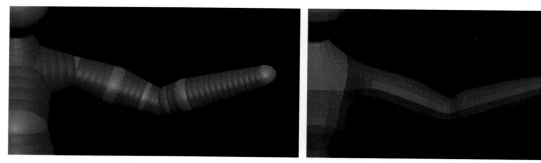

Figure 6.26: An extra ZSphere below the elbow, and another between the elbow and forearm joint, will further define the transition between the upper and lower arm.

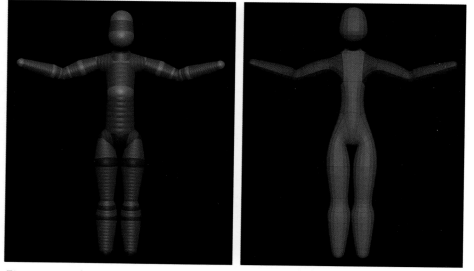

Figure 6.27: The ZSphere chain as it appears so far

Making Hands and Feet

Next, let's add hands to our ZSphere figure. There are several approaches to making hands, some more complex than others. More involved approaches can offer animation-friendly topology right out of the adaptive skin, while less complex procedures offer a hand mesh that is ideal for sculpting with minimal effort.

With the addition of topology tools in ZBrush 3, I find it is best to work with a simple ZSphere layout and build the animation mesh at a later time. This allows you to get to the sculpting phase faster, and the chances are a ZSphere mesh (much like any starting base mesh) will need to be tweaked for an animation pipeline. A simple process for making hands and feet follows.

1. Begin by drawing a hand sphere at the end of the arm chain. This new sphere will be the palm and all 5 fingers will be drawn from this sphere. Draw 5 spheres on this hand sphere. (Figure 6.28a)

2. Move the thumb sphere down slightly. This will allow the 4 finger spheres more space in which to flow into the hand and also creates a more realistic placement for the fingers (Figure 6.28b)

3. Press A to preview the skin. You will see the 4 fingers flow straight back into the hand and the thumb flows into the side of the hand and palm. You will want to draw new spheres at the tips of each finger now and pull them out with Move to create length. It is also a good idea to insert spheres in the middle of each finger to increase their resolution. Before you preview the skin make sure the Ires setting is 3 under Tool → Adaptive Skin. (Figure 6.28c)

This same process applies to feet as well. The key is keeping the Irs setting to 3 so the parent sphere is of suitable resolution to support the fingers or toes. The workflow shown here is ideal for creating fast and efficient base hand meshes.

Adaptive Skin Controls

Throughout this chapter we have been using the A key to preview our mesh. What this is doing is creating an adaptive skin based on the ZSphere chain. As you recall, adaptive skins are like polygon socks stretched over the ZSpheres. You can control how the sock stretches as well as how dense it is by altering the adaptive skin controls. These are found under the Tool → Adaptive Skin menu.

Here you will find several sliders. We'll go into some more detail on those you will use often. The Preview button will show a preview of the adaptive skin. This is what we have been displaying with the A hotkey. The Density slider controls how many subdivisions the skin will have. A setting of 3 will create a semi-smooth mesh of three divisions. The Mc and Mp buttons stand for Minimal Skin to Child and Minimal Skin to Parent, respectively (Figure 6.29). You can enable one or both of these buttons, or they can both be off. They control how skins are created where more than one ZSphere attaches to a parent—areas like hands, the torso, and the pelvis.

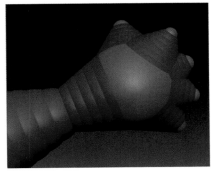

Figure 6.28a: The hand sphere drawn on the wrist

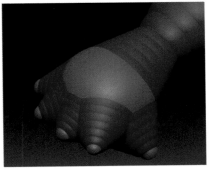

Figure 6.28b: The thumb sphere moved down slightly

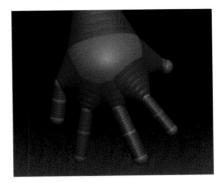

Figure 6.28c The ZSphere hand in preview mode

Figure 6.29: Minimal Skin buttons: Mc for Minimal Skin to Child and Mp for Minimal Skin to Parent

Minimal Skin to Child allows the child sphere to determine the connection points of the mesh but not to add new geometry. This accounts for the V-shaped transition seen in the crotch in Figure 6.30. Minimal Skin to Parent allows the parent sphere to determine the connecting points. Figure 6.31 illustrates how turning on Mp can change topology as well as curvature in the wrist.

The Mbr slider controls membrane curvature. This is the curvature of the mesh between ZSphere intersections. When set to 0, this slider has no effect. As you raise the value, the transitions between spheres will change.

Finally, there is the Make Adaptive Skin button 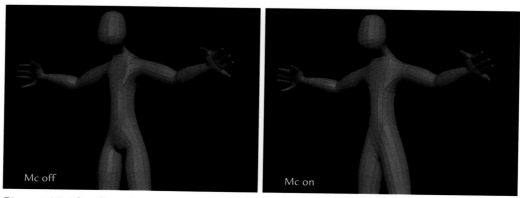. When clicked, this button creates an adaptive skin from the ZSphere chain based on the Adaptive Skin settings. This new mesh is stored in the Tool menu, where you can select it and sculpt on it. Before you start sculpting your ZSphere base mesh into a character, you must convert it to an adaptive skin using this button.

Figure 6.30: The effect of Minimal Skin to Child on the intersections of the mesh

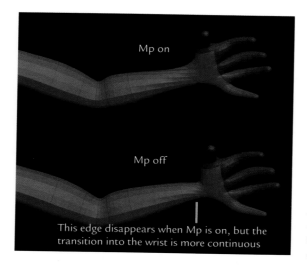

Figure 6.31: Minimal Skin to Parent can create a smoother transition into the wrist while removing the influence of the parent ZSphere on the topology.

Table 6.1: Options in the Adaptive Skin Subpalette

Menu Option	Description
Preview	Previews the adaptive skin.
Density	Sets the number of subdivision levels in the preview mesh as well as the resulting adaptive skin.
Ires	Intersection resolution controls the number of children a ZSphere can have before it is converted to a high-res sphere.
Mbr	Membrane resolution.
Mc	Minimal Skin to Child
Mp	Minimal Skin to Parent
Pd	Adjusts the lowest subdivision level of the skin when using Insert Local Mesh or Connector Mesh.
Make Adaptive Skin	Creates a polymesh based on the Adaptive Skin settings.
Insert Local Mesh	Replaces a ZSphere in the chain with a ZTool selected from the Tool menu.
Insert Connector Mesh	Replaces a connection between two ZSpheres with a tool selected from the Tool menu.

Adding Edge Loops to the Head

By adding a few more spheres to the head, we can give our model loops for the eyes and mouth as well as geometry to carry the nose. This ZSphere head is designed to allow for optimal edge loops for the eyes, nose, mouth, and ears.

Let's begin with the neck sphere already drawn on the torso. Draw the head ZSphere on the neck and move it up away from the body (Figure 6.32). Press the A key to preview this head mesh.

With X Symmetry on, draw two small ZSpheres for the eyes. Switch to Move mode and move them back into the head until they become concave holes instead of spheres (Figure 6.33).

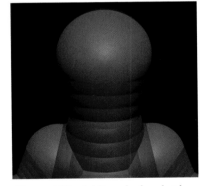

Figure 6.32: Adding the head sphere

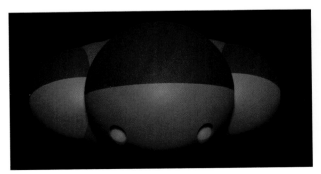

Figure 6.33: Making the eye spheres

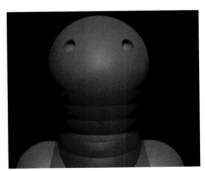

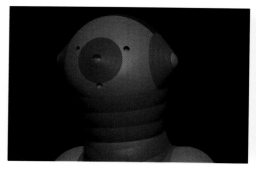

Figure 6.34: Creating the mouth, nose, and ears

Draw a mouth sphere. Again, move it into the head to create a hole. Likewise, create spheres for the nose and ears (Figure 6.34). Press A to preview the mesh. Because we have Ires set to 3, any sphere with more than three children will automatically become a higher-resolution mesh, creating the loops for the eyes and mouth as well as extra geometry for the ears and nose. While this mesh may look extremely basic, almost toonish, now it is absolutely effective as a base for sculpting any number of realistic characters.

That concludes the process of creating the ZSphere armature. You have now a solid base mesh you can sculpt on without ever leaving ZBrush. We'll sculpt in the major muscle forms and secondary forms of the face using the standard ZBrush sculpting tools, much as we did on the sphere in Chapter 2. ZSpheres work best as a quick and efficient mesh-generation tool. Part of the strength of ZSpheres is the ease with which you can re-pose and change proportions by just moving and rotating the chain. Figure 6.35 shows the figure re-posed and reproportioned.

Extreme changes to scale and placement of these spheres can yield a completely different type of character (Figure 6.36). It is also a simple matter to add in various parts. For instance, Figure 6.37 shows the same figure with centaur legs and bat wings.

Remember to press MakeAdaptiveSkin and select the new ZTool when you are finished editing the ZSpheres. A common error is to try and work on the adaptive skin preview mesh instead of saving a proper adaptive skin ZTool

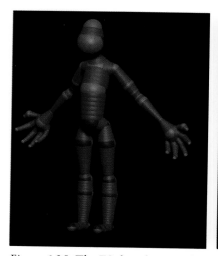
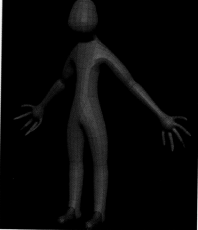

Figure 6.35: The ZSphere base mesh reproportioned and re-posed

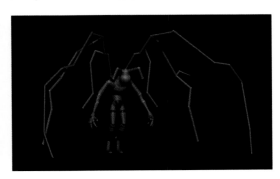

Figure 6.36: The same ZSphere chain rescaled and re-posed to create a more hulking monster type of character. No new spheres were added here—I only made changes to the existing spheres.

Figure 6.37: New appendages like wings can be added easily while existing limbs can be quickly reconfigured.

This concludes our look at building ZSphere bases for our characters. ZSpheres are a quick and powerful mesh-generation tool that can help speed up your sculpting workflow by freeing you from many of the more tedious base modeling tasks. The armatures built with ZSpheres are perfectly suitable for any kind of character or prop creation. Figure 6.38 shows a female figure sculpted from a ZSphere base by Ryan Kingslein. I encourage you to experiment with ZSphere modeling. With just a little practice, using the tools will become second nature and you will be generating base models in no time.

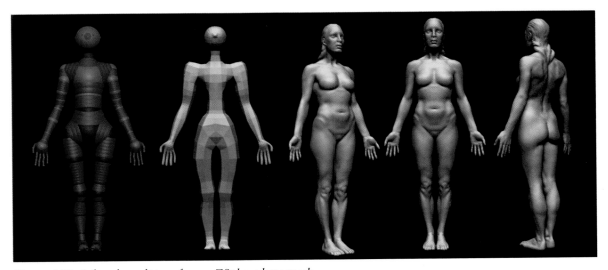

Figure 6.38: A female sculpture from a ZSphere base mesh

seven

Transpose, Retopology, and Mesh Extraction

In this chapter *we'll look at the ZBrush Transpose tools as well as the Topology tools. We have used Transpose in earlier chapters to move subtools, but we'll now take a more in-depth look and use Transpose as a dynamic posing tool. Using layers, we'll store multiple poses in one ZTool. We'll also look at the ZScript Transpose master for posing a model with multiple subtools.*

The Topology tools will be used to rebuild the underlying geometry of our ZTool while retaining all the sculpted details. This allows you maximum freedom when working in ZBrush since you can sculpt and even PolyPaint a model, and then use the Topology tools to rebuild the base mesh and project all your detail and painting. The topology tools are also useful for building accessories like costumes and armor parts for your models.

Moving and Posing Figures with Transpose

Transpose tools are accessible when you have a tool active in Edit mode on the canvas, but you leave Draw mode and enter Move, Rotate, or Scale by clicking the corresponding buttons at the top left of the screen (or using the Q, W, E, R hotkeys: Q is for Draw mode while W, E, and R are for Move, Scale, and Rotate, respectively).

In previous chapters we have used Transpose for moving subtools in relation to one another. Here we'll combine Transpose with masking and use it as an advanced posing tool. ZBrush allows us to create dynamic poses for our ZTools, store them in layers, and even maintain sculpting symmetry on an asymmetrically posed model. For a video demonstrating Transpose in action, please see the DVD.

The Action Line

The Transpose tool consists of a single modifier called the Action line. When entering a Transpose mode, this line will be apparent on the model (Figure 7.1); you can redraw this line by clicking anywhere on the object, then dragging and releasing. The length of the stroke determines the length of the action line, and the places that you start and end the line determine the pivots for rotation and scale operations. When you're drawing an action line, it will snap to the surface of the model underneath it and any previous action lines will be replaced. Note that by default the size of the endpoint circles will change to help illustrate how far one endpoint is from the viewer compared to another. This can help you spot when the transpose line is receding into space from the viewer.

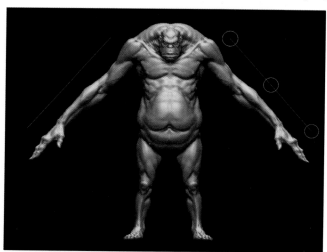

Figure 7.1: *The action line is an orange line with three circles that is visible when in Move, Rotate, or Scale mode. (Giant by Jim McPherson courtesy of Gentle Giant Studios and Secret Level/Sega)*

Transpose can be used with symmetry on or off; in Figure 7.1, both arms have an action line applied in Symmetry mode, if we turned Symmetry off, the line on the left arm would vanish.

You can reposition the action line by clicking and dragging on the line itself or on the yellow rim of the center circle. The circle endpoints can be adjusted by clicking on the circle, not inside the circle, to move them in the plane of the screen (X and Y directions only).

To center an endpoint in a joint, Shift-click-rotate to snap the model to a front view and place the endpoint. Then, Shift-rotate-snap to an orthographic side view and pull the endpoints back to the desired placement (Figure 7.2).

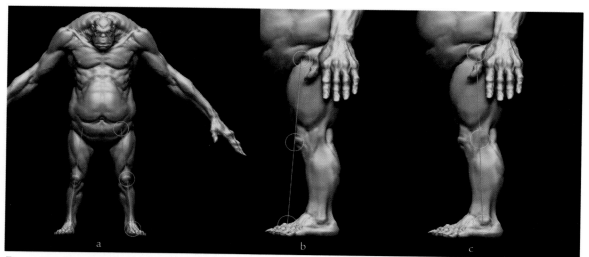

Figure 7.2: *To center a joint: (a) Draw an action line in the front view. (b) Snap to an orthographic side view. (c) Move the circles from the side to place them correctly in relation to the figure.*

To use the action line, click and drag from the center of one of the endpoints. You will know the endpoint is active when a red dot appears in the circle. With Move active  clicking in the center point will move the entire object, while clicking and dragging from one of the endpoints will scale the object proportionately as if the opposite end of the line were the world space origin (Figure 7.3). Holding down the Shift key while you drag will constrain the movement to a single axis.

Figure 7.3: Move with Transpose

To scale an object, make sure Scale is active at the top of the screen by clicking the Scale button or pressing the E hotkey. Click and drag an action line on the model. Place one endpoint where you want the center of the scale or the origin to be. The polygons under this endpoint will not move. By clicking and dragging in the other endpoint away from the origin, you will scale up the model. By dragging toward the opposite endpoint, you will scale it down (Figure 7.4). To scale in a plane perpendicular to the action line, click in the center point and drag toward one of the endpoints. Dragging to one end will thicken the figure; dragging to the other will thin it.

The Alt key will produce alternate effects in Transpose mode. Holding down the Alt key while scaling a figure will affect the parts of the model closest to that endpoint more. This could have the effect of lengthening the legs while leaving the rest of the figure relatively unchanged. Alt-dragging the midpoint will increase the scale effect between the midpoint and the last touched endpoint.

To rotate the model with Transpose active, enter Rotate mode by pressing the R hotkey or by clicking the Rotate button . Draw an action line and drag one of the endpoints. This will rotate the entire model around the opposite endpoint. If you click and drag in the center midpoint, the model will rotate around the axis of the action line itself.

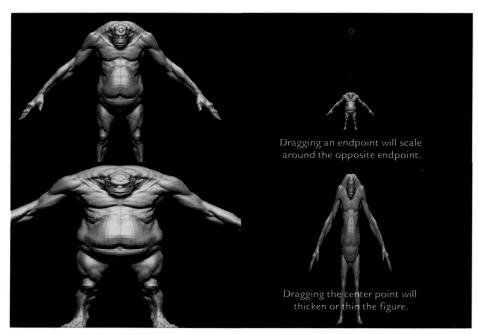

Dragging an endpoint will scale around the opposite endpoint.

Dragging the center point will thicken or thin the figure.

Figure 7.4: Scaling with Transpose

When rotating in Transpose it is sometimes important to keep the action line straight and perpendicular to the viewplane. To do this, start the action line on the model but drag off the model to release. This ensures the line snaps to a plane perpendicular to the viewplane, thus allowing you to make accurate rotations in X, Y, and Z (Figure 7.5).

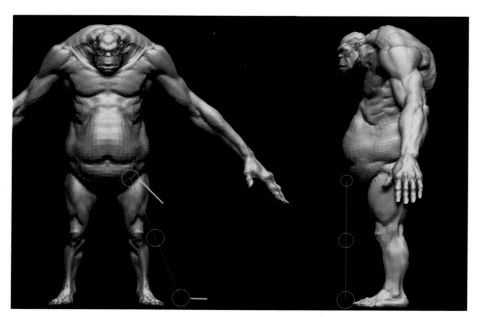

Figure 7.5: Drawing an action line from the figure to the background will create the line in the current view orientation, ensuring it is a straight line. Clicking the endpoint will then let you place it where desired.

Topology Masking

Figure 7.6 shows a figure with an action line drawn down the arm. If we enter Rotate mode and drag the endpoint, the entire figure will rotate. This is where masking comes in handy. By masking everything but the arm, the unmasked areas will rotate around the opposite end of the action line. Masking can be accomplished with the same methods we have discussed so far (Ctrl-clicking to paint masks or using a marquee).

Figure 7.6: Rotating an unmasked figure is a global operation. With the body masked, only the arm rotates.

In Transpose mode, there is another powerful masking option called topology masking. Topology masking creates a mask on the model based on the underlying edge flow (Figure 7.7). In a base mesh with evenly dispersed quad geometry and edge loops that flow down the appendages, this makes masking limbs quick and easy. The topology generated by ZSphere models is especially effective with this masking technique.

To mask by topology, hold down the Ctrl key and drag the arm. Notice that the line produces a mask that dynamically grows with the stroke. With the entire arm masked, Ctrl-click off the model and invert the mask so the arm is now unmasked. The edge of the mask can be blurred or sharpened using the Ctrl and Shift keys

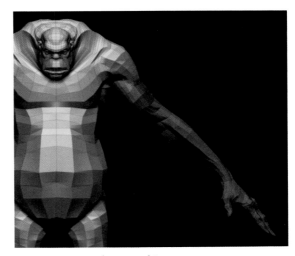

Figure 7.7: Topology masking

(Figure 7.8). Ctrl-click the masked area to blur it and to create a more natural deformation; Ctrl+Alt-click to sharpen the masked area. This can also be accomplished with the blurMask and sharpenMask buttons under Tool → Masking. You can adjust the amount of blur or sharpening that is applied when you Ctrl-click by choosing Preferences → Transpose. Topology masking is only accessible when Move, Rotate, or Scale mode is active.

Figure 7.8: By Ctrl-clicking (left), you can blur a mask; using Ctrl+Alt-click (right), you can sharpen it.

Posing a Figure

When posing a character, keep in mind some fundamental concepts. Where is the character's center of balance, where is the weight of the character placed in relation to the center, and how is the character's anatomy changing over the pose (meaning the extension and compression of the muscles)?

In Figure 7.9 I have labeled the skeleton, the center of balance, and the weight distribution on this character. The red lines represent the underlying skeleton. Notice that the left

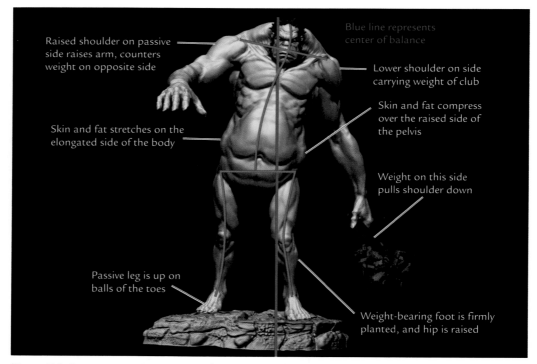

Raised shoulder on passive side raises arm, counters weight on opposite side

Blue line represents center of balance

Lower shoulder on side carrying weight of club

Skin and fat compress over the raised side of the pelvis

Skin and fat stretches on the elongated side of the body

Weight on this side pulls shoulder down

Passive leg is up on balls of the toes

Weight-bearing foot is firmly planted, and hip is raised

Figure 7.9: Important points to note when posing a character

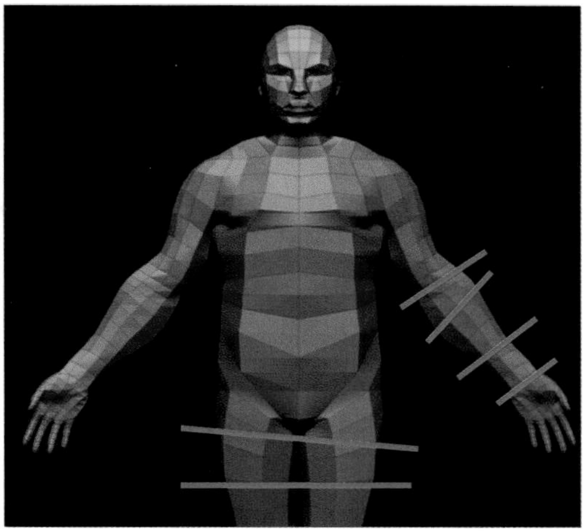

hip is raised with the weight being placed on the left leg. This shifting of weight across the center line is called *contrapposto*. The blue line represents the center of gravity; this is always a straight plumb line and is not necessarily in the center of the figure. Notice that the line of the hips is at an angle opposite that of the shoulders.

In this section we'll use the information you have learned about Transpose and topology masking to pose a character ZTool. We'll store this pose in a ZTool layer much like we stored detail passes in Chapter 4. This allows us to always return to the neutral posed version of the character.

1. Start by loading the `demosolider.ztl` file from the default ZTools folder. This is one of the ZTools that comes installed with ZBrush. This particular mesh is well suited to topology masking because of the edge layout. Notice in Figure 7.10 how the arms and legs are all com-posed of repeated rings moving up the length of the limb.

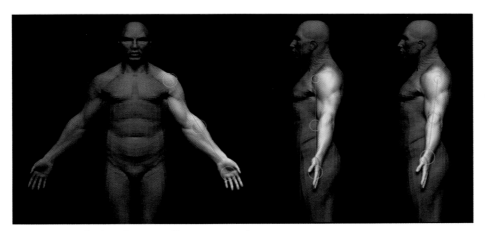

Figure 7.10: Evenly spaced topology rings are best suited for the topology-based masking tool.

2. Open the SubTool menu under the main Tool menu and delete all the subtools, leaving just the body. Divide up to the highest possible subdivi-sion level and create a new layer. Name this layer **pose**. Remember that layers can only be created at one subdivision level, so always make them at the highest possible poly-gon count. Changes made at lower subdivision levels will still store in the active layer.

3. Step down several subdivision levels. Transpose posing is more difficult when the mesh is dense. It is not necessary to have thousands of polygons when you are simply posing the model.

4. Ctrl-drag a mask from the arm to the chest. This is masking by topology. You may also enter Draw mode (the Q key) and paint the mask directly as you would normally. Once the arm is masked, invert the mask so that the body is masked and the arm unmasked by Ctrl-clicking the background.

5. With the arm unmasked, draw a transpose line from the shoulder to the wrist. Move to a side view and place the endpoint where the arm should pivot (Figure 7.11).

6. You can now rotate the arm using the endpoint on the action line.

Figure 7.11: Placing the action line to rotate the arm

7. Repeat this process for the legs, but this time turn on X Symmetry with the X hotkey. Notice how two action lines are created, and you can move the legs together (Figure 7.12).

8. Let's add a forearm twist. Mask down to the elbow and draw an action line from the elbow to the wrist. Click in the wrist endpoint, then Alt-drag in the center point. Since we clicked in the wrist endpoint, the rotation will be concentrated in the forearm and give us a nice twist (Figure 7.13).

9. We'll use bone posing for the elbow bend. Bone posing is a built-in skinning algorithm that stretches faces on one side of a pivot while compressing them on the other. This helps approximate the deformation of skin and muscle around a skeletal joint (Figure 7.14). Draw a transpose line from the shoulder to the elbow. Be sure there are no active masks. Alt-drag in the last endpoint, the one at the elbow. This will bend the arm, but it will have the effect of bulging the bicep and stretching the elbow skin. This kind of built-in skinning algorithm helps you quickly create natural poses.

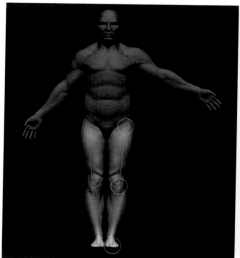

Figure 7.12: The legs rotated with Symmetry on

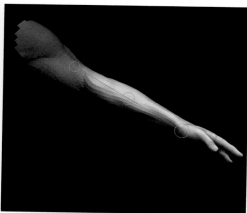

Figure 7.13: The forearm twist added

Figure 7.14: Masking and rotating with Transpose can create unnatural bends (a, b). Bone posing used to bend an elbow creates a more natural effect (c).

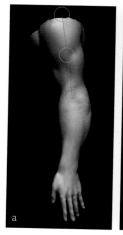

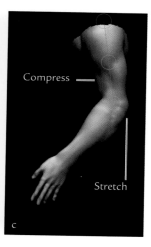

10. When you have finished posing the character, step back to the highest subdivision level where you created the pose layer. Under Tool → Layers, turn off the pose layer by clicking the eye icon. The figure will now return to its default pose. If you click the eye icon again, the figure will return to its pose.

Figure 7.15 shows a figure posed entirely with Transpose.

Adjusting the Intensity slider can have unexpected results since the blend is closer to a blend shape deformer than rigged animation. The figure will blend between its two positions by letting the vertices take the shortest path. The Intensity slider works exceptionally well when storing blend shapes for facial animation in layers (Figure 7.16). ZBrush can be used to sculpt facial animation targets; adjusting the intensity on the layer allows you to export different intensities of targets as well as blend target layers together.

Figure 7.15: A character posed with Transpose

Figure 7.16: Intensity to control facial targets

When posing your figures, keep in mind some artistic considerations. Most important is to maintain a sense of weight distribution over the center of balance. Make sure you know where the character is balanced; otherwise it will not appear to have weight and may look like it is simply floating in air. Also keep a sense of gesture while you pose. Gesture, as you recall, is the most important aspect of effective figure work.

Posable Symmetry

Although many parts of the body change during posing, there are others that it would be ideal to be able to sculpt with Symmetry turned on—such as the face or the bony masses of the body, like the pelvis and ribcage. ZBrush's *posable symmetry* feature lets you keep Symmetry on when posing a model asymmetrically. This symmetry is calculated based on the topology, so your model must have symmetrical topology for it to function. To use posable symmetry, click Transform → Activate Symmetry and click the Use Posable Symmetry button (Figure 7.17). Your cursor will turn green, alerting you to the fact you are in posable symmetry mode. This is a great tool for sculpting fingers, faces, or any other areas that maintain a level of structural symmetry when posed.

Figure 7.17: The posable symmetry feature is found in the main Transform menu.

Transpose Master

Transpose Master is a plug-in from Pixologic that allows you to pose meshes with several subtools. Transpose itself will only pose a single subtool at a time; Transpose Master will create a new ZTool with all the subtools combined into a low-resolution proxy model. Using masking to selectively isolate parts, you can pose the entire character, and then with the click of a button, you can transfer this information to the original ZTool.

You can download Transpose Master from http://www.zbrushcentral.com or http://www.pixologic.com. Install it as you would any other ZBrush plug-in, and use these steps to pose a complex model using Transpose Master:

1. Load the Demosolider.ztl file from the default ZBrush ZTools directory. This time don't delete the subtools. Make sure the ZTool is active in Edit mode on the canvas. If you have installed Transpose Master, you will now have a Transpose Master menu under the ZPlugin menu. This menu consists of two buttons: TPoseMesh and Tpose>SubT. TPoseMesh will create a new proxy ZTool of your character with all subtools as a single object. This proxy will be created at the lowest subdivision level, and it is this mesh we'll pose. The TPose>SubT button will transfer the pose from the TPoseMesh to the original multisubtool mesh.

2. Click the TPoseMesh button. The script will now generate a proxy posing mesh. The subtools and the main figure will all be one object, but each subtool will have its own polygroup to make hiding and masking easier (Figure 7.18).

Figure 7.18: The original ZTool is shown on the left; the proxy posing mesh is on the right. The proxy posing mesh created by Transpose Master is polygrouped for ease of masking and selection.

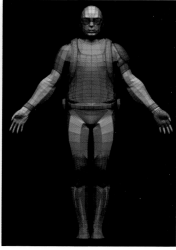

3. By using masking in conjunction with polygroups, you can effectively pose the proxy mesh with the attachments. In this example, you'll pose the legs. The leg consists of the leg itself, the kneepad, and the boot. Ctrl+Shift-click the body to hide all other polygroups, and then mask down to the right leg. Ctrl+Shift-click the background to view all polygroups again, and using the masking marquee, mask the attachments, leaving the boot and kneepad on the left leg unmasked. Remember, you can isolate polygrouped parts with Ctrl+Shift-click to make masking easier. Once the rest of the parts are masked, the leg and its accessories are ready to transpose (Figure 7.19).

4. Draw an action line down the leg and pose by moving the endpoint. Notice that the unmasked accessories follow as they too are linked to the action line since the proxy mesh is a single polygon object (Figure 7.20).

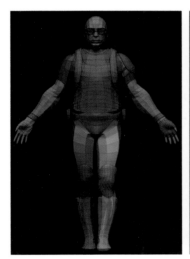

Figure 7.19: Masking other accessories

Figure 7.20: Posing leg

Figure 7.21: The final proxy pose

5. Repeat this process for the arm, masking all other parts of the body and posing the arm and its accessories. Note that the undershirt is masked to the shoulder so that the sleeve will deform with the arm as it raises.

6. The head follows the same process for posing. Mask all but the head and those accessories you want to pose, using a Transpose action line pose as desired. When posing fingers, you'll find it helpful to hide all the other accessories since they will not be moving; this saves the trouble of repeatedly masking them. Figure 7.21 shows the final proxy pose of the demo solider character.

7. You are ready to transfer the pose from the proxy mesh to the original ZTool. Under ZScript → TransposeMaster, click the TPose → SubT button to transfer.

Retopology

The ZBrush Topology tools allow you to build new geometry directly on top of an existing ZTool. You achieve this by making chains of ZSpheres that represent the polygon edges using the original ZTool as a template or base. Building new geometry in this way makes it possible to create costume elements that are custom fit to your characters. It is also possible to use the projection feature to shrink-wrap your new topology to a high-res Ztool, effectively capturing all your sculpted details while completely rebuilding the underlying topology. This is a huge advantage since it is not possible to change topology in a ZTool without losing all your sculpting detail. There are two reasons you may want to change the model's topology: You might want to adjust edge flow to remedy polygon stretching or loss of detail, or you may want to create an animation-ready mesh for use in an external animation and rendering package.

This tool allows you to start a character from just a polygon sphere and carry it all the way through to PolyPainting. By using projection in topology, you can project not just sculpted details but painted color as well. In the following section we'll rebuild the topology of the head from Chapter 2 into a mesh that can be animated. The process of rebuilding a model's geometry is called retopologizing, or more commonly remeshing. For a video of this tutorial please see the DVD.

Preparing for Remeshing

When you're trying to build an animation-ready mesh on your ZTools, it is often useful to have the topology planned out ahead of time using the PolyPaint tools. By PolyPainting the edge flow on the head first, you can work out topology issues ahead of time. Having the edge flow drawn on with PolyPainting allows you to trace the lines when you are using the Topology tools, which is simpler than trying to plan and execute a remesh on the fly.

1. With the head sculpt in Edit mode, turn on Colorize under the main Tool → Texture menu. Select the Standard brush and make sure only RGB is on.
2. Select white in the active color palette. Choose the main Color menu, and click the Fill Object button. This will fill the colorized head with white so you can draw the edge flow plan over it in black.
3. Switch the active color to black and turn on X Symmetry by pressing the X key. Begin by drawing on the eye and mouth loops, as Figure 7.22 shows.
4. Establish the main loops you want in the topology around the eyes, mouth, and overall face. Edge loops assist in animation, ensuring the mesh can be deformed naturally with minimal stretching. Usually you want major forms to be contained with edge loops (Figure 7.23).

When drawing complex areas like the ear, switch to red. Drawing these edges in red makes them easier to spot in tight areas.

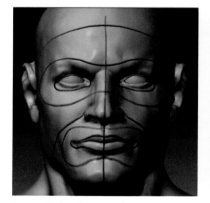

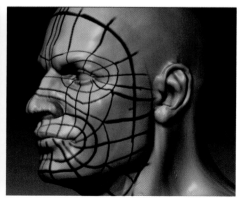

Figure 7.22: Starting loops

Figure 7.23: Topology sketch continues, taking care to loop the major forms and keep everything a quad

When planning the topology, try to keep all faces quad or triangle. ZBrush will not make a face with more than four sides; it will instead create a hole in the mesh.

5. Continuing with the Simple brush, sketch in the remainder of the topology (Figure 7.24). When you are done, save the ZTool. The PolyPaint color will save with the file here.

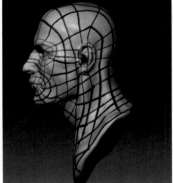

Figure 7.24: Topology sketched in

When planning the edge flow for an animation mesh, keep in mind how the character will move. The areas on a face that are the most mobile are the eyes and mouth, so naturally these areas are edge loops to allow a more natural movement from the face. There are many schools of thought on proper topology for a face and body, and most studios or setup artists have their own preference. The best way to learn about topology is to look at the meshes of others and experiment building your own. Gnomonology (`http://www.gnomonology.com`) has animation meshes available for purchase, and many online forums offer free samples. Sculpting facial animation targets and applying them in Maya will help illustrate what kinds of topology work best. Just like with sculpting, experience is key to getting a handle on this discipline.

Using the Topology Tools

Now that we have the topology planned out in the form of a PolyPainted template, we are ready to start using the ZBrush Topology tools. The Topology tools are based on ZSphere chains, so we'll start by creating a ZSphere as the root. Follow these steps to remesh a character head:

1. Drop any tools and clear the canvas. Make sure that the head ZTool with the PolyPaint topology is loaded in the Tool menu but not active on the canvas. From the main Tool menu select a ZSphere ■ . Draw a single sphere on the canvas and enter Edit mode.

2. This sphere will be the root of your topology chain. You'll link this sphere to the mesh you want to use as the base for your Retopology. With the ZSphere on the canvas in Edit mode, open the main Tool menu and dock it to the side screen by clicking the radial button ■ .

Figure 7.25: The Rigging menu is where you load the ZTool for retopology.

3. Scroll to the bottom of the Tool menu and you will find the Rigging menu (Figure 7.25). Click Rigging to expand this menu. Click the Select Mesh button to open the Tool palette; from there, select the head ZTool. This will link the head tool to the root ZSphere and specify it as the base for your topology tools (Figure 7.26).

4. Under the main Tool menu, click the Topology menu to unroll it (Figure 7.27). Click the Edit Topology button. The ZSphere will now disappear and the head will be visible. There is a small red circle in the center of the head (Figure 7.28); this is the root ZSphere (Figure 7.29).

Figure 7.26: The head ZTool is placed in the same world space as the root ZSphere

Figure 7.27: The Topology menu.

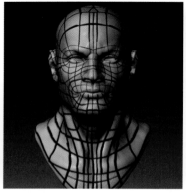

Figure 7.28: When edit topology is active, the root ZSphere disappears and the ZTool is ready to accept new topology.

Figure 7.29: The root ZSphere appears as a red circle; make sure you deselect it or your topology could have problems.

When drawing topology, make sure the root ZSphere is not selected. After each face is drawn, double-click on the background to make sure the root sphere is not selected. Failing to do this can create floating faces and other random geometry that connects to the center of the model.

5. Change to the Fast Shader and raise the Ambient modifier under Material to get rid of shadows to make it easier to see the edges as you draw them. Turn on X Symmetry and start to trace the topology drawn on the model. Draw a four-sided face and double-click off the model surface (Figure 7.30).

6. Continue drawing from one of the previously placed points. These points are actually ZSpheres. While drawing topology, click the A button to preview the mesh you are creating. Click A often so you can catch mistakes early (Figure 7.31). The A button is the same adaptive skin preview used in ZSphere modeling. You can adjust the resolution of the preview mesh under Tool → Adaptive Skin → Density (Figure 7.32). This will be an important setting when we are ready to project the detail from the original ZTool.

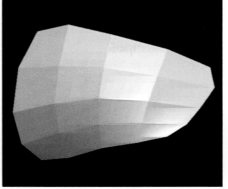

Figure 7.32: The Density slider in the Adaptive Skin menu allows you to increase the resolution of your preview mesh and ultimately the ZTool you generate.

Figure 7.30: Drawing quads over the template   Figure 7.31: A preview adaptive skin

7. Continue to trace the PolyPaint plan layout, and check the adaptive skin preview often. The best method I have found is to draw single quads, gradually building up the surface. If you try to connect too many faces at once, you will sometimes link to the wrong ZSphere, causing problems when generating a polymesh later (Figure 7.33). You can use Move mode (the W key) to move points on the surface to even them out.

Figure 7.33: A mis-linked ZSphere quad chain

Figure 7.34 shows the completed remesh. At this point we are ready to create an adaptive skin. If you want a quad mesh without the ZTool detail, all you need to do at this point is click Tool → Adaptive Skin → Make Adaptive Skin.

8. For this example, you want to retain the sculpted details of the original ZTool with the new topology as level 1. To do this, choose Tool → Projection. Turn on Projection under the Tool > Projection menu, and under Tool → Adaptive Skin, raise the Density slider to 6. This represents the number of subdivision levels the resulting ZTool will have. If there are not enough, then all the detail will not be apparent.

9. Click the Make Adaptive Skin button. The new ZTool will generate and load into the Tool menu. Select it and save. Figure 7.35 shows the topology with detail reprojected. Notice that the color transfers as well as the sculpted details.

Figure 7.34: A completed remesh. Note that when you project the detail from the polypainted ZTool to the remeshed head the color will transfer as well. This is a valuable feature when transferring details from a finished character to a new mesh.

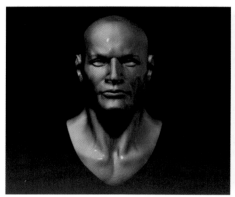

Figure 7.35: The reprojected head

If at any point you want to save your retopology and return to it at a later date, save it as you would any other subtool under Tool → Save As. When the tool is loaded later, draw it on the canvas and enter Edit mode. Select Tool → Topology and turn Edit Topology off, then back on. This will enable you to continue to draw and delete points on the surface.

Importing Topology

Topology does not have to be built in ZBrush. You can import a low-polygon mesh generated in another application and use ZBrush's project feature to re-create your ZTool with the new topology. The typical workflow is to export the highest resolution of the ZTool that your modeling application can open. Using the high-res as a template on a layer, build a low-resolution envelope mesh on top (Figure 7.36). This is an ordered mesh where each point sits just outside the surface of the high-res.

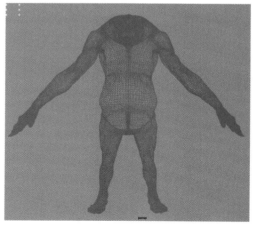
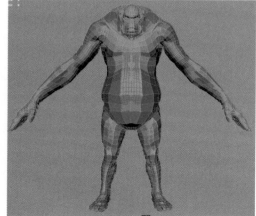

Figure 7.36: Building an envelope mesh in Maya

We'll look at an example where we just want to change one aspect of the low-res mesh. We'll export the original level 1 topology from ZBrush and reproject it in ZBrush. This technique will work for an entire rebuild of topolopgy as well.

1. From the Tool menu load the original ZTool as well as the low-resolution remesh. Figure 7.37 shows the original mesh that we want to change to remove triangles and redirect edge flow, and the reworked low-res cage built in Maya.

2. Draw a ZSphere and enter Edit mode. From the Rigging menu, select the original ZTool.

3. Under the Topology menu, click the Select Topo button ▓Select Topo▓ . This will open the Tool palette and allow you to select the imported low-res mesh and convert it to topology. Select the low-res cage and click Edit Topology under the Topology menu. This will load the imported mesh as topology and allow you to further edit and project the mesh to the original ZTool (Figure 7.38).

4. Using Alt-click, delete some edges by clicking the points. These can be redrawn as desired (Figure 7.39).

5. When you are ready to generate a new Ztool, follow the same procedure as before: set your adaptive skin density, and turn on Projection. Then click Make Adaptive Skin to generate a new ZTool.

Figure 7.37: Original topology and topology imported as an OBJ and loaded

Figure 7.38: Deleting unwanted faces   *Figure 7.39: Redraw topology*

Project All and the ZProject Brush

ZBrush offers other options for transferring sculpted detail from one mesh to another. Importing topology as shown earlier is one of the more difficult approaches. If you have a low-res mesh you want to project onto an existing ZTool and you don't need to further edit the topology, you'll find an option under the SubTool menu called Project All that makes this simple.

The ZProject brush also allows you to brush the projection effect across the surface with control over the intensity. Project All is a button in the SubTool menu that allows you to project the detail from one subtool onto another. Follow these steps to use Project All and the ZProject brush.

1. Load the original ZTool and the low-res mesh into ZBrush. Append the low-res as a subtool to the original high-res ZTool (Figure 7.40).

2. With the low-res mesh selected, subdivide as high as the original ZTool. For example, if the original sculpt was 1 million faces, you want to divide the low-res cage at least as high. Once this mesh is subdivided, click the Project All button under the SubTool menu (Figure 7.41). This will project the currently active subtool onto the other, inactive tools.

3. With two meshes in the same world space as we have here, it is an ideal way to transfer detail to other meshes without the complexity of topology tools. Click the Project All button and your mesh will capture the original ZTool detail. Figure 7.42 shows the new mesh. The original ZTool has been hidden for clarity.

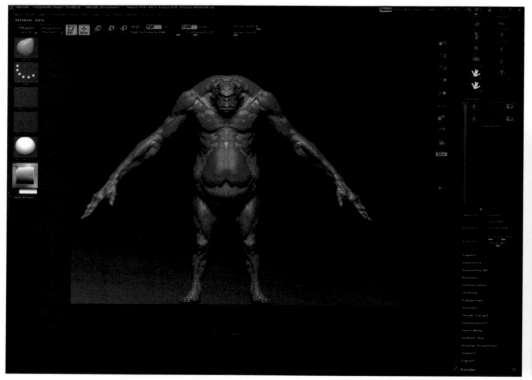

Figure 7.40: Original ZTool and remesh loaded as subtools

Figure 7.41: The Project All button is located in the SubTool menu.

4. In some cases, errors will occur. Errors are especially prone to happen when the low-res mesh does not match the high-res closely enough. These are simple to fix using the ZProject brush. From the Brush menu select the ZProject brush (Figure 7.43). Make sure ZAdd is on and both subtools are visible. Make the projected mesh with the error active. Turn on transparent mode with the Transp button on the side tray at the right.

5. Step down a subdivision level and stroke with the ZProject brush. This will have the effect of snapping the erroneous points to the surface. It is often helpful to smooth, then project and alternate between ZAdd and ZSub, depending on how deep into the mesh the points penetrate. Figure 7.44 shows the process of correcting this armpit defect. The ZProject brush works by projecting or pulling

Figure 7.42: Projected topology

faces directly down the Z-axis, so you will need to rotate around the figure as you work, snapping the vertices to the high-res with the brush.

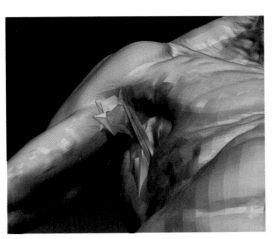
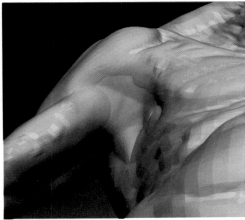

Figure 7.43: ZProject brush

Figure 7.44: Minor errors can be corrected with the Smooth and ZProject brush. Be sure Transparent is on.

Topology Tools Advanced Applications

The Topology tools are often applied to 3D scan data imported into ZBrush. This could be a scan of an actor or a clay design maquette. Figure 7.45 shows a character I roughed in as a clay maquette for the Secret Level/Sega game Golden Axe.

This clay maquette was photographed and scanned using a Cyberscanner 3D scan. The maquette photography was used as the basis of a Photoshop painting (Figure 7.46). The scan data was retopologized in ZBrush and used as a base to further sculpt into the final product shown in Figure 7.47.

Figure 7.45: The Shade clay maquette. (Image courtesy of Secret Level /Sega and Gentle Giant Studios.)

Figure 7.46: This Photoshop paint over design was created from the maquette photography.

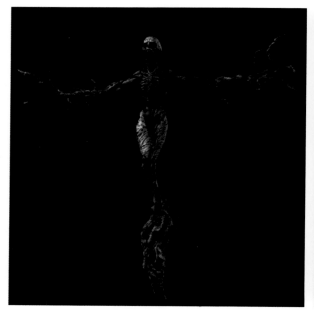

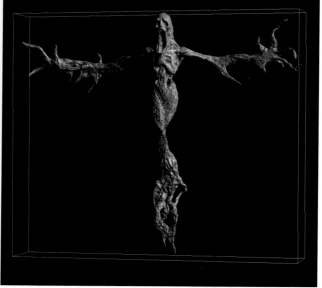

Figure 7.47: The final digital asset started in ZBrush from the scan of the clay maquette. The concept painting was projected as a color map and further refined. (Image courtesy of Secret Level/Sega, Gentle Giant Studios. Shade character by Scott Spencer and Jim McPherson.) The second image shows the initial scan data before retopology and sculpting in ZBrush.

Building Accessories with Topology Tools and Mesh Extraction

The Topology tools can be used to rebuild existing ZTools, but they are also useful for generating entirely new subtools based on your ZBrush sculpts. By turning off the Projection option, you can build new geometry that sits perfectly against another ZTool.

One example might be making a helmet or armor for a character by using the Topology tools to build it directly on the character. When you're building accessories with this technique, the resulting ZTool will have an ordered lower subdivision level and multiple divisions. In this section we'll build armor for a character. The ZTool used for this demo is available on the DVD as `warrior.ztl` (Figure 7.48).

1. Load the character ZTool into the Tool menu but don't draw it on the canvas yet. Select a ZSphere and draw it on the canvas. Enter Edit mode. Under Rigging, click the SelectMesh button and select the character ZTool (Figure 7.49). You are now ready to draw topolology, but instead of rebuilding the mesh, you want to create an accessory custom fit to the character's body. The process of drawing edges is the same, but we won't project detail from the high-res to this new topology.

2. Since this character was sculpted in a pose, you cannot use X Symmetry. You'll draw the outlines of the armor on both sides instead of relying on X Symmetry. If this character were in a bind pose, X Symmetry would be possible. While drawing, keep your topology all quad or triangles where necessary (Figure 7.50). Be sure to check your adaptive skin preview often by pressing the A key (Figure 7.51).

Figure 7.48: Using this ZTool from the DVD, we'll create accessories using Topology tools, mesh extraction, and ZSpheres.

Figure 7.49: The character ZTool loaded as a rigging mesh

Figure 7.50: Drawing topology for the chest plate

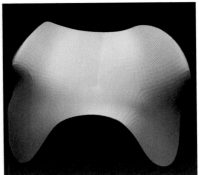

Figure 7.51: Check the resulting mesh often by pressing the A key.

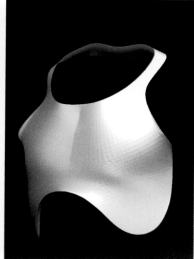

Figure 7.52: Continuing the armor around the back of the neck

Figure 7.53: The skin thickness slider

3. Once you've drawn the helmet mesh, switch from Draw mode to Move mode and start to move points on the surface to even out their distribution and make sure the armor looks as you want it. Continue a strip of polygons over the shoulders and the back of the neck (Figure 7.52).

4. Once the topology for the chest plate is complete you will notice the mesh generated has no thickness—it is a simple polygon plane. To correct this, turn on skin thickness under Tool → Topology. This will generate a mesh with an actual thickness to it instead of a flat plane (Figure 7.53). Raise this value to .2 and preview the mesh by pressing the A key. You will see the armor how has a thickness to it (Figure 7.54). By pressing Shift+F to enter Frame mode, you will see that ZBrush automatically polygroups the front, back, and thickness of the new part separately.

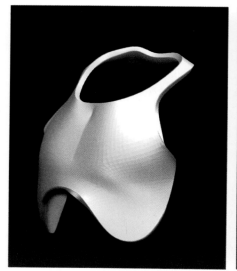
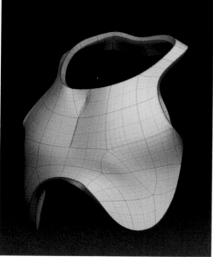

Figure 7.54: The chest plate with thickness. ZBrush polygroups each part by default.

5. Make some final tweaks to the shape of the armor. Using the Move tool, pull points away from the surface to change the shape of the armor (Figure 7.55).

6. When you are ready to generate a ZTool from this topology, raise the adaptive skin Density slider to 4 and click the Make Adaptive Skin button. This will create a new ZTool in the menu for the chest plate with four subdivision levels. Return to the original head character and append this part in as a subtool. It should fit perfectly and be ready for further sculpting (Figure 7.56).

When drawing topology for drapery, you can use the same methods as you would with polygon modeling to localize details and create drapery forms. In Figure 7.57, I have isolated the forms of two folds using localized detail in the mesh. By connecting two triangles with a line of edges, I can pull the line in and create the recess of a wrinkle.

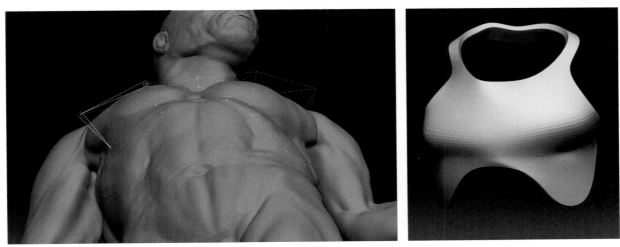

Figure 7.55: Moving points away from the surface to change the shape of the resulting adaptive skin

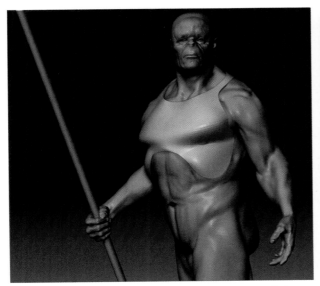

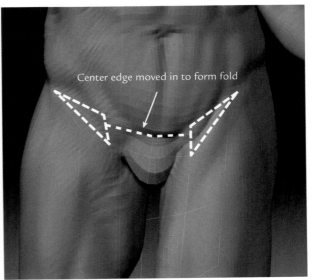

Figure 7.56: Character with chest plate part appended as a subtool

Figure 7.57: Creating topology for draped shapes

While drawing topology, you can switch to Move and increase the draw size of the brush to move multiple points together. In Figure 7.58, I am creating a sense of gravity by pulling down at the center of the folds.

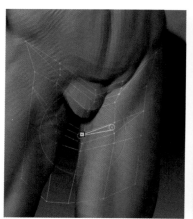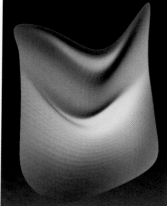

Figure 7.58: Adding gravity to the drapery

Figure 7.59: Masking the shape of the shirt on the body

Making a Shirt with Mesh Extraction

Using the Topology tools to make accessories results in an ordered, multiple-subdivision-level ZTool. It can be time consuming to lay out a mesh like this, especially when you want a high level of detail in the edges of the shape you need to create. To quickly generate new subtools from an existing high-res model, you can use mesh extraction.

Mesh extraction will create new geometry based on a masked area of your tool. The higher your subdivision level, the finer the mask will appear and the better the resulting extraction will be. Extracted meshes are typically very dense and consist of only one subdivision level, so you may decide to retopologize them later in the process to create a multi level ZTool as well as mesh that can be used outside ZBrush. Extracted meshes are fantastic for quickly generating complex shapes.

In this section, you'll make a ragged shirt for this character using mesh extraction.

1. Select the body subtool of the character mesh. Hide all other subtools by clicking the eyeball icon next to the currently active subtool.

2. Make sure you are at the highest possible subdivision level and paint a mask for the shape you want to create (Figure 7.59).

3. Under Tool → Subtool, you will see the Extract button (Figure 7.60). Set the thickness slider to 0.02. Leave E Smt and S Smt at the defaults; these control the resolution of the front and sides of the resulting mesh. Click the Extract button and a new subtool will be created based on the masked area (Figure 7.61). The surface can be smoothed and further sculpted.

Adding a Rope with ZSphere Subtools

By adding a ZSphere as a subtool, you can build new geometry that fits perfectly against another model. Let's use a ZSphere chain to make a rope to hold up the loincloth.

1. From the Tool → Subtool → Append menu, select a ZSphere to append it into the tool as a subtool. Scale the sphere and place it to coincide with the start of the rope (Figure 7.62).

2. Click and drag to draw new ZSpheres. Continue the ZSphere chain around the waist (Figure 7.63).

3. Preview the rope mesh with the A hotkey (Figure 7.64). To move spheres out so they lie closer to the surface, turn on Transparency with the Transp button to the right of the screen. This will allow you to see the spheres through the mesh. To scale all the spheres down, select Scale or press the E hotkey and click between the first and second sphere of the chain. Figure 7.65 shows the final ZSphere chain. To create a polymesh, click Tool → Adaptive Skin → Make Adaptive Skin.

4. This will create a new skin subtool of the rope in the Tool menu. Append the rope into the current ZTool. You can now hide or delete the ZSphere subtool. Figure 7.66 shows the final rope.

Figure 7.60: The mesh extraction settings under the Tool → SubTool menu

Figure 7.61: The mesh extracted shirt shown with other subtools hidden

Figure 7.62: Placing the first ZSphere for the rope

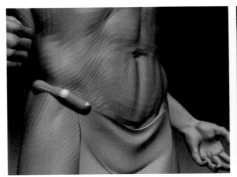
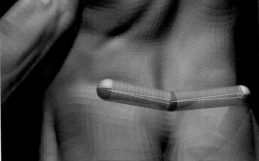
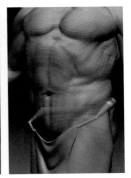

Figure 7.63: Drawing the ZSphere chain for the rope

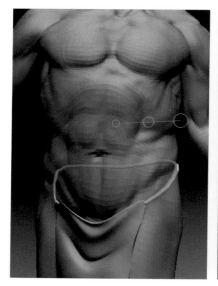

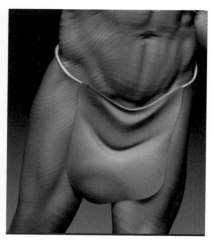

Figure 7.64: Preview the rope mesh.

Figure 7.65: The entire chain can be scaled by clicking and dragging between the first two spheres of the chain in Scale mode.

Figure 7.66: The final rope appended into the character as a subtool

That completes the building of armor and accessories for this character. Figure 7.67 shows the final character with some additional sculpting using the Pinch brush and some alphas or texture.

These techniques can be combined with the sculpting processes we have learned so far to quickly generate complex accessories for our characters. Topology and ZSphere-based costume elements are ready for use in other 3D applications. Mesh extraction accessories, on the other hand, would require being rebuilt with the Topology tools into an ordered mesh.

Figure 7.67: This character's armor was built in ZBrush using the topology tools.

Modeling Cloth: Wrinkles, Folds, and Drapery

Featured Artist: Ian Joyner

Modeling cloth can be a time-consuming and mind-bending experience. We all know when it looks wrong, but what makes it look *right*?

To start, make a plane and convert to Polymesh3d (so we can freely divide it). For this experiment, I'm using a sheet draped on a rod for reference; feel free to use images, but to really get the feel for cloth, it can be useful to have some form of "life model." I always like to try new techniques on a poly plane object. It is like a blank canvas; you can learn new brush features without worrying about topology or form, so you can see how the brush reacts to your settings. I will mention some settings I like, but I *strongly* encourage you to tweak these or try new ways.

Once we have a draped sheet and a poly plane, I divide it by one and on my reference I find a few of the major folds, up toward the top, where the eye of the fold is. When looking at how cloth drapes over an object, you will notice that central points radiate out, where the underlying form is causing tension, thus making dramatic folds. Since this is just a quick study, I grab the top two that overlap and mask them off on our poly plane.

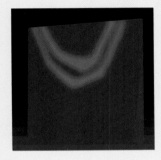

Once we have the mask, it may be a bit jagged, so I invert the selection by Ctrl-clicking off my object, and blur the mask by Ctrl-clicking *on* the object. Ctrl-clicking and Ctrl+Alt-clicking are great ways to sharpen or blur your selection, and by combining the two (blur a few times, sharpen a few times), you can soften your selection and get rid of the jaggedness.

Now that we have our first main folds masked, we need to make them drape. One of the first tricks I like to do for this is while the mask is still on, go to Snake Hook mode. You could use the Move (Tweak) brush as well, but I find Snake Hook is a little more organic for our needs. But to get it to have the right feel, and by that I mean tension in the middle, we need to do a few things. First we want to crank up our brush to maximum size, and turn the focal shift to about 40–60. For even more of that tension, we could add an alpha with a soft falloff, but this will work fine for now, as we are just blocking in our shapes.

Now we simply move the two shapes down and away from our plane (toward the camera). This is not the only way to achieve this effect. We could use the new gravity functions on a Standard brush, but I like pulling the points like clay. The next thing to do is invert our selection and smooth out the edges of the pull.

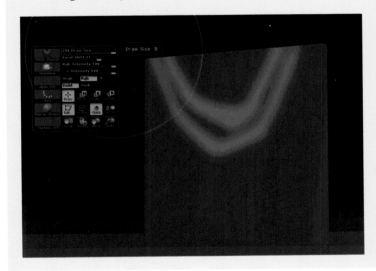

continues

Modeling Cloth: Wrinkles, Folds, and Drapery *(continued)*

That is the basic idea for our main bits of folding. Do this on a whole bunch of areas, and we'll go into a refinement stage and use a new tool, one of my favorites, the Pinch brush. The Pinch brush has a few uses in my workflow. The biggest one is using it for wrinkles and folds, and also tightening details. For this stage, we are going to use it to draw on some folds. First thing to do is change its settings. Turn the Brush mod up—something between 40 and 60 should do the trick; the next thing is to change the focal shift to something close to 70; and finally we'll add a nice soft alpha. This will make a nice pillowing effect as we draw.

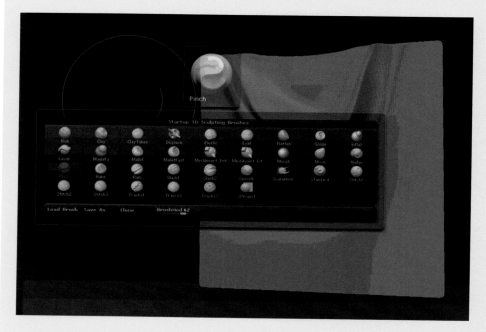

When making mechanical or cloth things, I like to toggle the LazyMouse mode on and off in the Stroke settings. This tool has a few options you may want to adjust as well, mostly in the stepping area, if you are getting a "dotted" look to your strokes.

Using a combination of the mask, with the Snake Hook brush to push and pull folds and cause nice overlapping, and the Pinch brush to not only sharpen some edges but add some indentations,

we begin to see the drapery we want. When using the Pinch brush, first use a low intensity, and draw along a few of our main fold lines. Holding down the Alt key, we'll cause the indentations and begin to add much more contrast to the shape of our subject.

It is fairly jagged at this point, so divide one or two times and we'll do a final cleanup. This is just a rough sketch to get used to the tools—feel free to take it further than I have at this stage. At this point, follow your reference, or just have fun with it. The only two brushes I used in this whole experiment were Snake Hook and Pinch, and though it could use some refinement, I think you can see the form taking shape.

OK, those are the tools; take it further to apply this to something with some form behind it. The final image shows a pair of pants made with the same process. You'll find it's easy, just using the Move, Pinch, and Inflate tools, to create some nice wrinkle effects. When I make wrinkles, Pinch with a high falloff is my weapon of choice, but I still use the other brushes to bring out certain details as well.

eight

ZBrush Movies and Photoshop Composites

In this chapter, *we'll be looking at methods of getting your work out of ZBrush. We begin by looking at the ZMovie function, which allows you to create videos directly in ZBrush. These can be captured work sessions or turntable animations of your work. In the second portion of this chapter, we'll look at exporting images from ZBrush and compositing them in Photoshop to create dynamic "renders" of our characters.*

ZMovie

ZBrush has the capability of recording your actions on screen as a movie. This recording can encompass just the document window or the entire screen, including menus. This is useful for training purposes or to showcase a technique. Recordings are stored in memory as a sequence of screenshots that may be saved as a ZBrush native format called a ZMV file or exported as a QuickTime video with any number of compression formats.

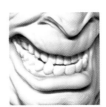

Recording the Screen

To record yourself in action, open the Movie menu from the top of the screen. Click the radial button ◉ to dock this menu to the side tray. Here you will find four recording options: Record, Turntable, Snapshot, and Time-Lapse. Record will record a sequence of frames based on the movie settings below. These can be recorded from the entire screen or just the document window. Turntable will record just the document window while rotating the ZTool around a user-specified axis. Snapshot will record a single screen capture. Time-Lapse records a frame

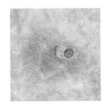

each time the mouse is released, thus creating a smaller file with faster playback. For this demo, we'll record the entire screen in real time.

1. On the Movie menu, click the Window button (Figure 8.1). This will record the entire ZBrush window. In the next line, click the Medium button. This will record frames that are half the size of your current document. If you want a larger video output, increase your document size and select Large for 100% of the document size.

Figure 8.1: These options allow you to specify what portion of the screen is recorded and the resolution of the video.

2. Click the Modifiers menu under Movie to unroll these options (Figure 8.2). The first slider is Frame Size, which specifies the scale factor for each frame. You set this by selecting Small, Medium, or Large in the previous step. By default, it is set to .5. If you set it to 1, the frames will capture at 100% of the document size. Leave this value at .5. Auto Zoom can remain at 0. Set Recording FPS to 20 and Playback FPS to 10. This slows down playback to a more natural speed. Leave the buttons Skip Menus, Antialiased Capture, and OnMouse on. If you want menus to be visible as you work (which may be desirable when you're demonstrating a technique), turn off Skip Menus—this will record menus as well as sculpting actions.

Figure 8.2: The Modifiers menu

3. Unroll the Overlay Image and Title Image menus by clicking on their names (Figure 8.3). The Overlay Image is a logo that will be overlaid on the movie. The default is the ZBrush logo, but you can load any image from the Texture palette by clicking the ZLogo icon. To turn this off, set the Opacity slider to 0.

4. The Title Image menu defines the image and text that appears at the start and end of the video. You can load an image from the Texture palette by clicking on the Z icon. Enter text by clicking the Text1, Text2, or Text3 buttons. Clicking these buttons opens a text entry box (Figure 8.4) that allows you to specify font size and enter text in the field. To disable this, set the FadeIn and FadeOut sliders to 0.

Figure 8.3: The Overlay Image and Title Image menus

Figure 8.4: The movie text entry field

5. When you're ready to record, click the Record button at the top of the screen. ZBrush will begin recording your actions. Perform a few strokes on the canvas; then when you are ready to end the recording, click the Pause button ▰▰▰▰▰. This will pause recording and allow you to either save the movie as a ZMV file, export it as a QuickTime movie, or resume recording from the last frame by clicking Record again.

Click SaveAs to save the video as a ZMV file. Depending on how long you recorded, this may be a large file. ZMV files are only viewable inside ZBrush. Load them by clicking the LoadMovie button under the Movie menu. The movie will play inside the ZBrush interface (Figure 8.5).

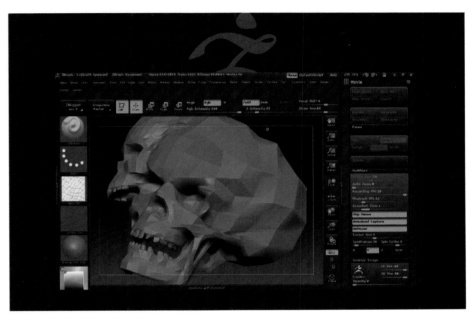

Figure 8.5: Movies play inside the ZBrush interface.

6. Once the ZMV is saved, you'll export a copy as a QuickTime file. To do so, click the Export button and specify a filename. Click SaveAs, and the QuickTime Compression Settings dialog box will appear (Figure 8.6). Select H.264 as the compressor, deselect Limit Data Rate To, and set the Quality slider to Best. Click OK, and your video will play as it exports. Do not press Esc or leave ZBrush during this process as it will cancel the export.

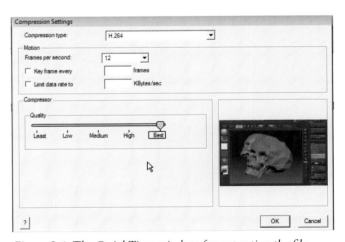

Figure 8.6: The QuickTime window for exporting the file

For the best-quality results, I recommend exporting MPEG-4 with no compression from ZBrush and applying H.264 compression in QuickTime Pro. Set the compression to None and the Frames Per Second to the recording FPS set in the Movie menu. This should be the default value in the menu. Set Depth to Millions of Colors + and the Quality slider to Best. These settings will create a very large file, but you will have better results by compressing to H.264 in QuickTime Pro.

Featured Artist: The Art of Steve Jubinville

This image caught my attention when it first appeared on ZBrush Central. The creature is imaginative in its design, and the render and composite are striking.

Turntable Animations

ZBrush comes with the capability of rendering high-quality rotations of your models. Turntables are a staple of most modeling reels and an ideal way to show off a sculpture in the round. While it is possible to do this in a third-party renderer, it is often faster to generate a rotation directly in ZBrush. You even have the option to add an overlay image of your name, logo or contact information. To create a rotation video, follow these steps:

1. Open the Movie menu from the top of the screen. Click the radial button to dock it on the side tray.

2. Under the Modifiers menu, set Recording FPS to 20 and Playback FPS to 20. At the bottom of the Modifiers menu is a SpinFrames slider. This determines the number of frames in a single rotation. To set this, determine how long you want a single rotation to be; in this example, use a 5-second rotation. If we are playing back at 20 frames per second, we need to multiply 20 by 5 to find the SpinFrames value. In this case, it is 100. Leave Spin Cycles set to 1 since a single rotation from ZBrush will loop when played back. There is no need to render more than one seamless rotation. You can set this value to –1 to reverse the direction of the rotation.

3. When you are ready to record, click the Turntable button at the top of the movie screen. The ZTool will rotate around its Y-axis. If the model seems to rotate in the wrong direction, change the Axis selection at the bottom of the Modifiers menu. The rotation video can be saved as a ZMV file or exported following the same steps as detailed in the previous section.

Keep in mind that only one movie can be stored in memory at a time. If a movie is stored or loaded when you record, the new frames will be appended to the end of the last movie. To clear memory, click the Delete button under Movie to start a fresh recording.

ZBrush to Photoshop

While ZBrush has a powerful renderer in its own right, when you combine it with Photoshop you can get high-quality images, especially when combining different materials as render passes and compositing them in Photoshop. The following technique is based on a workflow shown to me by Scott Patton of Stan Winston Studio.

This technique is based on exporting a single render from ZBrush with various material types and then compositing them together in Photoshop using blending modes to create a deep, rich image. For this demonstration, let's use the Fat Beast character from Chapter 3. I have PolyPainted the face, eyes, and teeth and applied a MatCap skin shader to the skin and the basic material to the eyes and teeth.

Figure 8.7: Turn off the Pro button and reconfigure the canvas to a portrait layout.

Setting Up the Canvas and Placing the Character

Because this is a portrait image, we'll reconfigure the canvas from landscape to portrait:

1. Open the Main document window and dock it to the side tray by clicking the radial button. Turn off the Pro button, which constrains proportions (Figure 8.7). Swap the Width and Height values so they read 720 wide by 960 high. Now click the Double button to double this document size to 1440 × 1920. ZBrush will notify you this is not an undoable operation. Click Yes.

2. If there were any active ZTools when you resized the canvas, they are now dropped to Pixols. Clear the canvas by pressing Ctrl+N. Let's now change the background from the default gradient to pure black. From the color picker, select black, and under Document, click the Back button. This assigns the currently selected color to the background. Turn Range and Center down to 0 (Figure 8.8).

Figure 8.8: Setting the document background to pure black

Figure 8.9: The perspective controls under the Draw menu

3. Switch your active color swatch back to white and draw the character ZTool on the canvas. Turn on perspective with the controls found under the Draw (Figure 8.9). Click the Persp button to turn on perspective (or press the P hotkey) and adjust the focal length until the character looks good. Lower focal length settings will give more perspective distortion, resulting in a fisheye effect. Note that these values are contingent on the scale of the particular model and will not be consistent between ZTools (Figure 8.10).

Creating Render Passes

In this section we'll create several versions of our character with different material settings. These various renders will be loaded into Photoshop and composited together:

1. Since it is important to maintain the exact same positioning between each render pass, now is a good time to store the character's position on the canvas. You could drop it to the canvas and create Pixols, but this would prevent you from making separate subtool passes unless you dropped each to a different layer. Storing the character's position is the easiest way to

Figure 8.10: The character placed on the canvas in perspective

Figure 8.11: Use
ZAppLink Views to
retain the character's
position on the
canvas.

ensure you can return to the same position if you accidentally move the character. Make sure ZAppLink is installed, and under the Document menu, open ZAppLink Properties (Figure 8.11). Click the Cust1 button to store the character position in the Custom slot. Save your views by clicking the Save Views button. For more information on using ZAppLink, see Chapter 5.

2. The first render pass we'll export is the standard skin shader. Click the AAHalf button on the right side of the screen  to antialias the document. Open the Main Document window and click Export. Save this render pass as SSS in PSD (Photoshop) format. Turn off Colorize under Tool → Texture, and save a version of the head with just the skin shading on. This will be used as a specular pass later in Photoshop. Save this file as `skinspec.psd`.

3. The next pass will involve flat color—just the color as painted on the surface with no shading information. From the Material palette, select Flat Color .

If you have filled an object with a material, the only way to change materials is to fill it with another. The default behavior of the ZTool displaying the currently selected material is overwritten. To revert back to this behavior, fill the object with the Flat Color material. From then on, whatever material is selected will be the one displaying on the character.

---

4. To fill the head with this material, select the Standard brush and turn on M at the top of the screen. Make sure RGB is off (Figure 8.12). Then open the main Color menu and click the FillObject button (Figure 8.13). Repeat this fill for each subtool and export the document as `flatcolor.psd` (Figure 8.14).

Figure 8.12: To fill an object with a material, make sure M is the only modifier on at the top of the screen.

Figure 8.13: Fill
with a material
by clicking the
FillObject
button.

Figure 8.14: The character file with the Flat Color material. All shading information is removed and only the painted color remains.

5. The next render is a shadow pass. This will assist us in faking an Ambient Occlusion style render. Turn off Colorize under Tool → Texture and fill the object with the Fast Shader. Open the Material modifiers and turn Ambient and Diffuse up to their maximum settings (Figure 8.15).

6. We also want to create a cavity map to allow us to isolate the sculpted details in Photoshop. To generate a cavity map, step down to the lowest subdivision level. Choose Tool → Texture and turn on Enable UV; then click the AUVTiles button to generate UV coordinates (Figure 8.16).

7. Step back up to the second-to-highest subdivision level. You want to capture just the fine details in the cavity map, so you won't generate it from the lowest level. Open ZMapper by clicking the ZMapper button on the upper left of the screen. Open the Normal & Cavity Map tab at the bottom of the screen and raise the Cavity Intensity slider to about halfway. You may also decide to raise Cavity Blur (Figure 8.17).

8. Click Create CavityMap. When the map completes, press Esc to exit ZMapper and export a document image of the cavity map on the character (Figure 8.18). This image will work best if you change your material to Flat Color. For a more in-depth look at ZMapper, see Chapter 10.

Figure 8.15: Raise Ambient and Diffuse to the maximum on the Fast Shader for the shadow pass.

9. The final passes are utility renders for depth and masking. The first pass will be a depth grab of the canvas. Recall from Chapter 4 that you can grab the depth information of the ZBrush canvas as an alpha. We'll do this now and use the resulting image as a mask in Photoshop for various effects, including simulating depth of field. Go to the main Alpha menu and click the GrabDoc button. This will grab a depth sample of the canvas with white values closest to the viewer and black farthest away.

A final version of this appears in Figure 8.19. This is sometimes called a ZDepth image. Be aware that the image will use the actual document resolution although you are displaying the document in antialiased half mode. When you use this image in Photoshop, you'll have to manually resize it by half.

Figure 8.16: Enable UVs, then assign AUV tiles.

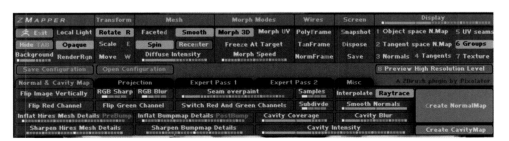

Figure 8.17: The cavity map settings

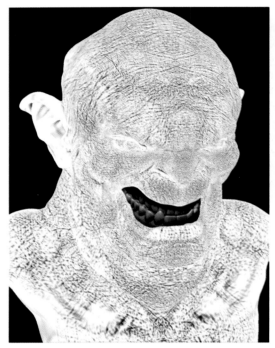

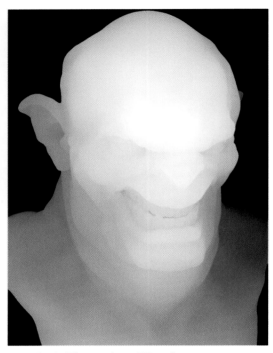

Figure 8.18: *The cavity map on the character will serve as a detail mask.*

Figure 8.19: *The resulting ZDepth image*

The remaining images are to be used for knockout masks if you decide to change the background, or if you decide to isolate the eyes or mouth subtools from the head. To create these masks, turn on MRGB at the top of the screen. This will fill the subtool with color as well as material. Select the color white and fill each subtool with white and Flat Color. Figure 8.20 illustrates this effect. Be aware that doing this will delete any PolyPainting you have applied to the surface!

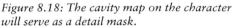

Here's an alternative approach: if you drop your character to the canvas by pressing the T key to leave Edit mode and then invoke ZApp-Link by pressing Ctrl+Shift+S, ZBrush will send a document to Photoshop that contains a shading layer, a Flat Color layer, and a mask.

Click the SysPalette button under the main Color menu and select green RGB value 0, 255, 0. Under the Document menu click the Back button to fill the background with chroma green.

Figure 8.20: *The character filled with white and Flat Color*

Figure 8.21: A chroma green mask created for the eyes, mouth, and background

Now select each subtool with the exception of the head (which will remain white). With green selected, you'll fill the eyes and mouth with the color green and the Flat Color material. This will make isolating these subtools much easier in Photoshop (Figure 8.21). Save this document as knockout.psd.

At this stage, you can save a ZBrush document of this character for future use, in case you decide to make changes at some point using the ZBrush 2.5D tools. These tools are covered in depth on the Chapter 1 bonus materials on the DVD. To save a ZBrush document, go to the main Document menu and click SaveAs. Save your document as a ZBR file. This is only a Pixol image and not a 3D model.

This concludes the process of creating our render passes. We are now ready to go to Photoshop and put everything together.

Photoshop Compositing

In the following sections, we'll take the render passes from ZBrush and composite them in separate layers. Using various blending modes, we'll create a rich and dynamic image much faster than we could by rendering in third-party software.

Loading the Skin Image and Adding Shadows

I have included the ZTool, skin material, and render passes on the DVD if you would like to follow along with this exercise. I encourage you to experiment with different settings and see what kind of results they yield.

1. To begin, load the sss.psd image into Photoshop. This is the image of the character with the Skin shader applied to the head and Basic material applied to the teeth and eyes. This will serve as our base (Figure 8.22).

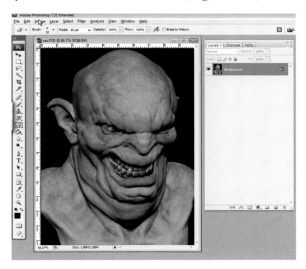

Figure 8.22: The sss.psd file loaded into Photoshop

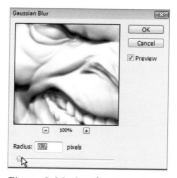

Figure 8.23: Set the Gaussian blur of this layer to 0.7 pixels.

2. Now load the `ambient.psd` file. This is the black-and-white image with only shadow information. Select the entire image and copy it.

3. Switch back to `sss.psd` and paste the image from ambient.psd into `SSS.psd`. `Ambient.psd` will now be a new layer in `sss.psd`; name this layer **ambient** and set the blending mode to Multiply. Lower the opacity to 44%. Apply a slight blur to this shadow layer by selecting Filter → Blur → Gaussian Blur. From the pop-up menu set the Radius to 0.7 (Figure 8.23). This layer will accentuate the shadows.

4. Open `flatcolor.psd`. Select the entire image, then copy and paste it into the `sss.psd` file. It will come in as a new layer (Figure 8.24). Set the layer blending mode for the flat color layer to Linear Burn and lower the Opacity setting to 60%.

5. The flat color layer has punched up the saturation and depth of the skin, but now we need something to mute this color a bit to make it feel more like translucent skin. Select the background layer (the original `sss.psd` file). Press Ctrl+J to copy the background as a new layer. Click and drag this layer to the top of the stack, and dial the Opacity setting down to 57%. The document now looks like Figure 8.25.

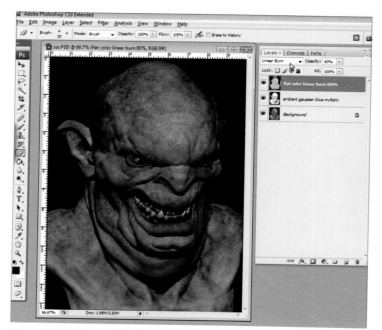

Figure 8.24: Setting the flat color layer to Linear Burn and dialing down Opacity to 60%

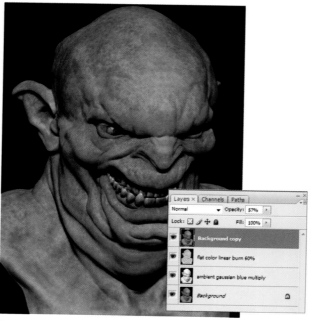

Figure 8.25: Copy the background as a new layer and set Opacity to 57%. This will help mute the colors introduced by the flat color layer.

Creating Selections with the Masking Layer

We'll now load the masking image we made earlier:

1. Load `knockouts.psd`. Copy and paste it into the working document. We'll use this document to create some saved selections. Using the Magic Wand tool ✦ , select the green swatch for the mouth (Figure 8.26).

2. With the marching ants active around this selection, choose Select → Save Selection and name this selection **Mouth**. Repeat this process, saving a selection for each eye and the background.

3. Now when you choose Select → Load Selection, you will find each of these saved selections ready for you (Figure 8.27). You can now delete the `knockout.psd` layer as we won't need it anymore.

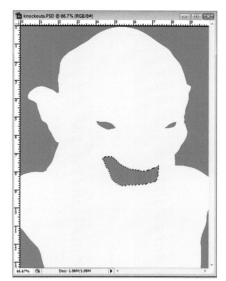

Figure 8.26: Selecting the mask for the mouth

Figure 8.27: Loading saved selections

Creating the Dead Eye and Specular Shine

We'll use the saved selection for the left eye to create a dead-eye effect:

1. Choose Select → Load Selection, select LeftEye from the dropdown menu, and click OK.

2. The left eye will now be surrounded by the Photoshop marching ants selection marquee. Make sure the background layer is selected and press Ctrl+J to copy the eye as a new layer. Name this new layer **eye** and move it to the top of the layer stack (Figure 8.28).

3. Select the eye layer and choose Filters → Artistic → Plastic Wrap. Adjust the sliders until you get a suitable dead-eye effect. Click OK when complete.

4. Now open the `skinspec.psd` file. This is the plain Skin shader with no Poly-Painting that we saved earlier. Copy and paste it into the document. Set the blending mode to Pin Light and the Opacity setting to 54%. It is also a good idea to add some noise to this layer by choosing Filter → Noise → Add Noise and setting Radius to 2.45 and Distribution to Uniform. This adds a shine to the surface of the skin (Figure 8.29).

Figure 8.28: Copy the left eye as a new layer and move it to the top of the stack.

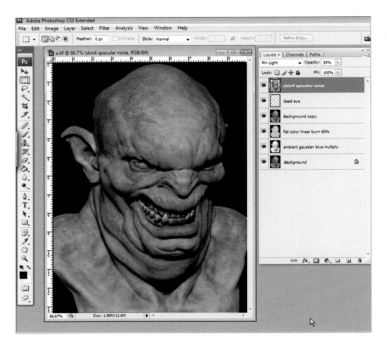

Figure 8.29: Adding a specular shine to the skin

Punching Up the Details

At this stage, we want to accentuate the skin details. To do this, we'll use the cavity map pass we rendered earlier.

Open the `cavity.psd` file and paste it into the active document. Set the blending mode to Multiply and Opacity to 37%. It is also a good idea to add a touch of Gaussian Blur to this layer. Keep the radius near 0.5. At this point the composite character looks like Figure 8.30.

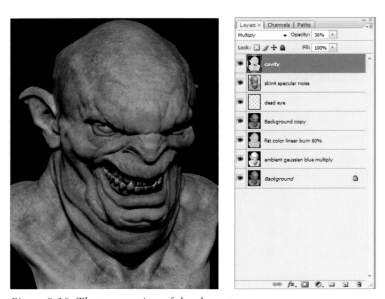

Figure 8.30: The progression of the character

Now all that remains is a bit of lighting, environment, and postprocessing. We'll create a new layer that consists of all the active layers collapsed into one. This will allow us to keep our previous layers and work on a new collapsed layer. Press Ctrl+Alt+Shift+E to create this new collapsed layer, and name it **collapsed** (Figure 8.31).

Finishing Touches

Let's add a cloud layer for the background as well as a depth-of-field effect to add to the realism of the image.

1. Load the background selection by choosing Select → Load Selection and selecting Background. Create a new layer and choose Filter → Render → Clouds. Turn the opacity down to 37%. Because the background selection was loaded, the figure will be matted out of the cloud background (Figure 8.32).
2. Create a new layer and name it **foreground clouds**. Clear any previous selections that may be active. Create a new cloud effect by clicking Filter → Render → Clouds.
3. Turn the opacity of this layer down to 25%. We'll want to selectively erase some of the clouds covering the face so they serve as more of a framing element than obscuring the figure.

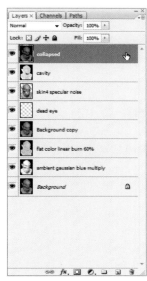

Figure 8.31: Collapsing the layers into a new layer

In Photoshop, it is always best to use masks to remove part of an image instead of erasing because the Eraser tool destroys pixels while a mask only hides then from view. You can always alter the mask if you decide you need more clouds in an area.

4. To create a mask, make sure the foreground clouds layer is selected and choose Layer → Layer Mask → Reveal All. This will create a layer mask attached to the foreground clouds layer.

5. The mask will appear as a white box next to the foreground clouds layer. In Photoshop, white appears to be transparent and black is opaque in a mask. Select the Paintbrush tool and the color black. Make sure the mask is selected by clicking it once in the Layer menu. A small rectangle appears around the layer mask when it is active. Start painting on the image, and you will notice it makes the cloud layer disappear while the mask begins to show your black strokes. To restore the cloud area, just switch to white. If you want to view just your mask, Alt-click the mask icon in the Layer menu and your mask will become visible (Figure 8.33); to restore the regular document view, Alt-click the layer mask icon again.

Figure 8.32: Creating a cloud background

6. Paint out the clouds around the face and eyes as this is the center of interest. You can let them remain around the shoulders and ears (Figure 8.34).

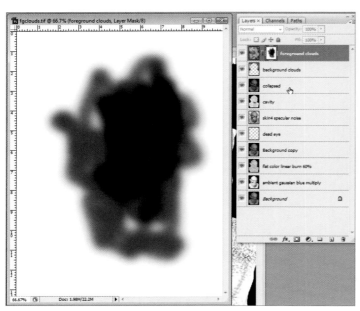

Figure 8.33: Alt-click the mask icon in the Layer menu to view your mask.

Figure 8.34: Foreground clouds

Depth of Field

Now we'll add a depth-of-field effect to the image using the depth.psd image that we exported from ZBrush:

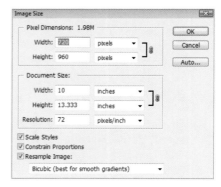

1. We need to resize the current file to the other document's resolution. Choose Image → Image Size and set the resolution to 720×960 (Figure 8.35). Remember that we were exporting documents at half size, but the Alpha menu exported this depth grab at full resolution.

2. Invert the depth grab by pressing Ctrl+I, then select all and copy the image to the clipboard. Select the collapsed layer and create a layer mask by clicking Layer → Layer Mask → Reveal All. Select the layer mask by Alt-clicking the layer mask icon and paste the depth grab into the layer mask (Figure 8.36).

Figure 8.35: Resize the depth grab to half its original resolution.

Figure 8.36: The depth grab inverted and pasted into the layer mask

3. We'll use this depth grab to calculate depth of field. Choose Filter → Blur → Lens Blur to open the setting box shown in Figure 8.37. Set the source to Layer Mask, Focal Distance to 15, and Noise to 4. Noise will help counteract the perfect look of a 3D render and add some imperfections to the scene.

4. Click OK and the filter will apply to the image. Now click the layer mask in the Layer menu and click the trashcan button 🗑 to discard the mask since you no longer need it. Once the mask is deleted, the depth-of-field effect will be visible in the document.

Lighting Effects

The final touch is a lighting effect to draw attention to the dead eye, the focal point of the image.

1. With the collapsed layer selected, choose Filter → Render → Lighting Effects (Figure 8.38).

2. Select Spot as the light type and place it with the Circular Light modifier. When you are satisfied with the light effect, click OK. Your final image should appear as Figure 8.39.

You can make further changes by handpainting details in Photoshop. Use the Dodge and Burn tools to accentuate shadows and highlights. You can even use the Liquefy tool to adjust the overall shape of the head. The possibilities are endless, and with this technique you can quickly create powerful renders with just ZBrush and Photoshop.

Figure 8.37: The lens blur filter settings

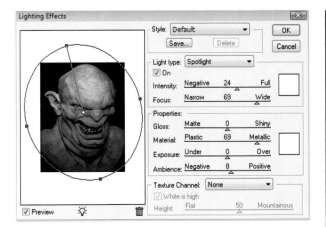

Figure 8.38: Using the Lighting Effects plug-in

Figure 8.39: The final Photoshop composite image

An Alternative Approach to Compositing: The Making of "Fume"

This section was contributed by featured artist Alex Alvarez.

Although Fume could have been created entirely in 3D, it would have taken much longer to produce. The workflow I'll describe keeps things quick and fun.

Between work and family, it can be hard to make the time to focus on a purely personal project, but I eventually decided to make some sort of humanoid portrait. I chose to box model a simple form in Maya (Figure 8.40). The problem with an older base mesh is that it will inevitably guide what I do, and for this project I wanted to be free.

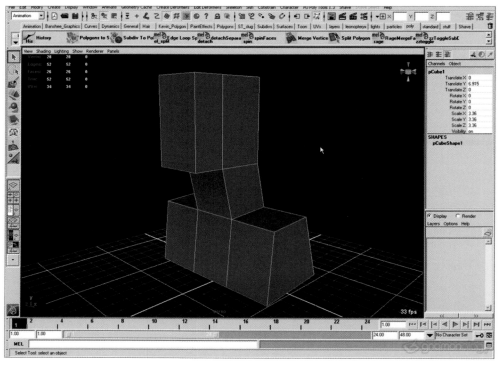

Figure 8.40: Simple Maya box model

I exported the simple box model to ZBrush, subdivided it a few times, and used the ClayTubes brush to block out the forms. I then retopologized the sculpt (Figure 8.41). Although I could have worked more on the sculpt before retopologizing, I wanted to be able to jump to Maya with a new generic humanoid base mesh. This would allow me to add thickness to the eyelids, a mouth interior, and position the necessary subtools (eyes, teeth, gums). In addition, the mesh would be generic enough at this point that I could use it as a start point for future characters in this style.

As should be the rule with any organized topology, I created the new base mesh in ZBrush following the anatomical forms defined in my initial rough sculpt. This can be tedious in Maya, but in ZBrush I actually enjoy it. Retopologizing a mesh is like solving a puzzle. It is, however, still time-consuming; this mesh probably took a couple hours. Once the topology was complete, I made the adaptive skin and exported it to Maya.

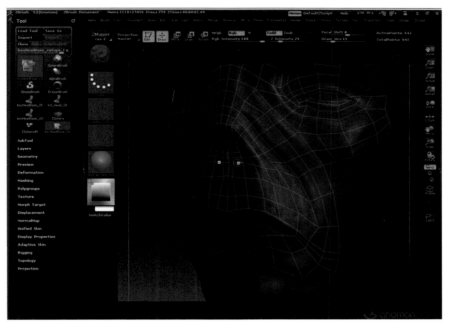

Figure 8.41: Retopologizing in ZBrush

In Maya I edited the base mesh, first by adding thickness to the eyelids and positioning the eyeballs. I then worked on the inside of the mouth, extruding edges inward to create a mouth cavity that extends down the throat a little. Even though the character in the final image has his mouth closed, at this point I didn't know where things were going and wanted to have that as an option. For the gums and teeth, I was tempted to create new ones (he would perhaps have a nonhuman number of teeth), but I got lazy and just grabbed something I already had and positioned/deformed the teeth to match the proportions of his mouth interior.

The final step before heading back to ZBrush was to lay out the UVs for the head using headus UVLayout (Figure 8.42). I chose to separate the head into three shells, for the head, neck, and mouth interior. The quality of the flattening in UVLayout is directly related to where you choose to cut things, and this worked pretty well. I then organized the UV shells in Maya for all of the objects (head, teeth, etc.), making sure that each mesh did not contain any overlapping UVs. I then exported each element as an OBJ.

Back in ZBrush, I imported the UV'd meshes and organized them into a single ZTool with six subtools: head, eyes, upper teeth, upper gums, lower teeth, lower gums (Figure 8.43). I next began the fun process

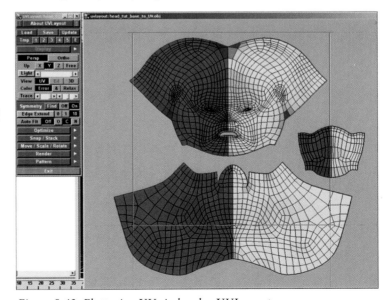

Figure 8.42: Flattening UVs in headus UVLayout

of sculpting and designing. The primary tools I used were ClayTubes, Rake, Standard, and Move. This was a freeform sculpting session where I just allowed myself to have fun and see where I ended up (Figure 8.44). I did jump to Maya a couple times with a high-res export of the head model just to test lighting and composition, in order to help determine where I should focus my time in ZBrush; there is little point in sculpting on the back of the head for a front-view portrait. For fun, however, I did end up spending some time on all sides of the sculpt, which also helped me "find" the character

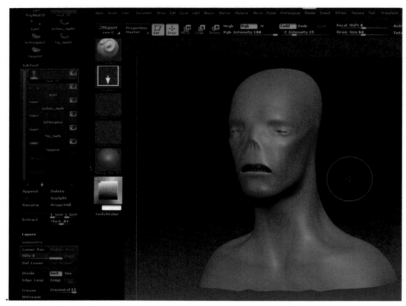

Figure 8.43: ZTool with subtools ready for sculpting

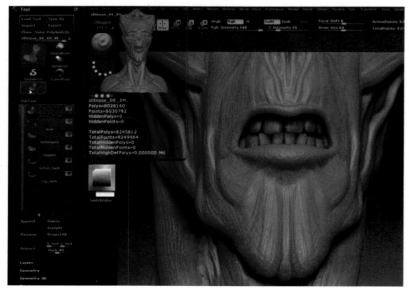

Figure 8.44: Detailed head sculpt complete at 8 million polys

Once I decided that the sculpt was pretty much done in ZBrush, I exported the subtools that had been modified back to Maya, with corresponding normal maps. For a still image, I do not bother with displacement maps, as I don't mind having a heavy mesh in Maya. The sDiv level that I send to Maya as an OBJ is determined by choosing the level that defines the silhouette of the character accurately. For Fume, the sDiv level ended up around 250,000 polys.

Back in Maya, I began by setting up Blinn shaders for each object and assigning the normal maps. I could share a single shader for both sets of teeth by moving the UV shells for the bottom teeth one unit to the right in U space (Figure 8.45). The top teeth UV shells were in 0–1 and the bottom were in 1–2. On the shader, the top teeth normal map was mapped to the bump channel, and the bottom teeth map was mapped to the Default Color attribute on the top teeth map. Then I unchecked Wrap U + V on the 2D placement nodes for both maps. Finally, I set Translate U on the bottom teeth 2D placement node to 1.

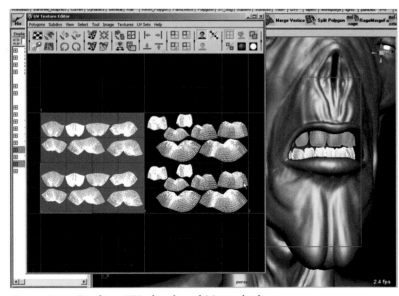

Figure 8.45: Stacking UVs for shared Maya shader

I had a basic Blinn shader on everything, and I began to do some composition and lighting experiments with mental ray. I started with some HDRi tests, trying out different HDR lightmaps (Figure 8.46). While these tend to look interesting, I never rely solely on HDR simply because I prefer to design my own lighting. For my final light rig, I created four directional lights and one spotlight. I liked the HDR tests that had strong rim lighting, so three of my directional lights were back lights. My spotlight was illuminating just the face from a high frontal ¾ with a small cone angle and high penumbra (edge softness). All of the lights featured raytraced shadows. During the lighting process, I also chose to create a quick skeleton and lattice rig for posing (Figure 8.47). I simply selected the objects, put them in a lattice, and skinned the lattice to a skeleton. This is a very quick solution for posing that takes only a few minutes.

Figure 8.46: Lighting study using HDRi

Figure 8.47: Lattice quick rig for posing

As I approached a light rig that I considered final, I decided to incorporate a cavity map into my Blinn shader for the head. I jumped back to ZBrush and, using the Cavity Mask option, filled the object with black. I then transferred the PolyPainted color to a texture that could be exported. In Maya, I assigned the cavity map to the Blinn shader color, and then adjusted the color balance to reduce the contrast in the image and make the effect subtler. So in the end, my final lighting/shader setup for Fume in Maya was rather simple: Blinn shaders, normal maps, one color map, and five lights.

Once I got to a point that I liked the lighting, composition, and pose of the character in Maya, I rendered a high-res and smoothly antialiased image with an alpha channel that I could bring into Photoshop.

In Photoshop, I experimented with a lot of different directions (Figure 8.48). I imported textures and tried out blending modes. I created gradient overlays to adjust lighting. I painted on layers with different colors and blending modes to colorize the render. Basically I was texturing the image in Photoshop instead of in 3D. This is a far quicker process and allows for many iterations to be produced in a short time. If you want to texture your character in 3D, you can use these 2D experiments as a guide.

After perhaps an hour of experiment, the idea for smoke and a cigarette emerged. I painted some smoke coming out of the top of his head and liked the idea. But to develop that idea, I need to either paint the smoke by hand, create it in 3D using dynamics, or use photos. I chose photography, the quickest option that would produce good results.

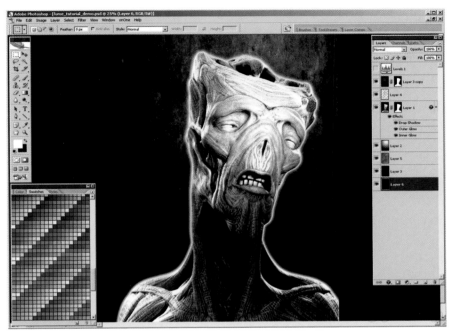

Figure 8.48: Color and texture study in Photoshop

Back in Photoshop, I experimented with some of the photos, compositing them using the Screen blending mode. Because they were shot with a black background, simply adjusting Levels gave me a perfect comp. I integrated seven smoke images by using the Liquify and Warp tools (Figure 8.49).

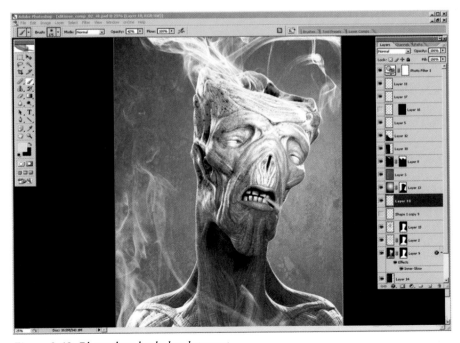

Figure 8.49: Photoshop look development

With the smoke mostly worked out, it was time to create the cigarette. In Maya I created a cube, extruded a face a few times to make it cylindrical, and positioned it in the mouth where I wanted it in relation to the teeth. I knew that I wanted my character to be biting the cigarette. I then flattened the UVs in Maya and sent the OBJ to ZBrush for detailing. I smoothed it a few times and then primarily used the Standard brush (drag rectangle) with various standard ZBrush alphas.

As I imported the cigarette from Maya, it was intersecting the teeth, so I added depressions to make it look like the teeth were clamping down on it (Figure 8.50). I also used the Move tool to give the cigarette a bit of sag. Once the image was complete in ZBrush, I sent an OBJ and normal map to Maya for final rendering. In Maya, I created a Blinn shader with no reflectivity and a broad and minimal specularity. I did not create any 3D textures for the cigarette; as with the head, I would do that later in 2D. I chose to render the cigarette separately from the head, so I created two new 4096×4096 renders. One render was of the head with the cast shadow of the cigarette but no cigarette (I achieved this by turning off Primary Visibility for the cigarette geometry). For the render of the cigarette, I set all of the shaders, except for the cigarette shader, to Black Hole matte opacity. This caused all objects to render as black in both the RGB and the alpha. I then took these two renders and integrated them into my multilayered Photoshop comp.

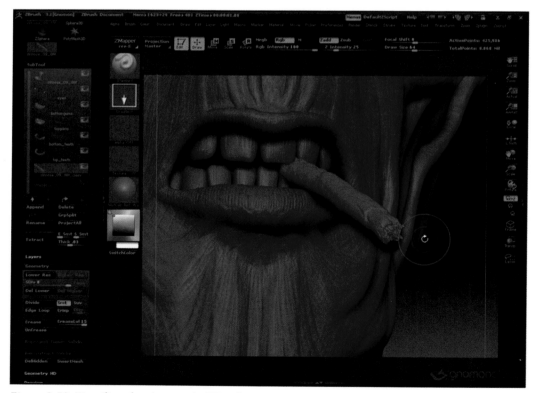

Figure 8.50: Detailing the cigarette in ZBrush

I created a couple overlay layers above the image to colorize the cigarette, adding a brown filter, the burned tip, and a brand label (Zufuhr brand smokes) using the Text tool and a little warping, and finally added more smoke coming off the cigarette.

With all of the elements in place, I felt my Photoshop composite needed some final color correction and contrast adjustments to make it appear stronger and less washed out (Figure 8.51). The main changes I made at this stage were creating a Levels adjustment layer for the entire composite and increasing the saturation of the background.

Figure 8.51: The final comp of Fume had 25 layers.

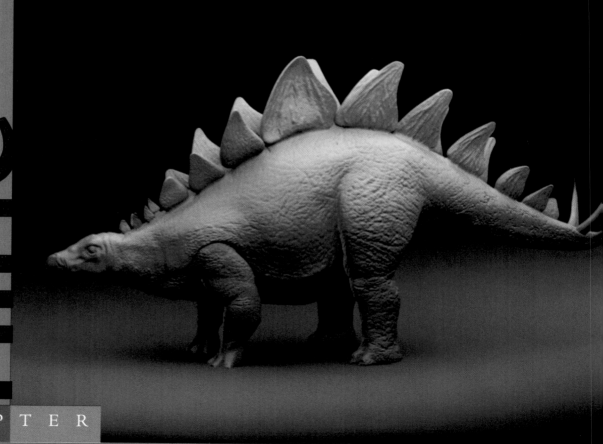

nine

Rendering ZBrush Displacements in Maya

After sculpting and painting *your character in ZBrush, you may want to transfer your work into another application such as Maya or 3ds Max for animation and rendering. Your final product may be for film, video games, or even print. By giving you a method of rendering your ZBrush work in other applications, Pixologic has opened the door for ZBrush to become a staple in professional entertainment industry pipelines.*

Although most applications cannot render millions of polygons, and at this time no application can animate a mesh with such a high polygon count, you can still use your ZBrush asset in a visual effects or game pipeline. By using difference mapping, you can re-create your high-polygon digital sculpture in a suitable renderer.

What's a Difference Map?

Before we proceed, it is important to understand the concept of difference maps and how they function. In this context, the term *difference mapping* refers to texture maps generated by calculating the difference between two surfaces, usually a high-resolution polygon mesh and a low-polygon counterpart placed together in world space so the program can find the corresponding point on the high-res mesh that matches the same point on the low-res mesh. ZBrush will calculate the differences between a high-res mesh and a low-res surface and produce a value appropriate for the kind of map being generated. The resulting map can be used in a third-party renderer to re-create the look of the highly detailed ZBrush model. ZBrush can create two kinds of difference maps: displacement maps and normal maps (Figure 9.1) In this chapter, we'll focus on displacement mapping.

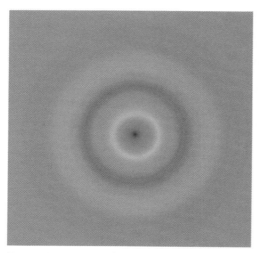
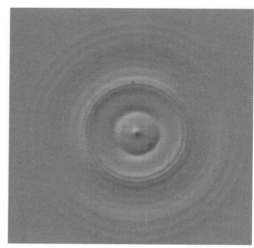

Figure 9.1: A normal map (left) and a displacement map (right)

Displacement Maps

Displacement maps create high-resolution details by physically displacing the geometry at render time. The model is sliced into millions of triangles by the renderer in a process called

tessellation. The surface is then pushed in or out based on a grayscale value in the displacement map. Some renderers perform subpixel displacement, which is a *re-tessellation* of the surface into micropolygons or microtriangles to support even finer details. The important thing to understand is that displacement mapping requires that the geometry be heavily tessellated at render time.

Because these maps create actual geometry, they are heavy on processing power and can involve long render times. They also offer superior results compared with any of the other mapping types since the rendered mesh is extremely dense and carries all the details of the surface and silhouette. This is in contrast to normal mapping, which only creates the *look* of a highly detailed surface without changing the underlying geometry or polygon count. See Figure 9.2 for an example of normal mapping versus displacement.

Figure 9.2: Two renders of the same character. On the normal mapping example at the top, notice how the internal forms appear highly detailed while the silhouettes still display polygon faceting. The image in the upper right shows the polygon mesh itself. The displaced render at the bottom contains all the fine details on the surface as well as a displaced profile with no faceting.

ZBrush also enables you to create bump maps by using the bump viewer material or by generating a displacement map for use as a bump map. In technical terms, bump maps and displacement maps are identical—it is the renderer that reads and displays them differently. Both are grayscale maps with white values representing height and dark areas representing depth. In application, however, bump maps differ from displacement maps in that they do not change the overall silhouette of the surface. Bump maps give the impression of surface detail where there is none by perturbing the surface normal of the mapped faces. Because bump maps don't require heavy subdivision at render time, they render much faster than displacement maps but do not provide high-quality results since the profiles are not altered. Bump maps can be extremely successful when combined with displacement maps. See the section "Applying Bump Maps in Maya" later in this chapter for more information.

Normal Maps

Normal maps are similar to bump maps in that they do not alter the profiles but they offer more realistic shading on the surface details. While bump maps perturb the surface normal, a normal map replaces it entirely with an RGB value. This vector value can represent the X Y Z coordinates of the surface normal of the high-res mesh and allows for highly realistic detailed surfaces but won't affect the low-poly faceting of the shape's edges. Normal maps are used heavily in video game applications.

Exporting Your Model from ZBrush

In this section, we'll discuss how to export your mesh from ZBrush as an OBJ file ready to import into Maya. We'll look at various options for UV mapping as well as methods of replacing the UVs on the ZTool before exporting geometry and displacement maps. For rendering, we'll be using the mental ray render plug-in. mental ray comes with Maya and offers extremely powerful rendering options for displacement mapping:

1. Begin by exporting the lowest subdivision level of your ZTool from ZBrush as an OBJ file. When exporting an OBJ from your ZTool, be sure you are at the lowest subdivision level or the level you want to generate your displacement map from.
2. You must verify some settings before exporting geometry from ZBrush. Under the Preferences menu, open the ImportExport submenu and turn off the iFlipY, iFlipZ, eFlipY, and eFlipZ buttons. These will flip the model's orientation when exporting from ZBrush. Turning off these options keeps the model's orientation and placement consistent.
3. To export the level 1 mesh, select Tool → Export and turn on Mrg and turn off Grp. The MRrg button will merge the UV points. If you left this button off, each UV would be an unmerged point and could cause problems later during rendering. Leave the Scale slider at 1. The slider will rescale the object on export, which can be problematic when you're trying to render accurate displacements.

UVs and Vertex Order

When generating displacement maps in ZBrush, it is important to be sure the UVs do not overlap at all. Overlapping UVs (which are easy to miss) will cause unexpected crashes when you are extracting your displacement map. You can avoid this problem entirely by using ZBrush AUV tiles or other automatic options for your mapping. This approach will remove any possibility of overlapping UVs, but as you will see, having UVs laid out in Maya instead will open up several workflow possibilities not otherwise available. AUV tiles are not human readable, which makes editing color maps in Photoshop nearly impossible.

Figure 9.3 is an example of overlapping UVs in the toes of a model. This problem must be corrected before the displacement map can be extracted. Otherwise, this small overlap could cause a crash. If at any point you crash while generating a displacement map, chances are extremely good that you have a minor overlapping UV.

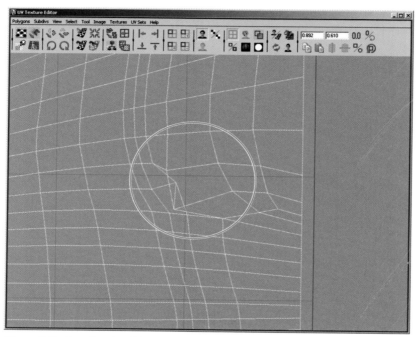

Figure 9.3: Overlapping UVs

Figure 9.4: UV Check button

Note that unless you are painting color maps with UV projection techniques, ZBrush is not concerned with UV coordinates This leaves you free to model and paint in ZBrush and then lay out UVs later or change your UV layout without losing all the work you applied to your model. ZBrush also offers a tool to check for overlapping UVs under the Tools palette: select Tools → Texture and click the UV Check button (Figure 9.4). Clicking this button will highlight in red on your model any overlapping UVs, so you know where to look for errors back in Maya. When performing an inspection like this in ZBrush, be sure to rotate your models to view all surfaces.

It is also possible at this phase to place your UVs outside the 0 to 1 texture space. This will allow you to use polygroups to organize your mesh in ZBrush for easy masking and hiding as well as enable you to maximize texture space and extract maps for each body part instead of a single map for the entire model.

Figure 9.5 shows an acceptable UV layout for a model. The UV shells are all in the dark gray square, which represents the 0 to 1 range. This will generate a single map in ZBrush that applies to the entire mesh. The multiregion layout in Figure 9.6 will allow you to interactively hide parts of the mesh using the UV Groups option (as discussed in Chapter 3). This layout will also enable you to generate multiple displacement maps for your mesh so that you can spread the body parts out across multiple maps, thus giving more texture space to the displacements. For example, the head, torso, legs, and tail may each have a displacement map at 4096×4096 resolution as opposed to spreading the detail for the entire body over one 4096 map.

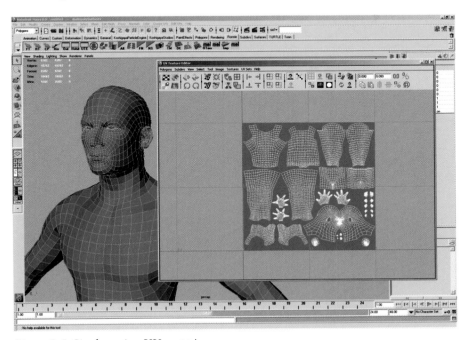

Figure 9.5: Single-region UV mapping

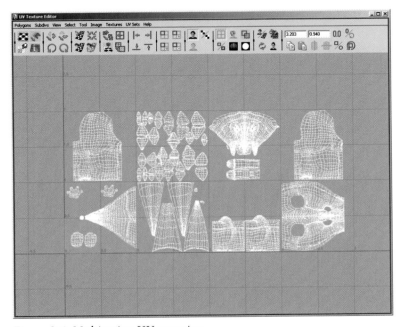

Figure 9.6: Multiregion UV mapping

If for any reason you need to change the UV coordinates of the model before generating maps, this is no problem. The process of transferring a model from ZBrush to Maya and back to ZBrush seamlessly is as follows.

You can move the OBJ file between applications as long as the vertex order remains unchanged. Vertex order is changed by cutting new faces, deleting faces, or reordering on import. Use the following process any time you transfer your model between Maya and ZBrush:

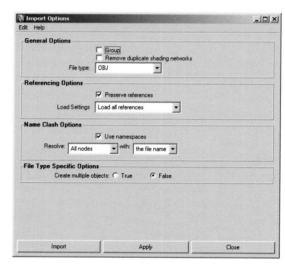

Figure 9.7: Import options in Maya. Note that Create Multiple Objects is set to False.

1. In ZBrush, select Tool → Geometry and set SDiv to 1. Export by choosing Tool → Export. Be sure the iFlip and eFlip options are off and Mrg is on.
2. Save the mesh as an OBJ file.
3. In Maya, choose File → Import ⌐ and select OBJ for the file type (Figure 9.7). Make sure that Create Multiple Objects is set to False. If True is selected, Maya will not preserve the point order and your model will not reimport into your ZBrush.
4. Make any positional or UV changes you want and export the OBJ again. This means you can move faces, repose characters, or change UVs, but you can't change topology.
5. In ZBrush at subdivision level 1, choose Tool → Import and select the new OBJ file. The UVs will automatically update to the ones in your new OBJ file. You can verify the updated UVs by using the Morph UV option in ZMapper, as described in Chapter 5.

If you import a model into ZBrush and the vertex order has changes, it may appear to import fine. The problem manifests when you try to step up subdivision levels. The mesh will explode, as shown in Figure 9.8.

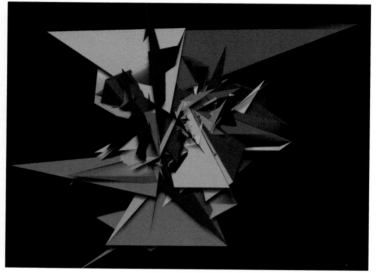

Figure 9.8: Changing the vertex order outside of ZBrush can cause meshes to explode.

Generating Displacement Maps

ZBrush is capable of creating 16-bit and 32-bit maps in single-channel grayscale or three-channel RGB. You also have the option to break displacements apart into multiple 8-bit maps if the renderer of your choice does not support 16-bit. In this section, we'll discuss how to create the two most useful kinds of displacement maps, 16-bit and 32-bit. Regardless of the type of map you generate, it is important to be aware of the shape of the base mesh from which you generate compared to the mesh on which you will render it.

ZBrush is a multiresolution editing tool, meaning that changes you make at the higher subdivision levels will telegraph back down to the lowest subdivision level, somewhat changing the shape of the original mesh. In some cases, you may want to access your original mesh shape again; for example, you may want to generate a displacement map against the shape built in Maya, as opposed to the somewhat different level 1 shape that will result after sculpting in ZBrush. To do this, follow these instructions:

- To ensure that you can return to the original Maya shape in ZBrush after sculpting, store a morph target before you begin sculpting: simply press Tool → Morph Target → StoreMT before you start modifying your model. After sculpting, you can use Tool → Morph Target → StoreMT to switch back to the original shape. An alternative way of doing this, which does not require storing a morph target, is simply to reload the Maya model after sculpting as the level 1 mesh of your sculpted model. This approach will work as long as vertex ordering has not changed (which should be the case as long as you have not added or removed points or edges). The morph target method is generally preferred because some programs can, on occasion, alter the order in which they write model vertices on export, even when the model has not changed at all.

- It is also important to note that using tools like the Transform → Nudge and Transform → Pinch Brush will make changes to the mesh that will not necessarily translate well into the maps created when setting a DPSubPix value as opposed to those generated using Adaptive mode (these settings will be discussed in detail later). This explains why in many cases when using these tools on your mesh, you'll find it beneficial to use the slightly shape-modified level 1 mesh for your base in Maya as opposed to the original morph target. In any case, always apply your displacement map to the geometry you generated it from in ZBrush. If you use the original morph target be sure to export this mesh to Maya for displacement.

- If you find that areas that have been pinched together are creating undesirable effects in the render, try using the Reproject Higher Subdiv button under Tool → Geometry. Reproject Higher Subdiv will allow you to relax the underlying edges while maintaining the sharp edges. This tool is discussed in depth in Chapter 2.

> If your base mesh is already rigged and cannot be changed in Maya, export the ZBrush level 1 mesh as an OBJ import into your Maya scene, and add it as a parallel blend shape to reshape the original mesh to the level 1 form exported from ZBrush.

Making 16-Bit Maps

If you plan on using a displacement map for detail transfer, as in Chapter 3, you must use a 16-bit map. For all other rendering, I recommend using 32-bit, which is described in the next

Figure 9.9: The Create DispMap button under Displacement

section. There are situations where a 16-bit map may be needed in a pipeline. These cases include pipelines that don't support 32 bit (these are rare these days) and the increased overhead of multiple 32-bit maps in a single render. For your own personal renders, I recommend using 32 bit as much as possible; the results will always be far superior to 16-bit displacement.

Generating a 16-bit map in ZBrush is simple. To do so, follow these steps:

1. Step down to your lowest subdivision level in ZBrush. Make sure the mesh has UVs that do not overlap.

2. Select Tool → Displacement and set MapRes to 2048 (this value can be higher or lower, but multiples of 2 are recommended, as in 1024, 2048, or 4096). Set your DPSubPix to 1 and click Create DispMap (Figure 9.9).

The difference between DPSubPix and Adaptive mode is in how the displacement map is generated. DPSubPix mode is a global subdivision value. With DPSubPix set to 2, for instance, when ZBrush generates the map it subdivides the entire mesh two more times in memory, thus allowing you to create a crisper, higher-quality map. Adaptive, on the other hand, is a feature-based displacement mode. This means that as the map generates, ZBrush will subdivide only those areas of high detail. For this reason, adaptive mode is sometimes faster than DpSubPix. Both map types have their benefits.

---

3. The map will generate and appear in the Alpha palette when it is complete (Figure 9.10).

Figure 9.10: Once the map completes generating, you can find it in the User Alphas section of the Alpha palette.

4. Before this map can be rendered in ZBrush, you will need to process it using the DExporter options in ZBrush. This map is a single-channel grayscale image while Maya requires a three-channel RGB image for displacement. You will also need to flip the map in the V direction since the texture space between ZBrush and Maya is different.

5. From the Alpha palette, select the newly created displacement map. Under the main Alpha menu, click the DE Options button (Figure 9.11). This will load the Displacement Exporter interface (Figure 9.12). This screen allows you to specify the file settings for the displacement map you want to export from ZBrush. For rendering in mental

ray for Maya, select R16 and set the Status switch to On. Each of the boxes at the top of the DE Exporter screen represents a selection of file type presets. R16 is the slot for RGB 16 bit. Enter the following settings:

Figure 9.11: The Displacement Exporter can be accessed via the Alpha menu from the buttons pictured here.

Setting	Value
Channels	1
Bits	16 bit
Vertical Flip	Yes
Scale	A.D. Factor
Ch1 Range	Full Range
Ch2 Range	Full Range
Ch3 Range	Full Range
Ch 1 Res	Full
Ch 2 Res	Full
Ch 3 Res	Full

6. Click the Export Current button to export a RGB displacement map based on the settings you just entered. A file browser dialog will appear. Browse to the location you want to save the displacement map and click Save.

You have now generated a 16-bit map from your ZTool and prepared it for rendering in Maya. You can move ahead to "Setting Up Single 32-Bit Displacement Renders in Maya" or read the next section for details on generating a 32-bit floating-point map.

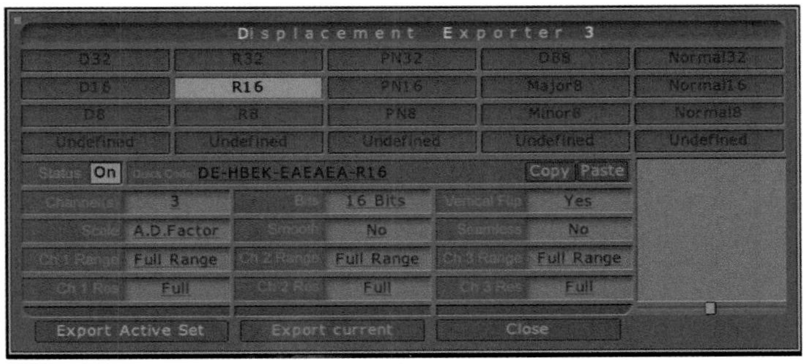

Figure 9.12: Displacement Exporter settings for a 16-bit map

Making 32-Bit Floating-Point Maps

You can only export 32-bit floating-point maps using the Alpha Displacement Exporter menu found under ZPlugin → Multi Displacement 3. They can be exported from ZBrush but not reimported, so if you plan on using a displacement map for detail transfer as in Chapter 3, you must use a 16-bit map. For all other rendering I recommend using 32 bit whenever possible.

The 32-bit floating-point maps generated in ZBrush should not be edited in an external editor—doing so may alter the map in undesired ways.

You can access this plug-in from two places in the ZBrush interface: under the Alpha menu (Figure 9.11) and in ZPlugin → Multi Displacement 3 (Figure 9.13). Although it is possible to export 32-bit maps from the Alpha menu, we won't use this button to do so in our example. This is because if you generate your map using the facilities in Tool → Displacement and then export it from the Alpha → DExporter menu, you will get a 32-bit map without real-world scale.

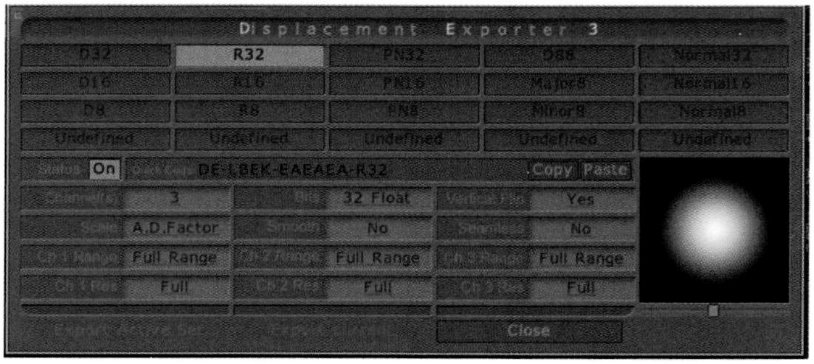

Figure 9.13: The Displacement Exporter can also be accessed via the ZPlugin menu under Multi Displacement 3.

If you generate a map from this menu for an object imported into ZBrush, the map will not appear to render correctly in the outside application. The reason is that ZBrush scales your model to one ZBrush unit multiplied by your Unify Scale setting in your Preferences palette. When you export the geometry, it will return to the original scale as the imported model. Maps generated using the Tool → Displacement menu will be baked with the internal ZBrush scale. On the other hand, to generate a map with the original object scale baked in, we need to use the Multi Displacement 3 plug-in found under the ZPlugin menu.

> The importance of having real-world scale baked into a 32-bit map is to simplify the rendering process. Sixteen-bit maps record only that one point is higher than another point; 32-bit maps record the relative height of the highest point and depth of the lowest point in relation to the overall scale of the object. This means that your settings in Maya will remain consistent for all 32-bit displacement maps you render. At the same time, 16-bit maps require some rescaling of values to achieve proper renders.

The original function of Multi Displacement 3 is to generate multiple maps based on UV region, but if your UVs are all in 0 to 1 space, it will create a single map as you'd expect.

This method is also useful if you have set up UV regions outside 0 to 1. Multi Displacement 3 will generate maps automatically based on each separate region. For example, a model with four UV shells in four separate regions will get four separate maps. Since the Alpha Gain is consistent between the maps, there will be no seams when these maps are applied to the mesh and rendered in Maya. This allows for higher-quality displacements since more texture space is allotted to each part instead of the whole character's displacement being contained in a single map.

> Suppose your base mesh is already rigged and cannot be changed in Maya but you want to displace the ZBrush level 1 mesh that has been slightly altered by sculpting. In this case, export the ZBrush level 1 mesh as an OBJ, import it into your Maya scene, and add it as a blend shape to reshape the original mesh to the level 1 form exported from ZBrush.

Multi Displacement 3 has several menu options:

GetMeshInfo Shows you how many UV regions are in the model. This corresponds to the number of maps that will be generated. A single UV region (UVs laid out in 0 to 1) will generate only one map and only one tile will be shown when you click this button.

Create All Starts the map generation process.

Create Missing Examines the export folder and generates maps that are missing.

Udim Specifies the number of regions in U (left to right); leave this set to 0.

Initial File Index Specifies the number assigned to the first map generated. Leave this set to 1001. The setting will increment as each file is generating, thus giving them unique names. The last digit will correspond to the UV region in which the shell lies, starting from left to right.

MaxMapSize Specifies your map resolution. Set this to 4096 or 2048. Lower numbers will be faster but result in lower quality.

MapSizeAdjust Set this to set to 0. This slider will automatically adjust the map resolution based on UV space. By setting it to 0 all maps are generated at the resolution you specified in MaxMapSize.

DpSubPix Governs the quality of the map generated. It specifies the number of times the mesh is "subdivided" as it generates. Set this to a value above 0: 1 subdivides once, 2 twice, and so on. Be aware that this will be memory intensive the higher it is set.

Overpaint Border Thickness You can leave this setting at 8. This setting creates an overpaint at the UV border and can help to avoid seam issues in some renderers.

Export Options Opens the Displacement Exporter dialog menu.

The Displacement Exporter allows you to export alphas from ZBrush as various kinds of displacement maps and even normal maps. Even though you can create normal maps with Multi Displacement 3, I recommend using ZMapper for the higher level of control it offers. Each option slot can be turned on independently and allows you to specify settings for each map type.

To create a 32-bit floating-point map with Multi Displacement 3, follow these steps:

1. Click the main ZPlugin menu and open Multi Displacement 33. Set MaxMapSize to 2048 and MapSizeAdjust to 0. Also, set DpSubPix to 1.
2. Choose Export Options to open the Displacement Exporter window. Select the D32 option and set the 32-bit export options listed here:

Channels 3
Bits 32 Float
Vertical Flip Yes
Scale A.D. Factor
Smooth No
Seamless No
Channel 1 2 and 3 Range are all set to Full
Channel 1 2 and 3 Res are all set to Full

These are the ideal settings for a 32-bit floating-point-map to render in mental ray for Maya. Your Multi Displacement 3 Export options should look like Figure 9.13. Click Close.

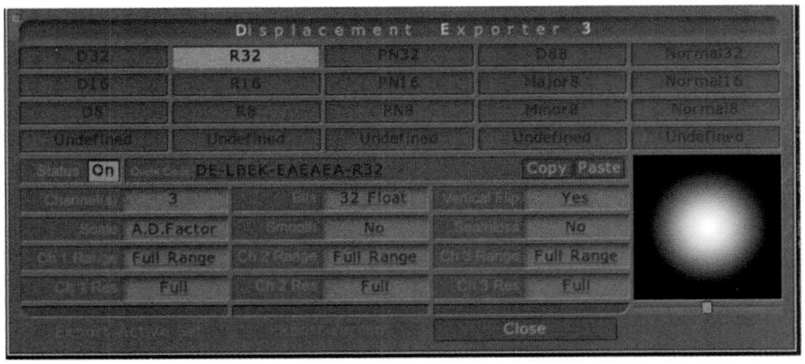

Figure 9.13: The Export options for a 32-bit floating-point-map

3. You may now generate your mesh based on SubD level1. If you decide to generate off a level higher than 1, be sure to export an OBJ file of that subdivision level to displace in Maya. Click the Create All button. A file browser will open. Select the folder in which you want to save the resulting displacement map. ZBrush will generate and then export the map based on the settings you specified.

Processing Displacement Maps for Use in mental ray

It is important to remember that with the Displacement Exporter there is no reason to open your map in an external image-editing software and resave it. In many cases this will destroy the floating-point data and render the map useless.

Maya provides a nice utility called `imf_info.exe` in the `Maya/bin` directory. You can use this program at the command line to read detailed information about your displacement map.

`imf_disp.exe` is another utility that will display maps and offer information on them. This utility features a graphic interface.

Your displacement maps will perform far better, faster, and with more stability in mental ray if you convert them to the mental ray native file format, `.map`. The difference is especially apparent with higher-resolution maps. Maya will process the render at a noticeable speed increase in many cases, and crashes are less common when working with larger map resolutions. Using the `.map` file format will also increase your speed at render time because `.map` files use mental ray's memory-caching features. Taking care with how mental ray handles memory will speed up renders and make for far better performance.

---

mental ray comes with another command-line utility called `imf_copy`, which will allow you to convert TIFF files to the `.map` format. To run this utility, open a command window in the folder where your TIFF files are located. Use the following command line to convert to `.map` format:

```
imf_copy -p originalfile.tif newfilename.map
```

To open the command window on a Windows machine, choose Start → Run and type **command**.

Perform this conversion on all displacement maps you plan to use. The maps will cache in memory and render faster and with fewer crashes. Included on the DVD is a Windows batch file to automate this conversion process. Simply drag and drop your TIFF files onto the `convertfile.bat` icon, and they will convert and save in the original location.

Setting Up Your Scene for Displacement

Whichever map type you decide to use, follow these steps to prepare your model to be displaced in Maya. Before we begin, you must load two plug-ins in Maya. The OBJ exporter is a plug-in that allows ZBrush to read the OBJ file format. The mental ray renderer is also a plug-in we'll load at this stage so it will be available when needed.

To load the mental ray plug-in, select Windows → Settings and Preferences → Plug-in Manager. This opens the Plug-in Manager window (Figure 9.14). The OBJ plug-in is called objExport.mll and the mental ray plug-in is called Mayatomr.mll. Click the Loaded check box next to each to load them now; you may also want to click Auto Load so they are available every time Maya starts.

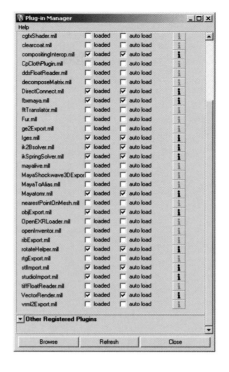

Figure 9.14: The Plug-in Manager window

> At the time of this writing, Autodesk has released Maya 2008. This new release has several changes to the core functionality of rendering, which can cause problems with displacement maps. This chapter addresses Maya 2008–specific settings in notes like this.

Setting Up Single 32-Bit Displacement Renders in Maya

In this section, we'll import the level 1 mesh to Maya, set up displacement shaders, and start rendering. We'll use a single displacement map to represent the entire character. In the next section, we'll look at using multiple displacement maps for a single character.

1. Import the level 1 OBJ into Maya. Make sure Make Multiple Objects is set to Off in the Import Options dialog box. With the mesh selected, press Ctrl+A to open the Attribute Editor. In the shape node, turn off Feature Displacement (Figure 9.15).

2. You now need to add a Subdivision Approximation to the mesh to tell mental ray how to subdivide at render time so there is enough geometry to support the displacement detail you need. To do this, use the mental ray Approximation Editor. Choose Window → Rendering Editors → mental ray → Approximation Editor (Figure 9.16). This control panel lets you specify how much you want to subdivide the mesh at render time. The higher the subdivision, the easier it is to pull fine details in your render.

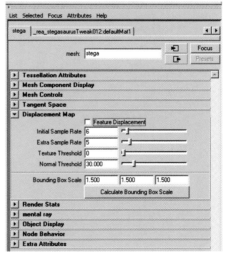

Figure 9.15: Deselect the Feature Displacement option.

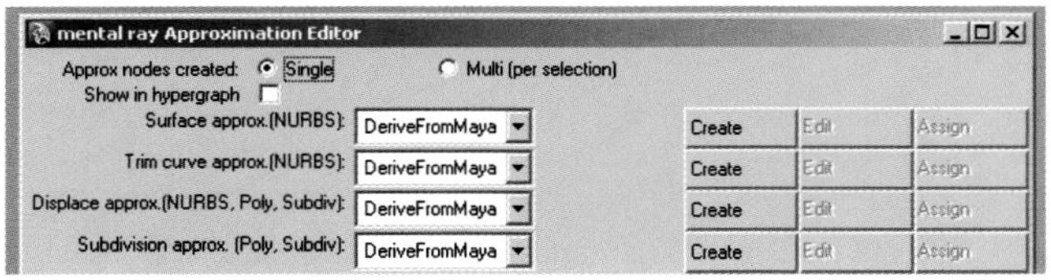

Figure 9.16: The mental ray Approximation Editor

3. Be sure that Show in Hypergraph is checked and click the Create button next to Subdivision Approx. The Edit button will now become active; click this to open the options in the Attribute Editor.

4. Change the Approx Method to Parametric. Set the N Subdivision setting to 4 and press Enter. This will be a good start, but this value can be increased as you render to find the best balance between surface-detail quality and render time. The N Subdivision setting controls the fineness of the surface tessellation at render time.

Maya 2008–Specific Setting: CCMesh

Maya 2008 has introduced a change to the approximation method, which converts surfaces to a CCMesh instead of the original method of using subdivision surfaces. The supposed advantage of CCMesh primitives is the ability to work with arbitrary edges while subdivision surfaces are limited to triangles and quads. Traditional quad layouts are still nevertheless recommended.

Although this new approach is intended to be faster, it can create seams in displaced renders with versions of Maya 2008 previous to SP1. Autodesk has released a Service Pack to address this issue which can be downloaded from the Autodesk site. If you find there are seams in your render, you may need to convert the CCMesh to a Subdivision Surface. To correct this, you will need to enter some Maya Embedded Language (MEL) in the command line at the bottom left of the screen:

```
addAttr -ln "miExportCCMesh" -at bool mentalraySubdivApprox1;
```

Be sure the approximation node matches the one in your scene. To set a MEL button for this command, enter the text into the Script Editor, then highlight the text and middle-mouse-button (MMB) drag it to the shelf. Maya will create a button that will execute this line of code when clicked. If you have only created a single subdivision approximation in your scene, it will work fine.

This change to the basic functionary of subdivision approximations was discovered and posted by ZBrushCentral member Marco Tronic. His research on this topic saved many people a lot of trouble with trying to use this new feature. This solution was discovered on ZBrush Central by the user Marco Tronic. Maya has also changed the default method of alpha detection which when left unchanged can cause bloated renders.

To change the luminance settings, go to Window → Settings and Preferences → Preferences, and select Rendering. Change the preferred renderer to mental ray and check the box marked Use Maya-style alpha detection on file textures.

On the DVD, you will find a script which automates the conversion of all SubdivisionApproximation nodes in a scene as well as changes in the Alpha as Luminance values. Follow the same process of MMB dragging the script to the shelf to create a button for future use.

Subdivision Approximations

In mental ray, the Subdivision Approximation tells the renderer how densely to divide the mesh at render time. The denser the mesh, the better your fine details will appear in the final render. I'll describe this as if your displacement map is pressing through the mesh you are rendering—the finer the mesh, the better the details will appear. Consider the mesh with a Parametric subdivision approximation set to 1 to be like burlap. There is not enough fineness to this surface to pick up all the detail of the displacement as it presses through. An Approximation setting of 3 is close to a cotton, which may show some detail but not the finest forms. A subdivision setting of 5 is like wet silk. This will show all your fine detail from the displacement map. These numbers may vary depending on the original low-res polygon count, but the analogy applies.

Another Approximation option is Spatial. It's more complex than Parametric but it has a few interesting options, including the length control and the View Dependent box.

Select Spatial as the Approx Method and set your Min to 3, Max to 6, and Length to 0.01. These are a good starting point, but all these settings may be adjusted to help achieve better renders. The Min and Max settings tell mental ray the minimum and maximum number of triangles to subdivide your model into at render time. The Length value tells mental ray the longest any triangle edge can be and helps ensure that large protrusions and areas of high displacement render well. The lower this number is, the smaller the triangles in the mesh. I find I get the best results with this set to 0.01 to 0.001, but it depends on how much RAM you have available.

mental ray will overrun RAM and crash if these settings are too high. The finer the mesh is subdivided, the more detail you can see from the displacement. High settings are not always necessary, and you will need to experiment with these values to find the right combination for each render. In cases where you have a displacement map that contains more form and fewer fine details, these settings can be lower. In most cases, I find Parametric is just fine for my rendering needs.

Creating a Displacement Shader

Now we'll create a shader for using a 32-bit floating-point map in Maya. If your initial OBJ file has all its UVs in the 0 to 1 range, or if it was mapped with AUV tiles inside ZBrush, you only have one displacement map from ZBrush, and you will only need to create one shader and apply it to your mesh. For rendering multiple maps, see the following section, "Setting Up Multimap 32-Bit Displacement Renders in Maya."

1. Open the Hypershade by choosing Window → Rendering Editors → Hypershade.
2. Create a Blinn material by dragging it to the workspace from the left window. I use a Blinn shader because it has a specular channel and this slight highlight helps spot finer details on the displaced surface.
3. MMB-drag a displacement node over the material. Select Displacement Map from the Connection Editor window that appears (Figure 9.17). Double-click the displacement node to open the attributes. You need to tell the shader it will use a file for displacement. Click the checker box to the right of the Displacement attribute. This will bring up the Create Render Node window. From this window, select File from to create a file node and connect it to the Displacement node.

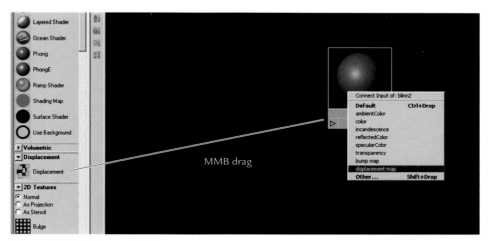

Figure 9.17: Making a shader

This creates a file node in which you can place your displacement map. You can graph your shader by selecting Blinn. Then in the Graph menu, select Input and Output Connections.

Your shader graph will now look like the one shown in Figure 9.18.

4. In the file node, you'll add the displacement map. The File Node options should open automatically in the Attribute Editor when you click the File button; if not, double-click

the file node in the Hypershade. The File Node options will be visible now in the Attribute Editor. Click the folder next to the image name to browse to the .map displacement. You may also want to turn off filtering at the top of the screen for the file node. It defaults to Gaussian, and in some rare instances this may cause artifacts. When using ZBrush maps for displacement or bump, it is a good idea to turn off this filtering if you get unexpected results from your rendered surface.

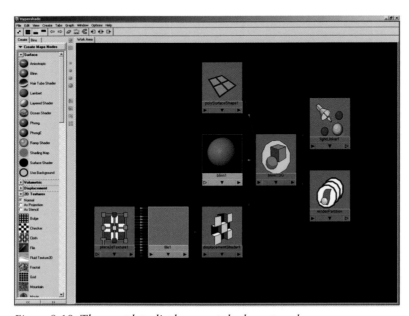

Figure 9.18: The complete displacement shader network

5. In the Attribute Editor with the file node open, click on the Color Balance heading and set Alpha Gain to 2.2 and Alpha Offset to –1.1. These settings account for the fact that ZBrush creates a map where 50% gray is no displacement but Maya sees black as no displacement. We need to shift that value to allow the mesh to be pushed in and pulled out by the map. Because we are using 32-bit floating-point maps, the Alpha Gain and Alpha Offset will be consistent for all maps created by Multi Displacement 3 in ZBrush.

Maya 2008–Specific Setting: mental ray Alpha Detection

If you are using Maya 2008, there is a change to the way that mental ray reads alphas and luminance in file textures. Choose Window → Settings and Preferences → Preferences → Rendering; from the dropdown box select mental ray, and check the Use Maya Style Alpha Detection option.

Using Expressions to Rescale

Using expressions in the Color Gain boxes can assist when you need to rescale the object. Because real-world scale is baked into the displacement map, if you change the object scale in Maya the settings of 2.2 and –1.1 will no longer be accurate. You can correct for this by driving Alpha Gain and Alpha Offset with expressions.

For Alpha Gain, type in the following expression, replacing *objectname* with the name of the mesh in Maya: **= 2.2 * *objectname*.scaleX**.

Type this for Alpha Offset: **= - 2.2 * *objectname*.scaleX /2**.

Be sure to begin both lines with the equal (=) sign. This ensures that the Alpha Gain value scales with the object scale and that the Alpha Offset value follows accordingly.

6. I find it beneficial to set up a single spotlight or direction light raking across the surface of the model to help spot details that tend to be lost in flat lighting. If you have a comparison image, try to approximate the same lighting setup in Maya as you had with the single light in ZBrush. It is also helpful to lighten the color of your shader to be closer to the surface color of the model in your comparison image.

Setting Up the Render Settings

Next, we need to change a few settings in the Maya Render Settings window. Select Window → Rendering Editors → Render Settings to open your Render Settings window. If it is not already set, choose mental ray from the Renderer dropdown box.

On the mental ray tab is a rollout option called Translation. Open this rollout and set Export Verbosity to Progress Messages. This will tell mental ray to report useful information to the output window when it renders. This includes the final Triangle count, which when divided by two is the face count of your subdivided model at render time. Compare this to the final face count in ZBrush to determine how close to the ZBrush subdivision you are getting with your Approximation settings (Figure 9.19). This can assist in setting your N Subdivision value accurately. Now open the render view and initiate a render. You can keep the image in render view for comparison (Figure 9.20). Figure 9.21 shows how raising the Approximation settings will increase the quality of the fine details on the surface.

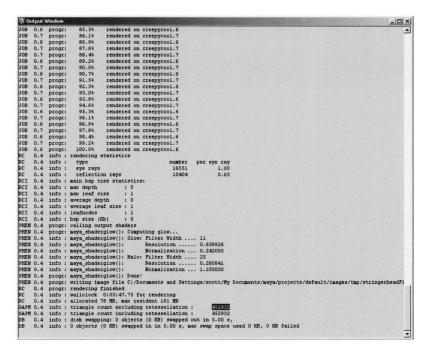

Figure 9.19: The output window: this mesh was divided to 452,932 triangles or 226,466 faces at render time.

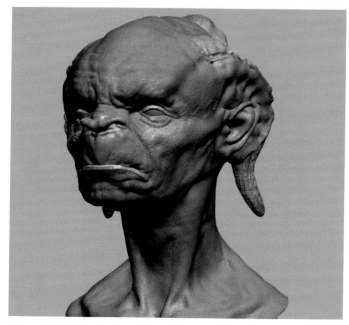

Figure 9.20: The final render with a single displacement map

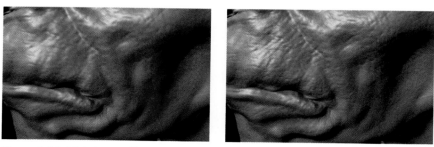

Figure 9.21: This image illustrates how a Subdivision Approximation setting that is too low will reduce the visible details.

Setting Up Multimap 32-Bit Displacement Renders in Maya

In this section we'll look at rendering a character using multiple displacement maps. Multiple maps are desirable when you need higher resolution in the finished render so you can spread the entire character's detail across multiple maps. With this technique, you can have 4096×4096 pixels of displacement detail for the head, arms, and body as opposed to spreading the texture space across the entire model.

To generate multiple maps with Multi Displacement 3, it is necessary to set up multiple UV regions in Maya. This simply means your UVs lie outside the standard 0 to 1 range, which is displayed in Maya by the upper-right quadrant in the UV Texture Editor (Figure 9.22). When your mesh has UVs that lie outside the 0 to 1 region, clicking the Create All button in

Multi Displacement 3 will start generating and exporting maps for each of these regions. Follow these steps to set up a ZTool with multiple UV regions:

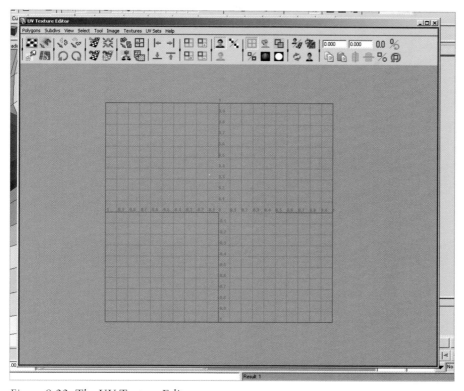

Figure 9.22: The UV Texture Editor

Figure 9.23: UV Texture Editor Grid Options

1. To display beyond just 0 to 1, select View → Grid ⌐ and raise the Length and Width value to 5. This value may be higher or lower as needed. You may also want to set Grid Lines Every *n* Units to 1 to visually clarify where each region begins and ends (Figure 9.23).

2. To shift UVs from 0 to 1, select a shell and in the Maya command-line editor or the Script Editor, enter the following MEL command (note the uppercase letters):

   ```
   polyEditUV -u 1 -v 0
   ```

   This moves the shell one unit to the right and 0 up or down. Repeat for each shell you want as a separate map or UV Group, placing each in its own quadrant. Increment the U number for the number of quadrants to move in each direction.

3. Once your UVs are placed, export the mesh as an OBG file. This mesh can be imported into ZBrush for sculpting. If you have already sculpted your character, this model can be imported into an existing ZTool, swapping the UVs.

   In this example, we created a separate map per body part to increase quality in the final product by allowing more texture space per body part and the use of multiple high-resolution maps. To assign the maps, we need to create a displacement shader for each map we'll apply to the model.

The model in this example has eight UV regions, so eight maps are generated. The resulting 32-bit TIFF files will be ready to apply to the mesh in Maya and should render exactly as seen in ZBrush. To make sure each map is applied to the correct region of the creature, open the UV Texture Editor.

4. Marquee-select one quadrant of UVs and choose Select → Convert to Faces (or press Ctrl+F9 on your keyboard). You can also select a few UVs from one shell and then choose Select → Select Shell to enlarge the selection to the whole UV shell. Now in the Hypershade, apply the shader with the corresponding map to the set of faces. You can quickly assign shaders to selected faces by right-clicking your shader in the Hypershade and selecting Assign to Selection.

5. Once the faces that correspond to the UVs in each region have their own displacement shader applied, you are ready to render. Because the Alpha Gain and Alpha Offset settings are the same for all maps, there will be no discernable seams between your maps (Figure 9.24). Be sure that the Alpha Gain and Alpha Offset values are correct for each file node on each shader.

Figure 9.24: The final render with multiple displacement maps

You can determine which map is for which quadrant by looking at the filename index number for each map: 1001 is for quadrant one, 1002 for quadrant two, and so on. Be sure to give your shaders descriptive names as you create them.

Setting Up 16-Bit Displacement Renders in Maya

Included on the DVD is a video demonstrating how to render 16-bit displacement maps in Maya. The process for setting up the shader is identical to that used for 32-bit maps. The difference comes in determining the Alpha Gain and Alpha Offset values for the displacement map file node.

Because a 16-bit map does not have real-world scale baked in, you must adjust the Alpha Gain and Alpha Offset values until the render appears correct. By using an expression for Alpha Offset, you can just adjust the Gain value and Offset will update. Set Alpha Offset to = - `filenodename.alphaGain /2;`. In this expression, replace `filenodename` with the name of the current file node. You can find this at the top of the Attribute Editor window when you select the file node (Figure 9.25). If the file node is called `file2`, use the expression = - `file2.alphaGain /2.`

Test-render your displacement. If your Approximation settings are correct, you will just need to raise the Alpha Gain value until the height of the displacement looks correct. Figure 9.26 shows the Pixologic displacement test head. This figure illustrates a ZBrush render of the test head on the left and a Maya render of the same head on the right. By adjusting Alpha Gain to increase the level of displacement, we can dial into the right settings. The render scene file for this test head is available on the DVD. Simply open the scene file in Maya and render.

Figure 9.25: The file node name can be found at the top of the Attribute Editor. This node is named `file2`.

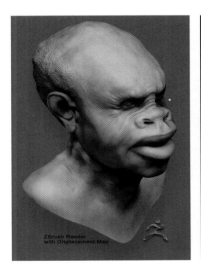

Figure 9.26: Pixologic test head rendered in Maya

Applying Bump Maps in Maya

In most cases, you will want fine details on your mesh such as pores and small wrinkles. You can add these into the geometry itself, and ultimately the displacement map, but that's not always the most efficient approach. With some preplanning, the finer details can be added in a bump map and rendered over the displacement in mental ray. This takes a huge load off the renderer since you don't have to subdivide nearly as high to get lower-frequency forms to appear. A good rule of thumb is if your detail will change the silhouette of the model, displace it. If it is not visible in the profile, add it as a bump map detail instead. ZBrush has a great tool for making bump maps in the Bump Viewer material. For more information on the Bump Viewer material, see Chapter 4. It is also possible to load your displacement map into the bump channel.

You can also generate a bump map for your finer details in ZBrush by simply extracting a displacement map from a higher subdivision level than 1. On a five-division mesh, try extracting a displacement from level 3 and using this as your bump map.

1. To apply your bump map in Maya, open the Attribute Editor for the material on your mesh. Here you'll see a bump mapping slot. Click the checker box to the right of the attribute name in the Attribute Editor and select File from the pop-up window. This will create a bump2D node. You will see some options in the Attribute Editor for the bump2D node. Bump Depth is the "volume" control for the level of the bump effect in rendering. The initial value of 1 is usually too high, so start testing with a value of 0.5. Render and adjust the Bump Depth value accordingly until you get a satisfactory result.

2. Click the arrow next to Bump Value to access the file node, where you will load your bump map. Remember just like the displacement map, this is based in 50% gray, so be sure to set your Alpha Gain value to 1 and Alpha Offset to −.5 under Color Balance in the file node.

3. Render your model to view the bump map effect on the surface.

Figure 9.27: This character's fine details are carried entirely by bump mapping.

Figure 9.27 shows a character whose details exist only as a bump map. These can be indistinguishable from displaced fine details and in many cases superior since they require less render time to produce for the same visual effect. Figure 9.28 provides another example: the sphere on the left is fully displaced. The sphere on the right has a displacement map driving the form, while another displacement map loaded into the bump channel handles high-frequency details.

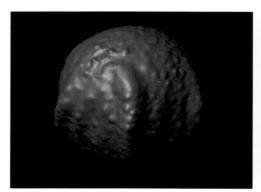
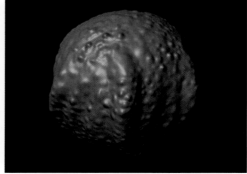

Figure 9.28: By using a displacement map in the bump channel, you can sharpen the fine details with minimal impact on render times.

Common Problems When Moving into Maya

When you're preparing a model for sculpting and displacement extraction in ZBrush, the mesh needs to be clean. By *clean*, I mean it should consist of all quads (or at least nearly all quads). Avoid triangles, poles (points where five edges or more meet), and n-gons (faces with more than four vertices). If you find you must have a tri, hide it in an inconspicuous area. Tringles and N-gons may cause artifacts at render time. You also want to ensure your vertices are all welded and that there are no nonmanifold or lamina faces. All of these mesh issues can be resolved with the cleanup tool. Follow these steps before you start sculpting on the model as they will potentially alter the vertex order of the mesh.

Figure 9.29: Cleanup Options dialog box

1. Select Polygons → Cleanup ⌐. to open the Cleanup Options dialog box (Figure 9.29).

2. If you choose Select Matching Polygons in the Cleanup Effect section and check only the 4-Sided Faces option, Click the Cleanup button and Maya will select all the quads in your mesh. You can then use Edit → Invert Selection to select the non-quad faces. Often, I will assign another color to these faces to keep them visible and continue working the topology until I have an all-quad mesh.

3. Still in the Cleanup Options dialog box, choose the Cleanup Matching Polygons (in Maya 8.0 this option is called Select and Cleanup) and select Lamina Faces and Nonmanifold Geometry in the Remove Geometry section. Click the Cleanup button, and this will resolve any of the issues that often arise when modeling with the Extrude tool. Cleaning up your mesh now can save a lot of headaches later on.

Troubleshooting Renders and Artifacts

In some cases you may see artifacts in your renders. If you see bloating in your render, then there is a mistake with the Alpha Gain and Alpha Offset values or the Alpha Detection setting in Maya 2008 is wrong (Figure 9.30). Usually you have forgotten to set one or both, or the Alpha Offset is not set to –½ Alpha Gain.

Small spikes on UV seams can be remedied by using the Smooth UV option under Tools → Displacement. Use this only when creating an adaptive map. It has no effect in DPsubPix mode. Many artifacts are caused by bad topology in the underlying mesh. Triangles, poles, or faces with more than four sides can result in surface errors (Figure 9.31). These artifacts should be hidden in inconspicuous places during the modeling process or removed completely. If you find such an artifact on your render, applying a smooth to the mesh before rendering can help (Figure 9.32). Doing so will increase render time, and you may want to lower your Approximation settings as a result.

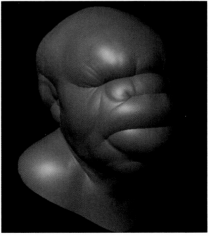

Figure 9.30: The bloating in this render is due to incorrectly set Alpha Gain and Alpha Offset settings.

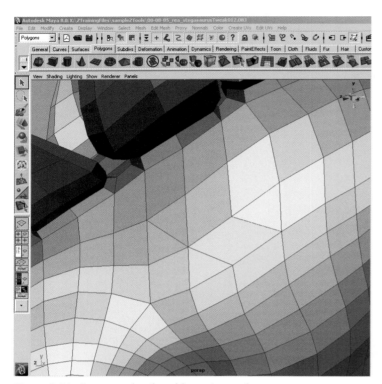

Figure 9.31: An example of problematic topology

Figure 9.32: Mesh artifacts in render

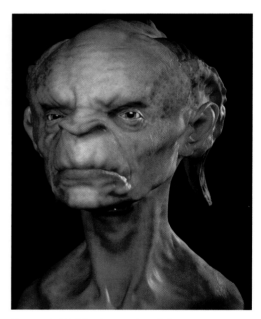

Figure 9.33: The Stingerhead character rendered with displacement and subsurface scattering

In this chapter, we explored the two major displacement map types that can be exported from ZBrush, and you learned how to set up models and shaders for displacement in Maya. By combining your texture map, displacement, diffuse, and bump maps with a subsurface scattering shader, you can achieve renders like the one shown in Figure 9.33. The ability to capture the high detail of your characters in other renderers allows you to take your work to the next level, breathing life and animation into your work. In the next chapter, we'll continue looking at difference maps in ZBrush by discussing normal maps.

Featured Artist: The Art of Damien Canderle

Damien is a freelance ZBrush artist whose striking renders have inspired many of us in the ZBrush community. I especially love the attention to color, light, and atmosphere in his final presentation.

ZMapper

ZMapper is a plug-in *that comes preinstalled with all versions of ZBrush after 3.0. ZMapper is a robust plug-in with many functions, including the ability to generate normal as well as cavity maps, and the ability to preview blend shape targets sculpted in ZBrush. In this chapter, we'll look at several uses for ZMapper.*

Normal Maps

ZBrush offers two methods of extracting your high-frequency details and then rendering them in an external application: normal mapping and displacement mapping. We have already discussed displacement mapping in Chapter 9.

Normal maps are color maps that represent the surface normal direction of any given point on the model. They allow a renderer to create the impression of a highly detailed surface on a low-polygon base. Figure 10.1 shows an example of a normal map and the rendered result on a model.

Normal mapping differs from displacement in one major way. While displacement mapping makes actual geometry at render time by subdividing the mesh, normal mapping creates the illusion of a highly detailed surface without changing the geometry. The benefit of this is speed, but the drawback is that the silhouette of the model will not change. In Figure 10.2, the sphere on the left is displaced while the sphere on the right is normal mapped. Note how the profiles are still angular on the normal mapped sphere.

For this reason it is imperative that the base model be optimized to best represent the overall profiles of the model when you will be normal mapping. If your low-polygon mesh is too low and does not represent the form of the high-res, you will end up with errors in your normal map at worst—or at least a normal map that is unconvincing when displayed on a faceted model.

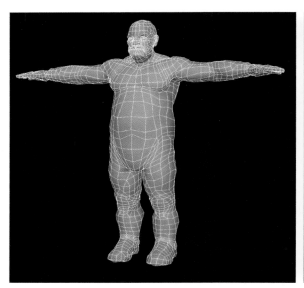 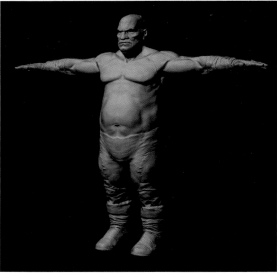

Figure 10.1: *This character is rendered with a normal map. This mapping method gives the low-polygon mesh seen on the left the appearance of high-frequency details, as shown on the right. (Image courtesy of Secret Level/Sega and Gentle Giant Studios.)*

Figure 10.2: *The model on the left is normal mapped while the right is displaced. Note the visible polygon facets on the silhouette of the normal mapped model (especially in the shoulder) and how the details do not translate into the silhouette. (Model by Jim McPherson)*

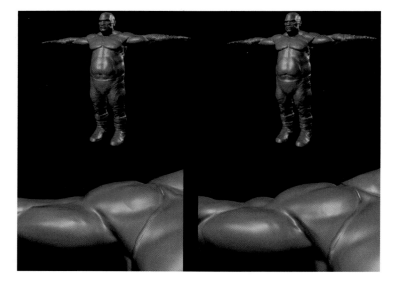

Normal maps offer a superb way to create the illusion of a highly detailed surface on a low-polygon base. Normal maps are actually generated from bump maps when processing; this process is invisible to the user but understanding it will help you understand the inner workings of the normal map.

A normal map is an RGB image file. Each channel of the map (R, G, and B) represents one of the three axes (X, Y, and Z). In Figure 10.3 the individual channels of a normal map have been isolated to help illustrate this. The Red, or R, channel represents the surface lit from the right; the G channel represents light from above, or the Y direction; and B is light shining down the Z-axis.

To create a normal map in ZBrush, you will use ZMapper. There is an option under the Tool menu (choose Tool → Normal Map), but this is legacy inclusion in the program and does not offer the same control as ZMapper.

ZMapper

ZMapper is a ZBrush plug-in that comes preinstalled in versions of ZBrush from version 3.0 and up. ZMapper allows you to create normal maps with a full level of control over all aspects of the algorithm. Since there are no published standards for how programs interpret normal maps, all applications interpret them slightly differently. By giving the user full access to the generation

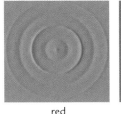
red

green

blue

process, ZMapper is an exceptional normal mapping tool. In addition to creating normal maps, ZMapper allows you to generate cavity maps, check blend shape animation, and check the UV layout on your model. Before we examine the ZMapper interface in depth, let's follow the process to load a ZTool and generate a tangent space normal map.

Figure 10.3: The individual channels of a normal map

Starting ZMapper and Generating a Normal Map

ZMapper is accessed by the ZMapper button in the upper-left tray of the user interface. Before ZMapper will launch, there must be a ZTool on the canvas in Edit mode. To load a model into ZMapper and generate a normal map, follow these steps:

1. From the Tool menu select a Plane3D tool and click the MakePolyMesh3D button. Draw the plane on the canvas and enter Edit mode by pressing the T key.

2. Open the main Tool menu, click the Morph Target menu to unroll it, and click storeMT to store a copy of the mesh at level 1. Subdivide a few times with Ctrl+D and create some sculpted strokes on the model. Notice in Figure 10.4 that the surface of the plane is deformed and the bumps have actual height.

3. When you have finished sculpting, step down to level 1. Click the main Texture menu and set your width and height sliders to 2048. Then click the New button. This will create a new 2048x2048 texture on the model. ZMapper will generate a normal map for whatever resolution texture is active when it launches. The plane already has implicit UVs, so you don't need to create those. In other cases, such as an imported mesh, you will always need to be sure the model has UVs.

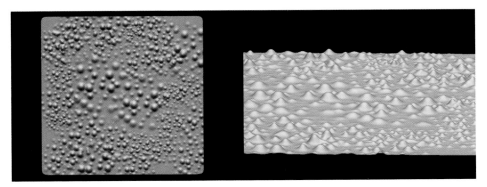

Figure 10.4: Sculpted plane

Figure 10.5: The Normal & Cavity Map tab

4. Click the ZMapper button to launch the application. The model will be spinning slowly at the center of the screen, and ZMapper's interface will appear in the document window (Figure 10.5). You can use the Tab key to show or hide the ZMapper menu.

5. Your model will default to having Spin on. This causes it to rotate on its axis after you move the model. Disable this now by clicking the Spin button in the Mesh column.

6. In the Display column, click the Tangent Space Normal Map button. Expand the Normal & Cavity Map tab by clicking its tab at the bottom of the ZMapper interface. This opens the basic normal mapping options.

7. You will now see the Create NormalMap button. Click this and the map will start to generate. You can see it update pixel by pixel on your model in the ZMapper view.

8. When the map is completed, it will display in ZMapper. You can rotate around the model and check the display. You may even move the light. In the ZMapper main menu, click the local light button. This activates a light you may rotate around the model. To move the light in ZMapper, Shift+left-click to rotate and Shift+right-click to raise up and down. If you move the light close to the model, you may see it displayed in the ZMapper window as a yellow cube (Figure 10.6).

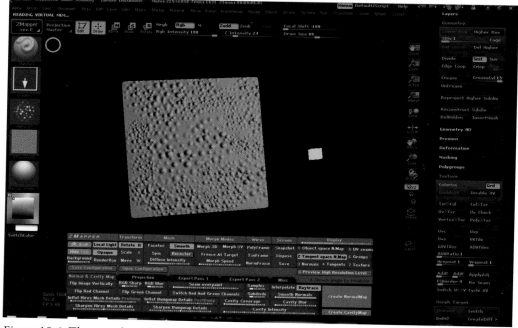

Figure 10.6: The completed normal map displaying in the ZMapper window. The yellow box is the movable light source in ZMapper.

9. Rotate around the mesh and note that the polygons have a slight elevation to them from your lowest subdivision level. We'll now switch back to the flat plane. Press Esc to exit ZMapper. Notice that the normal map generated is automatically loaded into the Texture menu.

10. Click the main Tool menu's Morph Target menu and select Switch. This will return the plane to its flattened state. Click the ZMapper button to launch the plug-in. Notice that the normal map still appears the same. Rotate the plane and see that it is indeed flat. The normal map gives the impression of depth and height (Figure 10.7).

Now you have completed the steps to making a basic normal map on a simple piece of geometry. We'll move on now to examine the interface more closely and experiment with some more in-depth examples.

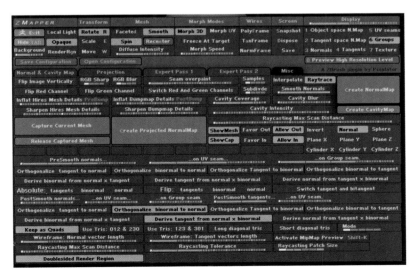

Figure 10.7: Normal map on a flat plane and a perturbed model

The ZMapper Interface

In this section, we'll examine the ZMapper interface (Figure 10.8). There are several tabs and menu options. This may look daunting at first, but you will soon see everything is in its place.

Navigation in ZMapper is similar to navigating in ZBrush itself. To rotate the model, drag the background. If the Spin option is on, the model will continue to move in the direction of the mouse movement when released. Panning is accomplished by dragging the background while holding the spacebar, and zooming is achieved by right-click-dragging the model or background.

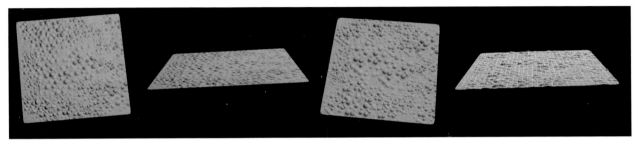

Figure 10.8: The ZMapper menu (here, with all the tabs locked open for a full view of the interface)

The ZMapper control panel is divided into two main sections. The upper controls remain consistent at all times. The lower tabbed controls are accessible from the various tabbed menus. These offer different menu sets for various aspects of the program.

The lower control tabs can be accessed by clicking the tab name. To lock a tabbed menu in the open state, Shift-click its name.

The upper menu is broken down into seven columns; see Table 10.1.

The lower control panel consists of several tabs. These control all aspects of the normal map generation process. The tabs and their function are explained in Table 10.2.

Table 10.1: Contents of the ZMapper Main Menu

Column	Controls
ZMapper	General controls for the ZMapper interface.
Transform	Controls navigation in ZMapper.
Mesh	Controls the mesh display in ZMapper.
Morph	Morph causes the model to dynamically shift between representations. Morph 3D will blend between the model and a stored morph target while Morph UV will unwrap dynamically to the UV map.
Wires	Controls the wireframe display of the model.
Screen	Allows screenshots to be stored and exported.
Display	Controls both the type of view in ZMapper as well as the type of the normal map generated (Tangent or Object space).

Table 10.2: Contents of the ZMapper tabs

Tab	Controls
Normal & Cavity Map	Normal and cavity map general settings.
Projection	Settings for generating a normal map between arbitrary meshes.
Expert Pass 1	The Expert Pass tabs allow fine-tuning of every aspect of the map-generation process. These are usually best left at the default settings unless you have specific technical needs in your engine.
Expert Pass 2	Same as above.
Misc	Various options that done fit in other menus. The most important two are Doublesided Render Region and Raycasting Max Scan Distance, both discussed later in this chapter.

ZMapper Control Types

The menus contain three kinds of controls: buttons, switches, and intensity controls.

- Buttons, such as Exit or Create Normal Map, are shaded in gray; clicking these causes an action to occur.
- Switches are shown in a darker gray. These turn an option on or off. The Spin switch will toggle the spinning rotation that is ZMapper's default display.
- Intensity controls govern the strength of an option or effect. The Morph Speed slider shows this value set to 0 on the left and 100% on the right.

ZMapper Configuration Files

Normal maps do not have a published standard in the same way that displacement maps do. This means that all programs interpret them with subtle differences. It is for this reason that ZMapper has so many options open to you. Luckily ZMapper also includes the ability to create and store configuration files. Config files contain all the pertinent settings for the application or engine in which you will render your normal map.

To open a configuration file, click the Open Configuration button to see the default files that come standard with ZBrush. Most major application settings are represented here. If you are rendering Maya, select Maya Tangent Space Node Best Quality. This will configure ZMapper will all the necessary settings for a tangent space map to display in Maya.

If you have specific needs for your own engine or map, you can set your ZMapper settings and then click Save Configuration. This will store these settings in a file that can be shared between artists in a studio so all maps are consistent in their settings.

Using the Render Region Feature

Often as you are generating normal maps, you may want to adjust settings and compare them to previous renders. You can save time by generating only part of the map at a time for comparison purposes. To do this, use the RenderRgn button under the ZMapper menu column.

The Render Region feature allows you to generate just a portion of the normal map so you can quickly evaluate settings. In Figure 10.9, Render Region is active. Notice the red rectangle; clicking in the corners allows you to scale this selection rectangle to the area you want to render. Clicking inside the double box lets you move the rectangle around. If you click and drag inside the box, you can further refine the render selection with a lasso tool (Figure 10.10).

Some settings may increase the time required to generate the normal maps. Adjusting the Raycasting Max Scan Distance slider, for instance, can increase the time it takes for a map to complete. You can enhance the efficiency of the render region by turning off Double Sided so only those areas facing the viewer are rendered. On the Misc menu tab, click Doublesided Render Region to turn it off (Figure 10.11).

Figure 10.11: Turn off double-sided rendering.

Figure 10.9: Render Region square

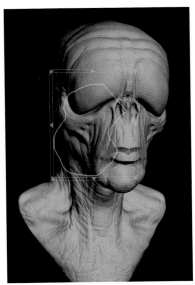

Figure 10.10: Render Region lasso

Let's use the render region to experiment with various normal map generation settings:

1. Turn on Render Region by clicking the RenderRgn button. Draw the rectangle around one side of the model, as shown in Figure 10.12.
2. Under Normal & Cavity Maps, raise the Sharpen Hires (high-resolution) Mesh Details slider. This will sharpen the detail as the map generates.
3. Click Create Normal Map. The map will generate for just the area inside the region (Figure 10.13). You can easily compare the result of these settings to the previous render on the other side of the face.

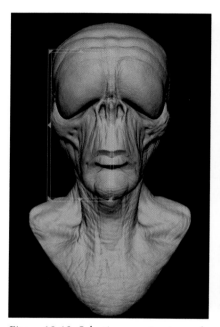 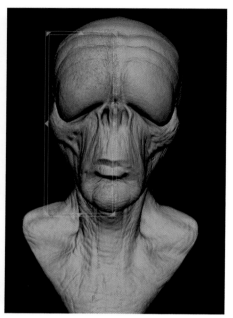

Figure 10.12: Selecting a region to render   *Figure 10.13: Region rendered*

Arbitrary Meshes

When transferring high-res details from one ZTool to a low-res mesh as a normal map the most common approach is to sculpt the high resolution model first. When this model is completed a low-res animation friendly model is made either in ZBrush or in another application. When building the low-res model always take care that the edges are placed on the highest and lowest points of the silhouette. This helps to ensure that while the internal forms will appear highly detailed by the normal map the overall outline of the character will not have an overtly faceted or low polygon look. Failing to make the most efficient use of your edges in the silhouette can be a dead giveaway to the low poly nature of the mesh and ruin the illusion of the high-resolution appearance.

This approach also allows you to finish sculpting before you have to worry about topology. ZMapper lets you generate normal maps between two separate meshes just as if they were one ZTool. In this section we'll load a design sculpt and a remeshed game mesh, and create a normal map between the two (Figure 10.14).

1. Load the original ZTool. We'll call this the design sculpt since the topology is not the final that you'll want to use as the base model. This should be a multi-resolution ZTool with all your sculpting applied. For this demo, load humanhead.ztl from the DVD.

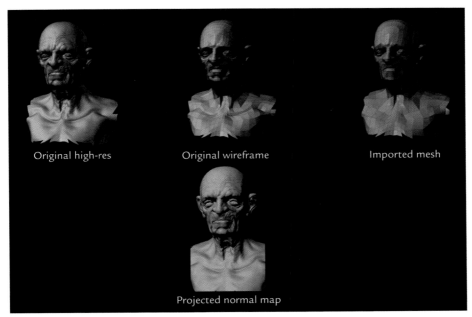

Original high-res   Original wireframe   Imported mesh

Projected normal map

Figure 10.14: Arbitrary mesh transfer allows you to bake details from one ZTool into a completely different low-res cage.

2. Choose Tool → Texture and click AUV Tiles to generate texture coordinates for the design sculpt. Launch ZMapper by clicking the ZMapper button.

3. Open the Projection tab at the bottom of the screen. You'll want to capture the details of this design sculpt and then project them into a new topology that follows the same overall shape of this mesh. Turn up Raycasting Max Scan Distance halfway. This is the length each ray will cast trying to find the difference between the two meshes: the design sculpt and the remesh (Figure 10.15).

Figure 10.15: Raise this slider to increase the length each ray casts.

4. Click the Capture Current Mesh button. The model will now be covered in red lines; these are the normals of the current mesh captured (Figure 10.16). Exit ZMapper by pressing the Esc key.

5. We now need to load the new mesh onto which we'll project this detail. I have created a lower-polygon version of the human head model, which is on the DVD. To import it into the current ZTool, select Tool → Clone to make a copy of the current mesh. Under Tool → Geometry, click Del Higher to delete the higher subdivision levels so there is only one.

6. Now import the `humanheadlow.obj` file into the current ZTool. This will ensure the pivot and scale remain the same while swapping topology.

An alternative method is to have the two meshes as subtools. After capturing the high-res details, switch to the subtool of the game mesh and re-enter ZMapper.

---

7. Open ZMapper again. Under the Projection tab, you can turn off Show Cap to remove the red normal lines. Click Create Projected Normal Map to generate a normal map between the design sculpt and the new topology. When completed, the map will display in ZMapper (Figure 10.17).

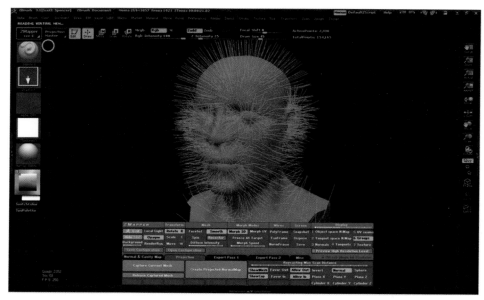

Figure 10.16: High-res mesh details captured

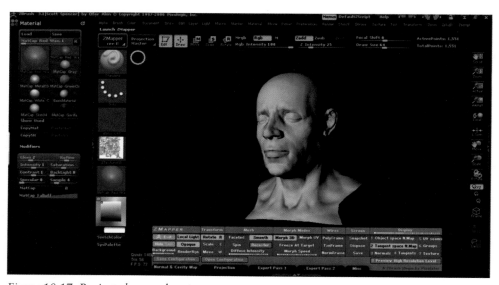

Figure 10.17: Projected normal map

Cavity Maps

Cavity maps are specialty textures that can be generated in ZMapper. They are essentially the blue channel of a normal map and represent dark shading in the crevices of the model. They can be useful as a multiply layer over a diffuse color map to accentuate details or as a diffuse map in Maya to help punch up the high-frequency details in a render. Figure 10.18 shows a cavity map. It is essentially a black-and-white map in which black represents the recesses and white is the high points.

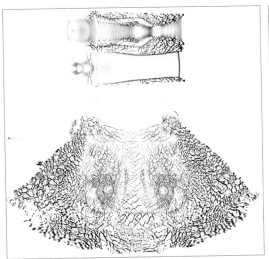

Figure 10.18: A cavity map

Cavity mapping is intended to help mimic Ambient Occlusion, but it is not by nature an Ambient Occlusion effect. It also has several other uses. Ambient Occlusion works by casting rays out from the surface of a 3D model. If a ray hits another surface before dying out, then a grayscale value is recorded that represents how far that ray traveled before being occluded. This is how Ambient Occlusion maps generate darker shadows in tight recesses like inside ears or under the brow ridge. The rays there intersect the next surface faster than, say, faces under the chin, which would record a lighter grayscale value.

Cavity mapping, on the other hand, just shades in recesses. It doesn't use advanced raycasting or calculate distances between surfaces. It is, however, useful as a diffuse map or a Photoshop mask or any other application where you want to isolate the high points from the low points on a surface texture. Figure 10.19 shows a cavity map and Ambient Occlusion map to help illustrate the differences.

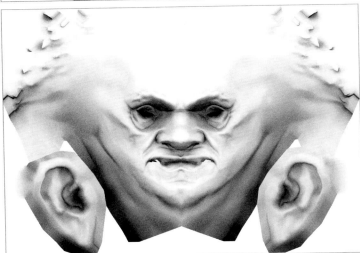

Figure 10.19: A cavity map and an occlusion map. The first image is a cavity map. Notice how the recesses are shaded while the Ambient Occlusion image shows a gradient shading into the recessed areas of the head.

Cavity maps are generated with ZMapper under the same Normal & Cavity Maps tab. To generate a cavity map, simply raise the Cavity Intensity slider to around the halfway point and click the Create Cavity-Map button (Figure 10.20). The map will generate on screen just as the normal map did before. When the map is completed, it will display on the model in ZMapper. Exit ZMapper and export the map from the Texture menu.

Figure 10.20: Cavity mapping options in ZMapper

Figure 10.21 shows a cavity map used in the diffuse channel of a Maya Blinn shader. The cavity map is perfectly suited to help accentuate the rendered details by governing how light is reflected back from the surface. The dark areas reflect less light, so they appear darker; the lighter areas have the opposite effect. This effect helps accentuate the recessed areas by limiting the amount of light they reflect, giving them a darker, more-shadowed appearance.

Figure 10.21: This character head was rendered in mental ray using a displacement map and a cavity map in the diffuse channel. The first image is the render without the cavity map; the second image is with the cavity map.

Using ZMapper to View UVs

You can view your UV in ZBrush by using ZMapper. To verify your UVs in ZMapper:

1. From the DVD, import the `body.obj` file. Choose Tool → Import and browse to the body file.
2. Draw the OBJ on the canvas and enter Edit mode by pressing the T key.
3. With the tool active on the canvas, click the ZMapper button in the upper-left corner of the screen.
4. At the bottom of the screen, you will see the ZMapper interface (Figure 10.22). For now we are concerned with the Morph UV button at the bottom.
5. The Morph UV button will cause the model to unwrap on your screen into its UV coordinates. Click the Freeze at Target button to freeze the UV display. Click and rotate in the interface somewhere off the model to rotate.

This process helps you quickly verify the UV layout on a ZTool. In ZBrush it is possible to swap UVs at any time by simply importing a new model into level 1. Press Esc to exit ZMapper. In the next section we'll change the current UV layout by importing a different UV set.

Figure 10.22: ZMapper interface

Rendering Normal Maps in Maya

In this section we'll generate a normal map in ZMapper using the Maya Tangent Space Node Best Quality configuration file. We'll then move to Maya where we'll set up shaders and render the normal map (Figure 10.23).

1. Open your ZTool in ZBrush. Draw it on the canvas and enter Edit mode. Step down to the lowest subdivision level. Assign AUV tiles by selecting Tool → Texture and clicking the AUV Tiles button. Create a texture in the main Texture menu. Set the resolution to 2048×2048.

2. Click the ZMapper button. From the ZMapper menu, click Open Configuration File. Select Maya Tangent Space Node Best Quality. This will automatically set up ZMapper for Maya. Click the Normal & Cavity Maps tab to open this menu. Click the Create Normal Map button.

3. When the normal map finishes generating, exit ZMapper by pressing Esc. The map will load into the Texture menu. You may notice it no longer displays correctly on your ZTool. This is because ZMapper was set to Maya configuration, which will flip the texture map vertically so it renders correctly in Maya. From the main Texture menu, export the normal map as a TIFF file. Open the main Tool menu and export level 1 of your ZTool as an OBJ.

When exporting OBJ files from ZBrush, be sure to adjust the following settings:

- In Preferences → ImportExport, make sure that all the iFlip and eFlip options are off (Figure 10.24).
- Under the main Tool menu, click the Export menu and make sure Mrg is on and Scale is set to 1.

This will merge your UVs on export. These settings will maintain your object scale and orientation.

Maya Normal Map Setup

Now that you are familiar with the process of generating the normal map in ZBrush, we are ready to move into Maya and render this character with a normal map applied.

1. Open Maya. Import the OBJ file of your level 1 mesh by choosing File → Import → ⅂ and selecting OBJ as the file type. Always be sure to set Make Multiple Objects to False (Figure 10.25).

2. Select the mesh, and under the Polygons menu, click Normals → Soften Edge. This will soften the edge normals and give the faceted model a smooth appearance (Figure 10.26). Right-click the model, and from the Marking menu, assign a new shader and select a Blinn (Figure 10.27). This creates and assigns a new Blinn shader to the object.

Figure 10.23: The normal map displaying on the character head in the ZMapper interface

Figure 10.24: Import export prefs and tool export prefs

Figure 10.25: Import options in Maya

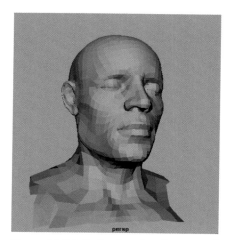
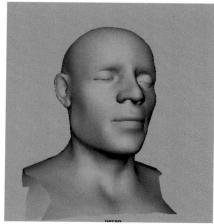

Figure 10.26: Softening the edge normals to give the impression of a smoother mesh

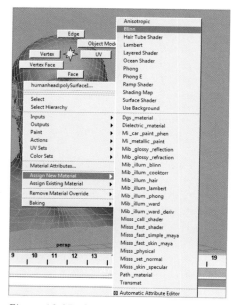

Figure 10.27: Creating a new Blinn shader

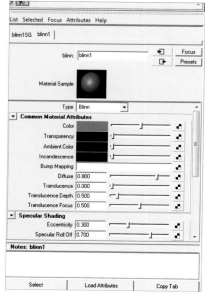

Figure 10.28: The Blinn shading node in the Attribute Editor

3. Press Ctrl+A to bring up the Attribute Editor. Select the Blinn shading node (Figure 10.28).

4. In Maya, normal maps are loaded into the bump channel. Click the check box next to the bump slot in the Blinn shader. In the Create Render Node window, select File (Figure 10.29) to attach a file node to the bump slot in the Blinn shader. This will open the bump 2D node pictured in Figure 10.30. Change the Use As value to Tangent Space Normals (Figure 10.31). This tells the renderer to interpret the bump map as a normal map and not as a grayscale map.

5. Click the downstream arrow next to the Bump value. This will open the file node driving the bump map node (Figure 10.32). Here you can load the normal map. Click the file browser menu icon and select the normal map exported from ZBrush.

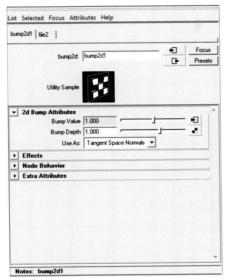

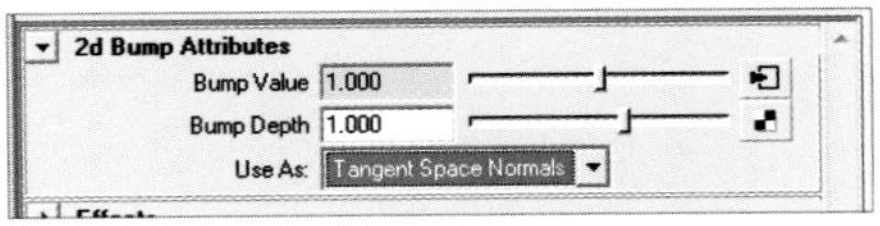

Figure 10.31: Set Use As to Tangent Space Normals.

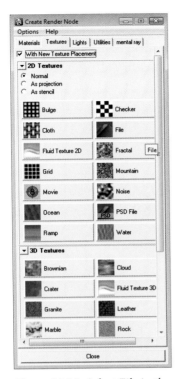

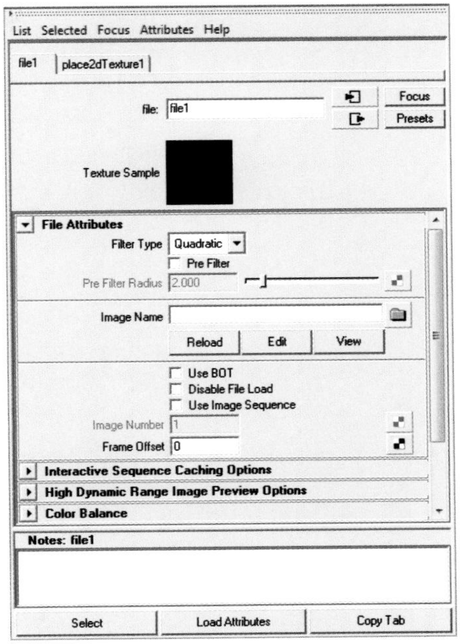

Figure 10.29: Select File in the Create Render Node window.

Figure 10.30: The bump2D node

Figure 10.32: The file node window in the Attribute Editor

That completes shader setup. Now create a directional light by clicking Create → Lights → Directional. Rotate this light to illuminate the model. You can switch to lit view by pressing the 7 key on your keyboard. Maya is capable of displaying the normal map in the viewport. To turn on normal mapping, click Renderer in the Viewport menu and select High Quality Rendering. Select Shading and click Hardware Shading. The normal map will now display in the viewport. The map can be rendered like this using hardware shading or through the mental ray renderer. Figure 10.33 shows this character rendered in the viewport as well as in the software renderer using Final Gather and Image Based Lighting.

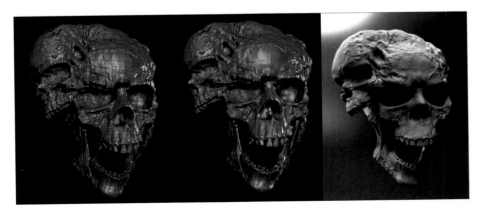

Figure 10.33: This character head is rendered with a normal map. The first image is the normal map with wireframe in the Maya viewport. The second image shows the normal map rendered in the Maya viewport. The third image is the normal mapped mesh rendered in mental ray with Final Gather and Image Based Lighting.

Figure 10.34: Selecting mental ray as the renderer

To render the normal map with mental ray, choose Window → Rendering Editors → Render View, and select mental ray as the renderer (Figure 10.34).

Congratulations! You have now created and applied a normal map in Maya.

Featured Artist: The Art of Joel Mongeon

Joel Mongeon's "Studio Wall" series caught my attention at SIGGRAPH (Special Interest Group on GRAPHics and Interactive Techniques) 2007. Taking a classic sculpture exercise and translating it into digital, Joe has created an exciting and inspiring image as well as demonstrated a valuable sculpting exercise.

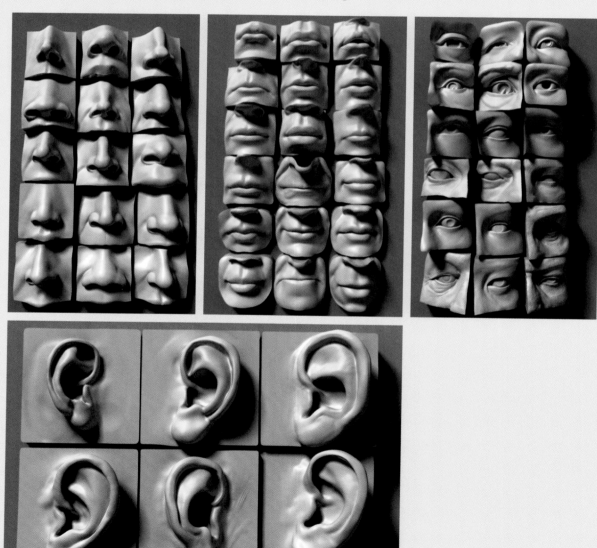

ZMapper for Blend Shapes

ZMapper does more than normal and cavity maps. It is also a useful tool for checking blend shape animation on targets sculpted in ZBrush. Blend shape animation is an animation technique in which two versions of the same model are added as deformers to a base. This allows you to blend between the different vertex positions to create a variety of shapes on a single mesh. It is most commonly used for facial animation. With its organic sculpting tools, ZBrush is ideal for sculpting facial animation targets. ZMapper allows you to view the animation between a base and your blend shape target.

For example, we'll use a human head that transforms into a monster. Both models are sculpted from the same base mesh. Load the human head base into ZBrush.

1. Load the base model into ZBrush. This is your neutral base (Figure 10.35). Store a morph target by choosing Tool → Morph Target (Figure 10.36). Under Layers, create a new layer and call it **blendshape1** (Figure 10.37).

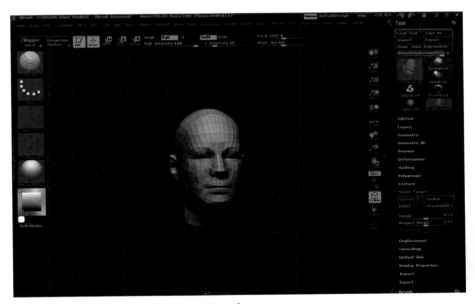

Figure 10.35: Base mesh loaded into ZBrush

Figure 10.36: Store a morph target

2. Using the standard sculpting tools, create a new character head from the base. These changes are stored on the blendshape1 layer since it is active. Change the human head into this beast (Figure 10.38). You can switch between this shape and the original with Tool → Morph Target → Switch.

Figure 10.37: Creating a new layer and naming it blendshape1

3. With a base head and a morph target stored, you can now check the smoothness of the animation between the two when they are exported to Maya, 3ds Max, or another application. ZMapper uses the same interpolation as any other blend shape animation software so you can easily check the skin for realistic deformations or look for erroneous stray movements in vertices.

4. Load ZMapper and turn on morph3D under the Morph Modes column. The model will now blend between the base shape and the stored blend shape (Figure 10.39). If there are any problems in the animation, they will be apparent now instead of much

later when the heads are exported to Maya and loaded into a blend shape deformer. You can even turn on Polyframe mode to check that the vertices all move in an evenly distributed manner (Figure 10.40). This is a huge time-saver and helps the sculptor use the tools to create subtle interesting skin deformations in blend shapes. Let's now add a new blend shape.

Figure 10.38: Human head base beast layer

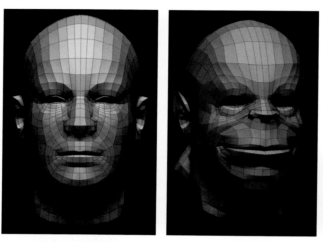

Figure 10.39: Morph 3D in action

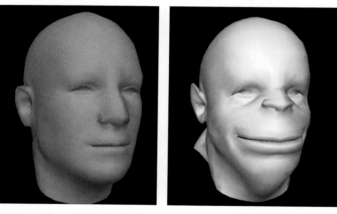

Figure 10.40: Use Polyframe mode to check the movement of edges during animation.

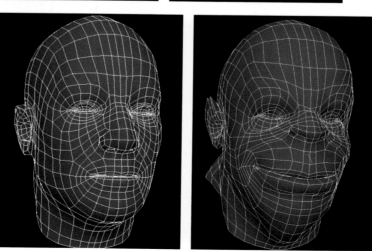

5. Export level 1 of your base head as an OBJ and call it **headbase.obj**. Turn off the blendshape1 layer. Switch to the morph target stored and click delMT so that the creature head is on your screen.

6. We'll now open the mouth and store this shape in a new layer as well as a blend shape. Storing the shapes in layers allows you to always access a morph target since ZBrush will only store one morph target at a time. Create a new layer; call it **open mouth monster**.

7. Using the Move brushes and masking, open the mouth. When the position is correct, click storeMT. Now you can open ZMapper and check the animation. Often when animating faces it is desirable to have the edges move slightly from all areas around the movement's center. This helps create the illusion of elastic skin instead of localizing the motion to a central point, which is very unnatural. Try using the Nudge brush to slide the skin of the cheeks back as the character smiles.

Raycasting Plateaus and Silhouette

Plateaus or flattened areas in your normal map represent points where the ray faded before it was able to intersect the high-res mesh. This occurs in areas of large protrusion where the high-res is pulled far away from the low-res cage. See Figure 10.41 for an example of this kind of map artifact. They will appear as blank spots in the normal map.

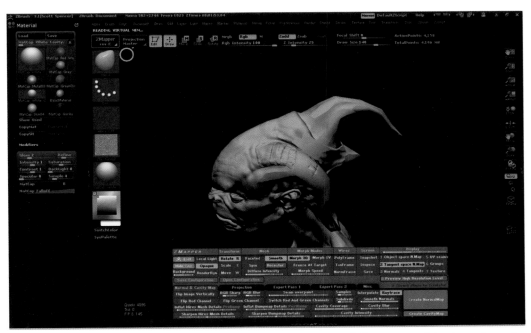

Figure 10.41: Plateau artifacts are caused by a high-res mesh that differs too much in shape from the low-res.

Figure 10.41:
Continued

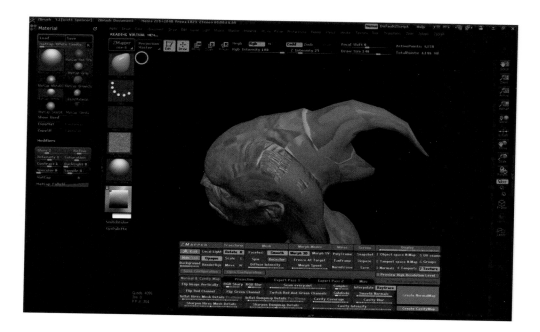

Figure 10.42: Raycasting Max Scan Distance slider

When this happens, the map will create a blank flat plane in the areas where the ray never intersected the second mesh. To correct, this you can simply raise the Raycasting Max Scan Distance, which allows rays to live longer and gives them more time to intersect the second mesh.

To correct for this, raise the Raycasting Max Scan Distance slider under the Misc tab (Figure 10.42). Figure 10.43 shows the effect raising this value has on the plateau areas of the map.

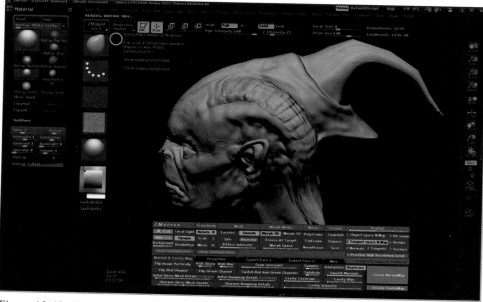

Figure 10.43: Correcting the plateau artifact by raising the slider

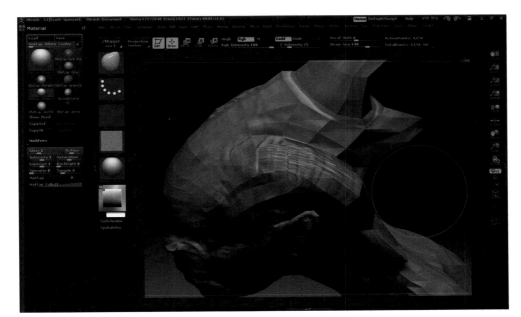

Figure 10.43:
Continued

Quick Reference to ZMapper

- Make sure the mesh has UV coordinates assigned.
- Create a texture at the resolution you want your normal map.
- If you are baking in bump detail, load the bump map in the alpha slot and adjust the displacement intensity until it displays correctly.
- For organic characters, use tangent space normal maps.
- Plateaus in the map can be corrected by raising the Raycasting Max Scan Distance slider.

CHAPTER eleven

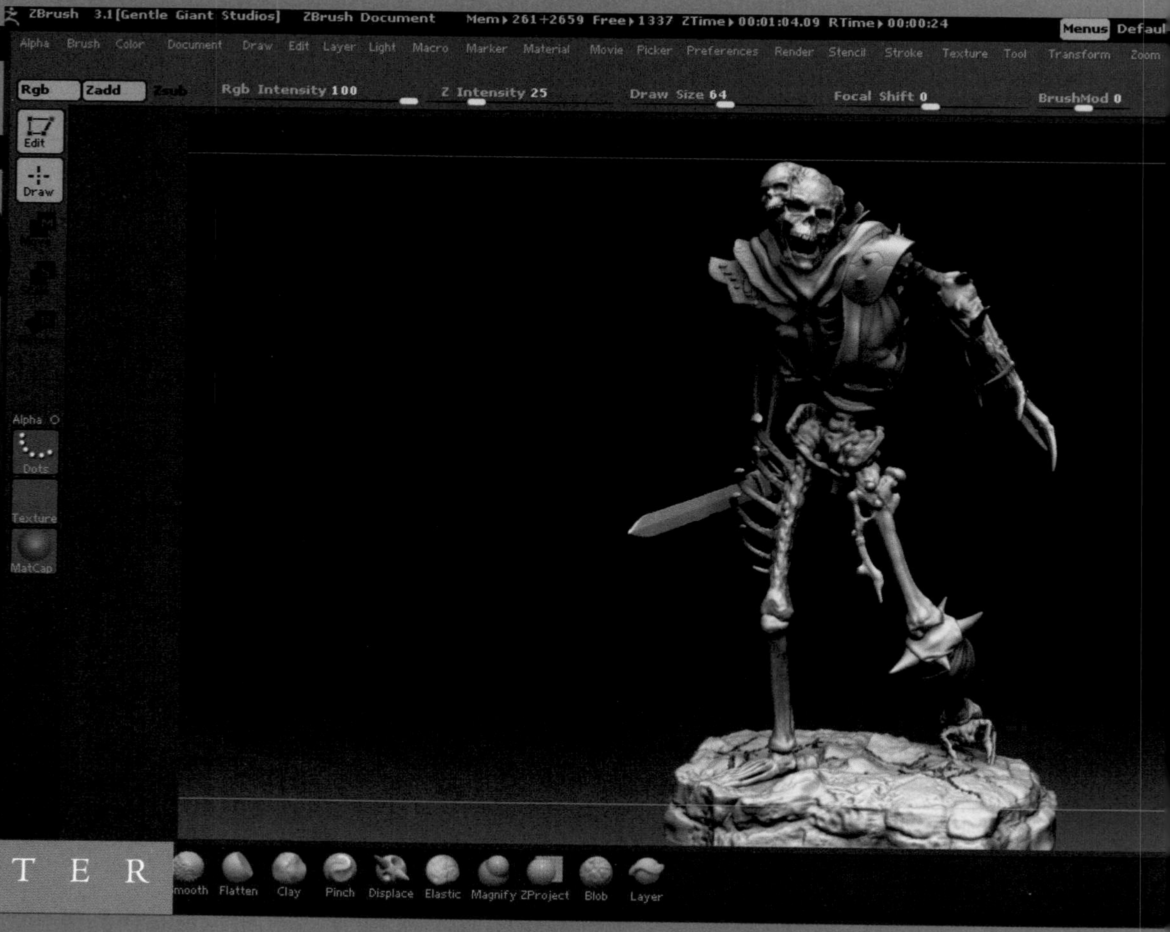

ZScripts, Macros, and Interface Customization

ZBrush gives you *a wide array of customization and scripting options. In this chapter we'll look at ZBrush interface building as well as ZScripts and macros. ZScripting is the built-in ZBrush scripting language, and using it requires some knowledge of programming. Macros are recordings of ZBrush actions saved as brushes and require no scripting skill. Macros can be a huge time-saver when you're creating custom brushes or menu options.*

Contrasting ZScripts and Macros

ZScripts are programs, written in a ZBrush scripting language, that allow the user to automate tasks inside of ZBrush. ZScripting is a macro-based programming language. You write a ZScript and it is interpreted by the program as it runs. Both are freely distributed via ZBrushCentral, and the user community is overflowing with great ZScripts.

Installing a ZScript is as simple as copying a file into a folder. For example, we'll use the incredibly useful AutoSave plug-in by ZBrushCentral member Svengali, which is included on the DVD. When you download a ZScript from the Internet, it will most often come in a ZIP archive. Extracting the archive will provide you with a single .zsc file or in some cases a data folder and a .zsc file. In the case of AutoSave, you will have a single .zsc file.

To install this ZScript, copy the file. You want to paste it into your ZBrush installation directory: /zbrush3/zstartup/zplugs. ZScripts copied into this folder will install automatically when ZBrush starts (Figure 11.1). Copy the AutoSave script to this location now. If ZBrush is running, close it and reopen the program now.

When ZBrush loads, you will have a new folder under the ZPlugin menu called Svengali. In the ZPlugin menu you will find several buttons (Figure 11.2). These buttons allow you to save a numbered iteration of a ZBrush document, ZTool, ZMovie, or a screen capture. This makes saving iterations of your model a simple one-button click.

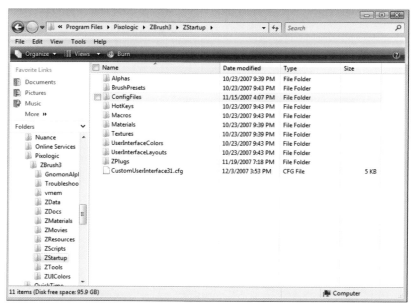

Figure 11.1: ZStartup folder

Figure 11.2: The Svengali menu

To use the program, load a ZTool and in the ZPlugin Svengali menu click the Model button. This will save the first iteration of the ZTool setting, the filename, and the starting number. In this case, the model name is _001.

Now when you click the m+ button, a new ZTool will save to the same folder with a new three-digit extension—in this case, _002. This ensures you save new copies of the file each time; if a file becomes corrupted, you won't lose your work (Figure 11.3).

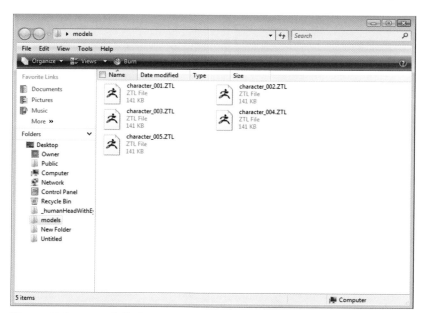

Figure 11.3: Iterated file list

These buttons can be easily docked to new locations in the interface or even assigned hotkeys. Later in this chapter we'll do just that while creating a custom interface.

Recording Macros

ZScripts are not limited to only those who can write programming languages. For repetitive tasks, ZBrush comes with a macro recorder. Macros are recordings of ZBrush actions stored as buttons. They can be used to store custom brush setups, and to perform common actions such as creating a polymesh sphere and preparing it for sculpting, or even loading a selection of tools or alphas. In this exercise, you will create a button to load a polysphere and prepare it for sculpting:

Figure 11.4:
Recording a macro

1. To record a macro, begin by clicking the New Macro button under the Macro menu (Figure 11.4). Any actions you perform in ZBrush after clicking this button will be recorded in the new macro until you click the End Macro button.

2. Click in the Tool menu and select the sphere3D tool. Click MakePolymesh3d and draw the sphere on the canvas. Orient the poles to the top and bottom of the sphere and turn on X Symmetry.

3. Return to the Macro menu and click the End Macro button. ZBrush will prompt you for a place to store the macro. Save it in the ZStartup/macros folder (Figure 11.5). Macros stored here will load with ZBrush at startup. The subfolder in which you save the macro will determine the heading under which it appears in ZBrush. I've saved this macro in the misc folder with the name createSphere.

4. Under Macros, click Reload All Macros. This will reinstall all macros in the ZStartup/Macros folder. Under the Macro menu in the misc selections, you will now find the createSphere macro button (Figure 11.6). Click this and the actions will replay, creating a sphere and preparing it for sculpting. It is possible to take this button and dock it elsewhere in the interface. We'll discuss interface customization later in this chapter.

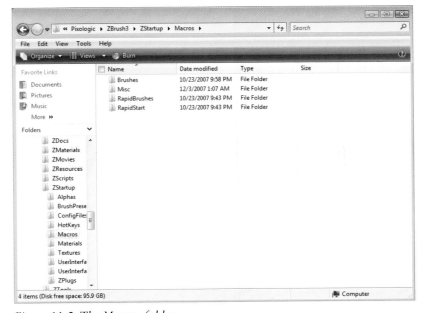

Figure 11.6: The
createSphere macro
button

Figure 11.5: The Macros folder

Now that you have created a macro for generating a polymesh sphere, let's try a different application of macros. Next you'll create a custom macro brush.

1. Click New Macro under the Macro menu. ZBrush is now recording.
2. From the Brush menu, select the Simple brush.
3. From the Stroke menu, select Spray. Turn the Color modifier down to 0.
4. From the Alpha menu, select Alpha 07.
5. Select the RGB red and turn off all modifiers on the brush but RGB.
6. End recording and save this macro under the macro brushes menu. Call it **Spatterbrush**.

You have now created a custom macro brush that mimics the spray brush from earlier in this book. By storing the brush setup in a macro, you can alter settings such as the RGB value, stroke settings, and even masking settings.

You can assign this brush a hotkey or dock the button elsewhere in the interface. When using macro brushes, it is always a good idea to create a new macro to return the brush to its default setting. To do this for the Spatterbrush, follow these steps:

1. Click New Macro to begin recording.
2. Select the Simple brush. Change Alpha back to off and the Stroke to Freehand.
3. Turn off RGB and turn on ZAdd.
4. In the Macro menu, click EndMacro. Save this macro in the Macros/Brushes folder as standardBrush.
5. In the Macros menu, click Reload All Macros. This will load the button under `Macros/ Brushes` for the Standard brush (Figure 11.7). Now when you select the Spatterbrush and want to switch back to the Standard brush, click this button. Otherwise, the Standard brush will retain the previous settings.

Figure 11.7: The standardBrush macro button

Anatomy of a ZScript

This section was contributed by featured artist Svengali.

Many ZBrushers use ZScripting as a simple recorder to capture all mouse moves, mouse clicks, and keyboard presses made while modeling. When the ZScript recording is stopped, it is saved to a text file. When reloaded for playback, the ZScript will faithfully reproduce the entire recorded modeling session. What a powerful teaching tool! Of course, a ZScript file created this way may also be viewed in a text editor to show how many ZScripting commands work.

But a ZScript can be much more. You can write original ZScripts that provide a way to do the following:

- Customize ZBrush with new buttons.
- Enhance ZBrush with new functionality.
- Automate and streamline tedious ZBrush processes.
- See into ZBrush's inner workings.

We'll examine the power of ZScripting by looking inside a sophisticated, practical script called ModelViews that presents a pop-up menu with buttons for saving and loading four, posed views of our model. ModelViews will teach us the purpose and advantage of subroutines and how easily we can create an autoloading ZBrush plug-in.

ZScripting Fundamentals

There are three main sections in any ZScript, simple or complex:

Variables Define and assign values to the global variables we'll use in the script.

Subroutines Name each of the subroutines and script their functionality.

Buttons The Main section is where we define the buttons and how they work.

You should also refer to the indispensable ZScript Command Reference (which can be found in the ZBrush Wiki at `http://www.zbrush.info`) for a more complete explanation of usage, syntax, and arguments. Here are some basic ZScript conventions and commands:

Comments Wherever authors of a script want to include information for users who are reading their script, they'll insert a comment by first typing **//** (double forward slashes), followed by informative details. ZBrush knows to ignore these comments when running the script.

Bracket pairs Every command must be enclosed in brackets ([]) so ZBrush will recognize the command or commands to process. Missing brackets can be hard to track down and will likely cause the script to abort, so be careful!

VarDef Before a variable can be used, it must be created and assigned a unique name. Along with naming it, the variable will be assigned a value (numeric) or text (called a *string* and enclosed in quotation marks).

VarSet Once a variable is defined, the script will use `VarSet` to assign a new value (or string) to the variable.

RoutineDef Subroutines are mini-scripts that are included in the larger script. Each is designed to do one job and is "called" each time that job needs to be done. Subroutines make it easy to organize your script. In fact, once you've designed and tested a subroutine, you can cut and paste it into other scripts, thus saving time and effort.

RoutineCall Once a subroutine is defined, you simply insert a `RoutineCall` command anywhere else in the script and the task gets done. When the called subroutine has finished, it returns to the command line following the `RoutineCall` and continues with the script.

IGet This versatile command lets ZScript test the status of various ZBrush buttons, sliders, and internal settings, such as reading canvas dimensions or detecting whether or not a certain button is clicked. You will use this command frequently in most of the ZScripts you write.

TransformGet This useful command retrieves the transformation values from the current model: X, Y, and Z values for position, for size, and for rotation angle. It takes nine separate variables to capture and store this information.

TransformSet This companion command applies new transformation values to the model, thus posing a new view of it on the ZBrush canvas.

Note This command sends a pop-up message to communicate with the user. (Later we'll find out a pop-up note may also include buttons that the user can click.)

Two final commands involve script flow control: the If command (used for testing/branching) and the Loop command (used to repeat the same group of commands a designated number of times):

If Tests whether a statement is True or False by comparing a known value with the contents of a variable or some internal ZBrush state or value. Then, depending on the answer, ZBrush chooses to execute one of two different sets of commands. Here's an example:

```
[If, A == 1,          // tests the value of A
   [VarSet, B, 10 ] // A does equal 1, set B to ten
 ,   // else           // Otherwise...
   [VarSet, B, 20 ] // A not equal 1, Set B to twenty
]
```

Loop This powerful command lets ZBrush execute the same list of commands a specified number of times. Loops (shown here) will be used several times in our second ZScript:

```
[Loop, 5,
   [VarSet, A, A + 10 ] // add ten to A for each loop
]
```

Before we move on to our script, let's look at two advanced groups of ZScript commands to see what they do.

The first group contains commands that use a memory block where variables can be safely stored. Normally, when you exit a ZScript, any values stored in script variables are lost. The next time you start the ZScript, the variables will all restart with their original values. With these memory commands, all variable values can be copied into protected memory (and from there, copied to a disk file) so they can be used again later in the modeling session or even on another day.

Managing Memory Blocks

The ZScript language provides several commands that define a memory block and refer to it using a unique name. Other commands read or write values to the memory block and will even save a copy of the memory block to a disk file.

MemCreate Creates the memory block (MemBlock) by assigning it a name and defining its size, which is always some multiple of four. For example, a MemBlock to hold 10 variables would be 4×10, or 40 bytes.

MemDelete As you would think, this command deletes the named memory block.

MemCreateFromFile This command creates a memory block too, but it then immediately loads the MemBlock with the contents of the named file, setting the block size based on the file size.

MemWrite Writes the value stored in the named variable to a designated position in the memory block. The position must also be some multiple of four since each variable is stored as 4 bytes.

MemRead Reads a value stored in the MemBlock into a named variable. Again, the position of the value is a multiple of 4-byte offsets into the memory block.

MTransformGet This powerful command carries out several steps when called. It reads the XYZ for position, XYZ for scale, and XYZ for rotation for the current model; then, without any other instructions, it automatically writes those nine values directly into the MemBlock at the designated offset. It's like the `TransformGet` command on steroids!

MTransformSet Likewise, this companion command carries out several steps as well when called. It looks into the named MemBlock at the offset designated, for nine variables (36 bytes). It then loads those values representing XYZ for position, XYZ for scale, and XYZ for rotation and uses these values to pose the active model on the canvas.

Making a ZScript into a Plug-In

Finally, let's take a quick look at the command that makes a script into a plug-in and how it would be used to create a button. A plug-in is a special ZScript that defines one or more button sets that are loaded automatically when ZBrush starts up. Most often these scripted buttons end up in a submenu of the ZPlugin menu.

ISubPalette This command is added at the beginning of the Main Script section before the `IButton` of the plug-in is defined. It designates for ZBrush a path to the Palette menu where the plug-in's button should be placed.

IButton Notice in the ModelViews script how the `IButton` is named: We must remember to include the path defined in the `ISubPalette` command as part of the `IButton`'s name. Thus the name becomes `ZPlugin:MyPlugin:ModelViews`, which places the button in the MyPlugin subpalette group. (A subpalette in ZBrush is essentially just a submenu. It is any menu heading that can be unrolled when clicked and contains other buttons.)

Anatomy of ModelViews, a Pop-Up Menu ZScript

In this ZScript, which is available on the companion DVD, we'll create a simple but useful little utility. While editing a model, assume we want to store and retrieve up to four views of it as we work. One easy way is to create a ZScript pop-up note that displays a menu like the one in Figure 11.8.

The logic of the ZScript is indicated in the flowchart in Figure 11.9. Only buttons for View 1 and Save 1 are included since the other three pairs work exactly the same way. Compare the flow of the diagram to the ModelViews script to see how the concept is turned into buttons and subroutines.

When we click the ModelViews plug-in button, it displays a pop-up menu note consisting of the menu title, four Save buttons, four View buttons, and an Exit button. Each time we click any one of the four Save buttons, data from the current pose of our model is stored into block memory (which is also saved to a disk file).

After that, each time we click the matching View button, the data is retrieved from block memory and the model is re-posed to the exact same view that was saved. To leave the menu, we click the Exit button and continue modeling.

An innovation for this menu project is the presence of a hidden button, right behind the menu title. Clicking on the title will display another pop-up note, which peeks at the data stored for our four model views in block memory. Another click brings back the menu.

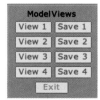

Figure 11.8: The pop-up box that will display from our script

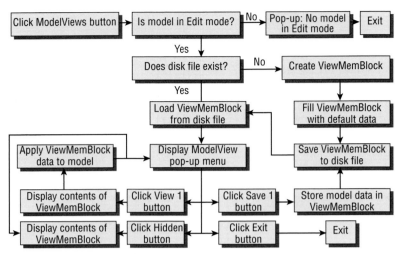

Figure 11.9: Code flow for the ModelViews script

In the following section, we'll forgo a line-by-line analysis as we deconstruct the ZScript called ModelViews. Instead we'll focus on the various subroutines that set up and manage menu operations.

Subroutines and What They Do

Each subroutine is designed to perform one operation. Look at the subroutine name to see the task it is doing, then follow along in the ZScript listing to see how it does what it does.

Some subroutines make calls to other subroutines to complete their own task. This division of labor is essential to writing efficient ZScripts.

Test3d subroutine Tests for active model, and does it in several ways. First it checks whether the Edit button is clicked, indicating that the model is in Edit mode. But there are other things we also need to check to see if a model is active. Any of the Transformation buttons (Move, Scale, or Rotate) may be clicked while the user adjusts the model with the Gizmo.

If the Test3d routine discovers no model in Edit or Gizmo mode, it displays a pop-up warning note for two seconds and then exits the script. Otherwise, the routine returns and the script continues.

LoadViews subroutine First it tests if the disk file named ModelViews.DAT exists. Why? Because the very first time this script runs, the disk file won't exist and it must be created by a call to another subroutine called ResetViews (described in a moment), which creates the ViewMemBlock of memory, loads it with default data, and saves it to a disk file.

Now, and every time this routine is called in the future, it will deliberately delete the block memory so it can re-create it using the MemCreateFromFile command, which loads in the data from the ModelViews.DAT file of the last saved views.

SaveViews subroutine Does what it says: saves the `ViewMemBlock` of memory to the `ModelViews.DAT` disk file.

ResetViews subroutine Creates a block of memory of 144 bytes and names it `ViewMemBlock`, a unique name only used by the ModelViews ZScript. Once created, this empty memory block needs to be filled with four "default" views, which will all be the same home view: your model centered in screen and facing front. A simple loop command is used to load in the four sets of data, one byte at a time. Look at the ModelViews script listing to see how it does this and look at the diagram (Figure 11.10), which

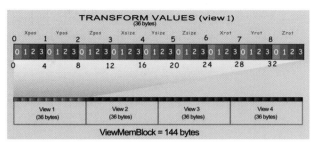

Figure 11.10: Memory block layout

visualizes the `ViewMemBlock` layout highlighting the nine data values for the first View. Finally, with a routine call to Save Views, the contents of `ViewMemBlock` are copied to the disk file.

ShowMenu subroutine At first glance, this subroutine can be a little overwhelming, but it really is simple and consists of three parts. The first part is dedicated to the appearance of the menu; in the other two parts, a loop is created to allow users to stay inside the menu until they click Exit.

Part One Defines the colors used when drawing the menu and buttons. The color is assigned using the [VarSet, Clr2, 0xc00000] command, which works like this. Following the standard hexadecimal prefix 0x (zero x) are six numbers. Each hex number will be between 0 and f in pairs representing red (c0), green (00), blue (00). For more on this 6-digit color concept, look in the ZScript Code Reference under the RGB entry.

Part Two Inside the loop, this part creates the menu using the `NoteIButton` command for the note background, and more `NoteIButton` commands to name and set up each of the buttons displayed on the menu. See the `NoteIButton` command in the Code Reference for more details on what each of the values designate.

It is important to point to the command line following the last `NoteIButton` command. It reads:
`[VarSet, Reply, [Note, , , ,0 ,0 ,0 ] ]`

This forces the note menu to be displayed and waits for the user to click one of the buttons. Once a button is clicked, the number identifying it is stored in the variable named `Reply`.

Part Three Consists of a series of `If` commands that test the value in the `Reply` variable. Let's look inside a few of these tests to see how the menu works:
• If the Exit button (10) was clicked, the script simply ends with an `Exit` command.
• If the Hidden button (11) was clicked, the script calls the `PeekMem` subroutine, which displays the contents of the memory in the `ViewMemBlock`.

- If one of the View buttons (2), (4), (6), or (8) was clicked, the script loads the ViewMemBlock from the disk file, then poses the model using data stored for one of the four views. If Reply equals (2), it uses the first group of nine values from the ViewMemBlock. Reply (4) will use the second group, and (6) or (8) uses the third or fourth group.
- If one of the Save buttons (3), (5), (7), or (9) was clicked, the script saves the view by inserting the appropriate nine transform values into the ViewMemBlock. Then the disk file is updated with the contents of the ViewMemBlock.

ShowMem subroutine When called, this subroutine displays a new pop-up note showing the contents of the ViewMemBlock consisting of the four Transform view groups. The subroutine returns to the menu when the user clicks the left mouse button.

FixRotateY subroutine This subroutine examines the model's RotateY setting and adds .01 to the value for RotateY, *only* if RotateY is set to zero. Without this adjustment, the MTransformSet command will mistakenly display the model in home position but upside down.

The ModelViews Button

In this ZScript, only one button is actually created. Note that the commands used to define the ModelViews button consist entirely of routine calls to four of the subroutines we've already examined. In order, these subroutines are: Test3d, LoadViews, FixRotateY, and, of course, ShowMenu.

This economy of commands for our button definition demonstrates the power of subroutines. Remember, these subroutines as designed may be reused in other ZScripts. Follow this approach in your own scripts and you'll quickly evolve an expansive library of subroutines that will streamline the design and writing of all your future ZScripts.

Making ModelViews into a Plug-In

The ISubPalette command in the script is used to identify the menu and subpalette path where the plug-in button (or buttons) will be created.

In our ZScript, the [ISubPalette,ZPlugin:MyPlugin] command names the ZPlugin palette menu and establishes a new subpalette named MyPlugin.

For a plug-in button to work, the subpalette path must always be used as part of the IButton's name.

It's important to save your ZScript as a .txt file in the \ZStartup\ZPlugs folder with all the other custom plug-in scripts. Before you can use the new plug-in there is one last thing left to do. It must be converted into a new file: ModelViews.zsc, a compressed format that removes all the comments from the script and encodes the commands in a form only readable by ZBrush.

Conversion happens automatically the first time you use the Load button in the ZScripts palette menu to run the ModelViews.txt file in the ZStartup\ZPlugs directory. After that, the new ModelViews button will be always be available the ZPlugs\MyPlug subpalette.

It is possible to customize your ZBrush interface to make the ModelViews button (or any of the other plug-in buttons) always available. To do so, you must first click the Enable Customize button in the Preferences:CustomUI subpalette. Then, holding down the Ctrl button, drag the ModelViews button from the ZPlugs menu onto an interface shelf area and press Ctrl+Shift+I. Remember to click the Enable Customize button again, and you are done. The custom buttons will appear whenever ZBrush is restarted.

Now ZBrush will always include the new ModelViews button on startup.

Debugging a ZScript

Writing scripts can sometimes be frustrating because the command syntax and script logic must be exactly right. However, ZBrush tries to help you in a number of ways when your ZScript contains errors.

Often a ZScript with syntax errors simply won't run. Sometimes a ZScript will run, but the syntax error is discovered only when a certain button is clicked. In either case ZBrush will pop up an error message with a guess as to the script lines containing the error, though this can be wrong, especially in the case of mismatched brackets.

By scrolling down the script's text displayed in the ZScript window, you will find a point where the formatted color coding stops and the text becomes black. This is the point where the error has likely occurred. Once you discover the error, you must go back into your editor to correct the original ZScript text and resave it. In ZBrush, reload the .txt version again via the ZScript palette menu to test the new version.

Plug-in ZScript errors are a special case, and here is a good tip to remember. You should always restart ZBrush after correcting and resaving a plug-in script you are debugging so a new .zsc version of the script is created and loaded. Each time ZBrush starts up, it regenerates fresh .zsc scripts for all matching .txt files it finds in the ZPlugins folder.

Recommended ZScripting References

For further study, I recommend the ZBrush online wiki, which has an extensive section on ZScripting for beginners and seasoned scripters. In the wiki you can also find the indispensable ZScript Command Reference. Keep that handy; you will use it often.

In fact, ZBrush itself has a built-in lexicon of ZScript commands that can be accessed by clicking the Cmd button in the ZScript palette. This opens a scrollable listing in the ZScript window, just below the canvas.

Finally, in Pixologic's ZBrushCentral Forum, you'll find a very active online ZBrush user community. Look for two forums (the ZBrush ZScripting Help forum and the ZBrush ZScript Utilities forum) where ZScripting questions are quickly answered and free ZScript plug-ins are posted by Pixologic and numerous script writers from the ZBrush user community.

Hotkeys

Any menu item in ZBrush may be assigned a custom hotkey. This is particularly useful for speeding up workflow and allowing you to remain centered on your task at hand rather than removing attention from your work and placing it on the interface.

ZBrush comes with many standard hotkeys already, such as T for Edit mode and F for re-centering the model. There are also some useful function key shortcuts new to ZBrush 3. Pressing the function keys at the top of the screen will bring up the various associated palettes listed in Table 11.1.

Pressing one of these function keys will instantly bring up the appropriate palette at the location of your cursor. This can be a huge time-saver when you're in the middle of a work session as the time it takes to move through the interface does add up over the course of a day. Other useful hotkeys can be easily found by simply mousing over an interface item. If there is a default key assigned, it will appear in the tooltip. Figure 11.11 shows the hotkey for Subdivide Mesh (Ctrl+D).

Table 11.1: The Default Palette Hotkeys

Key	Palette
F1	Tools
F2	Brush
F3	Stroke
F4	Alpha
F5	Texture
F6	Material

Figure 11.11: The hotkeys for certain buttons can be found by mousing over them and reading the tooltip.

Making Custom Hotkeys

Any interface item can be assigned a custom hotkey by simply holding down the Ctrl key and clicking the button. If another hotkey exists for this item it will not be replaced; this new hotkey will simply be added. When you Ctrl-click, a message will appear at the top of the screen asking you to enter a key combination to save as a hotkey (Figure 11.12).

If the key combination you press is already assigned as a hotkey, ZBrush will notify you with a warning box. By answering yes you will replace the existing hotkey with your new selection. If you specify no, the action will be canceled. To save your hotkeys for the next ZBrush session, click Preferences → Hotkeys and click the Store button.

Figure 11.12: Hotkey prompt

Customizing the Interface

ZBrush comes with several custom interfaces for you to choose from. You may find that one of the interfaces other than the default suits your working methods better. You can scroll through the various interfaces with the Load Next User Interface Layout button in the upper right of the screen (Figure 11.13). Clicking the Load Previous User Interface Layout will move back. Figure 11.14 shows a sample of some of the interfaces available.

Figure 11.13: ZBrush interface layout examples

*Figure 11.14: Some available
ZBrush interfaces*

Default

Minimal

Sculpt01

In addition to custom user interfaces, ZBrush offers several preset color schemes. You can change the colors in the Preferences → IColors menu, but for a quick harmonious color scheme try clicking the Load Next (Previous) User Interface Colors button (Figure 11.15). Figure 11.16 shows several of the custom color sets available to you.

Figure 11.15: Colors

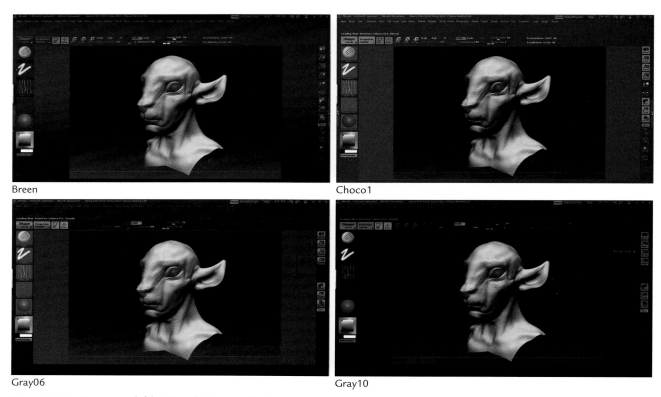

Breen   Choco1

Gray06   Gray10

Figure 11.16: Some available ZBrush Custom Color sets

Setting a Save Hotkey

In this section we'll use what we have learned so far to create a custom ZBrush interface tailored to our needs. This will include hotkeys, custom button positions, as well as a custom menu set. You may decide to create this based on the default menu set, or if there is another menu layout you prefer, simply select that one and follow the exercise. This will base your custom menu on this other menu layout.

1. To use these steps, you must have the ZPlugin quickSave script by Svengali installed. If you haven't already installed it, follow the instructions at the start of this chapter. Open the ZPlugin menu from the top of the screen and unroll the Svengali menu.

2. Ctrl-click the M+ button to set a hotkey for saving the iteration. Because the Alt button is used so much for navigation and sculpting in ZBrush, I tend to use it for hotkeys since my thumb is usually there while I work. I set my save iteration hotkey to Alt+S.

3. To save this new hotkey addition for future ZBrush sessions, go to the main Preferences menu and click Hotkeys to unroll that menu. Here you will click Save to store the startup hotkeys file, including the key we just set. See Figure 11.17.

Figure 11.17: Saving the hotkey

Now we have a hotkeys set to save iterations of our model. We'll still need to use the Model Save button to save the first instance of the ZTool to establish the filename. This would be a good button to move from this nested menu into the interface itself. To do this, we need to turn on Custom Interface in the Preferences menu:

1. Click the main Preferences menu and unroll the Custom UI submenu. Here you will find a button marked Enable Customize (Figure 11.18). Switch this on to allow you to move interface items around.

2. With Enable Customize on, the Ctrl-click function will not assign hotkeys. Instead, it will allow you to drag buttons from one interface location to another. Dock the ZPlugin menu on the side of the screen and open the Svengali menu. Ctrl-drag the Model button and place it on the top tray. As you drag a button over an area where it can be docked, you will see a rectangle appear (Figure 11.19). Release the button in the top tray. The Model button is now placed in the top tray for easy access (Figure 11.20).

Figure 11.18: Custom interface

Figure 11.19: Docking buttons

Figure 11.20: Placing the Model button

Setting the Interactive Light Hotkey and Button

We'll now place the button for Interactive Light into the main screen as well as set a hotkey for it. Again the hotkey will be centered on the Alt button.

1. Click the main ZPlugin menu and open the Misc Utilities submenu. Here you will find the InteractiveLight button for moving the light source with the mouse (Figure 11.21). This helpful utility is a prime candidate to be assigned a hotkey and placed within easy reach.

   Remember that the interactive light will only work with Standard materials and not the MatCap shaders since the lighting model is baked into the MatCap materials.

Figure 11.21: Misc Utilities

2. Ctrl-drag the InteractiveLight button from the ZPlugin → Misc Utilities menu and drop it into the top toolbar (Figure 11.22). Place it beneath the Model button.

3. To set a hotkey for this button, we need to turn off Custom UI. This is because Ctrl will drag buttons while in Custom UI mode and will not set hotkeys. Return to the main Preferences menu and turn off Enable Customize under Customize UI menu.

4. To assign a hotkey, simply Ctrl-click the InteractiveLight button. I set this hotkey to Alt+Q.

Another function I use often while sculpting is switching between a few of my favorite materials. I use Flat Color to check silhouette, Basic Material to interactively light, and White Cavity for brightness and detailing. To set hotkeys for these three materials, simply open the Material palette and Ctrl-click the material you want to assign hotkeys to. I assign Alt+1 to Flat Color, Alt+2 to Basic Material, and Alt+3 to White Cavity.

Figure 11.22: Interactive light

Figure 11.23: Naming your menu

Figure 11.24: The empty Scott menu

Figure 11.25: Scott brushes

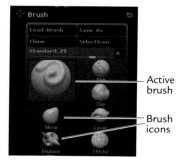

Figure 11.26: Brush selection

Figure 11.27: Creating a bar divider

Figure 11.28: Strokes

At this point, save your new interface and hotkeys. To do this, open the Preferences menu and, under the UI submenu, click Save. Under Hotkeys, click Save. This will store your custom UI as the default and the hotkeys added will be appended to the startup hotkeys file.

Making a Custom User Menu

In this section we'll create a new main menu interface item filled with custom menu options. Once this menu is set, we can assign it a hotkey, which will create a custom pop-up menu item containing your favorite items.

1. In the main Preferences menu, under the Custom UI heading, click Enable Customize.

2. Click the Create New Menu button. ZBrush will prompt you for a menu name (Figure 11.23). For this example, call this menu **Scott**.

3. A new menu named Scott will appear in the main menu bar. Tear this empty menu off to the side of the screen by clicking the radial button so we can begin to add new interface items (Figure 11.24).

4. First we'll add a couple of the most-used brush icons to this menu. From the Brush menu, Ctrl-drag the Standard brush icon to the Scott menu. In Figure 11.25, I have placed four of my most commonly used brushes in the Scott menu. Be sure that you drag the brush icons from the Brush *menu*, not from the main brush icon; the icon only represents the current brush selection (Figure 11.26). This is true for the Texture, Alpha, and Material menus as well.

5. Now add a divider between the brush section and the next selection of menu items. In the Custom UI section of the Preferences menu you will see several orange bars. These can be Ctrl-dragged into the interface to serve as dividers and blank spots. Ctrl-drag the long orange bar into the Scott menu, as shown in Figure 11.27.

6. Beneath this new divider, we'll place the icons for the Freehand and DragRect strokes. Use Ctrl-drag to dock these buttons, as shown in Figure 11.28.

7. The custom menu is now complete. You can continue to add items to your own menu. If you Ctrl-drag the Custom Subpalette item to the menu, you can even add a custom "subpalette." To name your custom menu, Ctrl-click it (Figure 11.29). Figure 11.30 shows my custom menu with a submenu that contains the Edit, Move, Rotate, and Scale buttons. This submenu can be collapsed just like any other submenu in ZBrush.

8. Now click the main Preferences menu and under Custom UI turn off Enable Customize. To save the changes you have made to the UI, click the Store Config button under the Preferences → Config menu.

9. The final step is to assign a hotkey to the custom menu you just created. This will allow you to invoke this menu at the cursor position anywhere in ZBrush, much like a marking menu in Maya. To assign a hotkey, Ctrl-click the menu name at the top of the screen and press the desired key or key combination. I set mine to Alt+W. Now I can access my custom menu from anywhere in ZBrush (Figure 11.31).

Figure 11.29: Naming the submenu

Figure 11.30: My menu

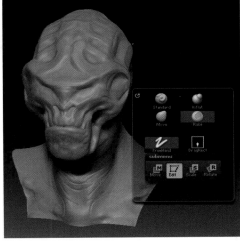

Changing Your Default Document

It is possible to change the size, orientation, and color of your default document window when ZBrush starts. This is a simple process:

Figure 11.31: My menu screen

1. Initialize ZBrush or create a new document by opening the main Document menu and clicking New Document (Figure 11.32). This will clear any tools and create a fresh document on which to work.

2. If you simply want a bigger document than the default size, click the Double button. This will double the current document size; the ZBrush default is 960×720, so this will create a document that is 1920×1440.

3. You may decide that you prefer a document that is oriented in portrait style rather than landscape. In that case, turn off the Pro button. This button constrains proportions. With this button off, you can enter exact image dimensions in the Width and Height sliders. To enter a value, click the slider to highlight the numbers and type the value you want. Try using a document that is 720×960. This will rotate the workspace 90 degrees.

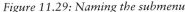

4. When the document dimensions suit you, it is possible to change the background color and gradient settings. To remove the gradient entirely and create a black background, select black from the color picker at the left of the screen and under the Document window, click the Back button. This assigns the currently selected color to the document.

5. To remove the gradient, simply turn the Range slider down to 0. Your document will now be solid black. Be sure to switch your active color back to white before drawing a tool on the canvas.

6. To set this document as the ZBrush default at startup, click the Save As button and save the document in the ZBrush3 installation folder at the following path: `Pixologic/ZBrush3/ZStartup/`. Be sure to name the file `startupdocument.zbr`. Now when ZBrush loads, it will default to this document's settings.

Figure 11.32: Click the New Document button.

Changing the Startup Material

In addition to changing the startup document size, you can change the default material. ZBrush loads with the MatCap Red Wax material selected by default. Follow these steps to change your default material:

1. Open the main Material menu and select the MatCap Red Wax material. Click the Save button and save this material as `RedWax.zmt` in `Pixologic/ZBrush3/ZStartup/Materials`. We are saving this material since we need to copy our preferred startup

shader into this slot. By saving the MatCap Red Wax material into the startup materials folder, you ensure that it will still be available when ZBrush starts.

2. From the Material menu, select the shader you want ZBrush to start with by default. In this case I selected the Basic Material. Click the CopyMat button under the main Material menu.

3. Select the MatCap Red Wax material again and click the PasteMat button to replace the RedWax material with the Basic Material.

4. Clear the canvas and set your document to the dimension you want the ZBrush canvas to be as a default each time you start the program. Select the Simple brush from the Tool menu and with just M and ZAdd active on the brush, create a small stroke in the corner of the canvas (Figure 11.33).

Figure 11.33: Adding a small stroke to the corner of the canvas with the new default material

5. Save this document as StartupDocument.zbr in the Pixologic/ZBrush3/ZStartup folder. Overwrite any previous startup document you may have saved. Restart ZBrush and you will find it loads with your new default material. The Red Wax shader will also still be available in the Startup MatCap Materials.

Congratulations! You have just completed building a complex custom user interface for ZBrush. Customizations like this can help you harness the power of this program and increase your speed greatly. Knowing exactly the options you want and having them at your fingertips can make working in ZBrush smoother, faster, and more efficient.

Wiley Publishing, Inc. End-User License Agreement